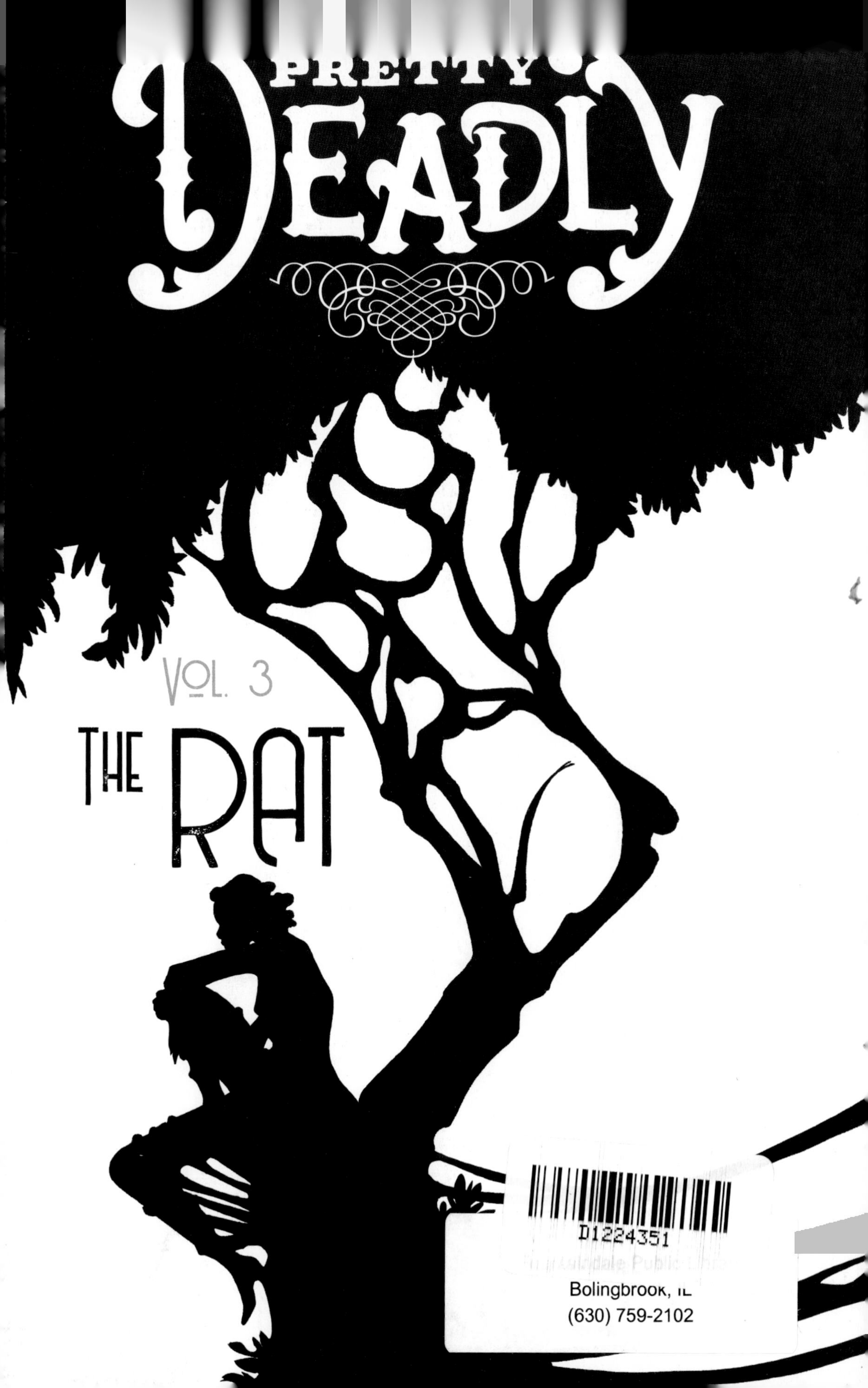
PRETTY
DEADLY
VOL. 3
THE RAT

IMAGE COMICS, INC. ROBERT KIRKMAN - chief operating officer ERIK LARSEN - chief financial officer TODD MCFARLANE - president MARC SILVESTRI - chief executive officer JIM VALENTINO - vice president ERIC STEPHENSON - publisher / chief creative officer JEFF BOISON - director of publishing planning & book trade sales CHRIS ROSS - director of digital services JEFF STANG - director of direct market sales KAT SALAZAR - director of pr & marketing DREW GILL - cover editor HEATHER DOORNINK - production director NICOLE LAPALME - controller IMAGECOMICS.COM

VOL. 3

THE RAT

SCRIPT
KELLY SUE DeCONNICK

ART & COVERS
EMMA RIOS

COLORING
JORDIE BELLAIRE

LETTERING
CLAYTON COWLES

DESIGN
LAURENN McCUBBIN

EDITOR
SIGRID ELLIS

MANAGING EDITORS
LAUREN SANKOVITCH
TURNER LOBEY

PRODUCTION DESIGN
TRICIA RAMOS

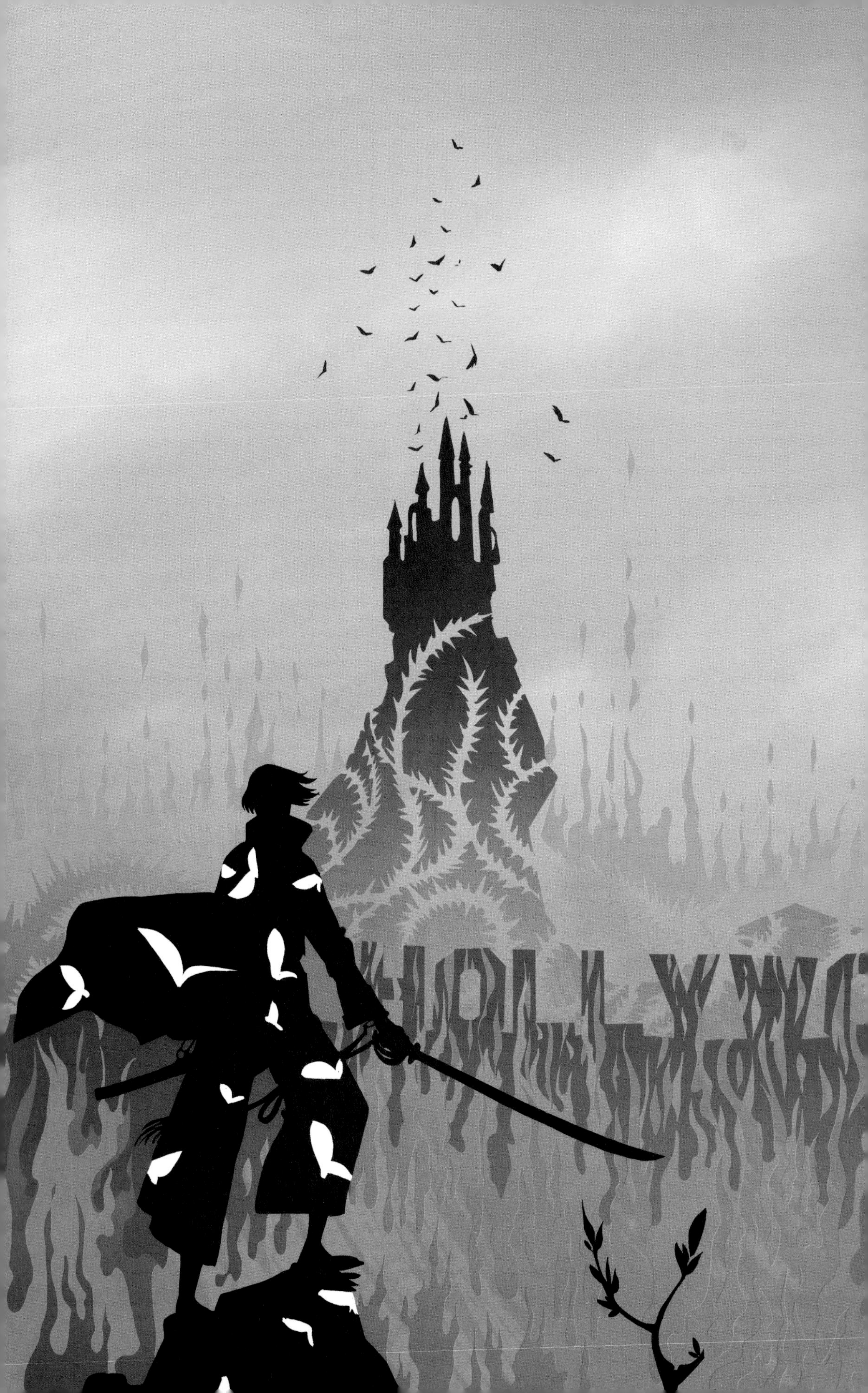

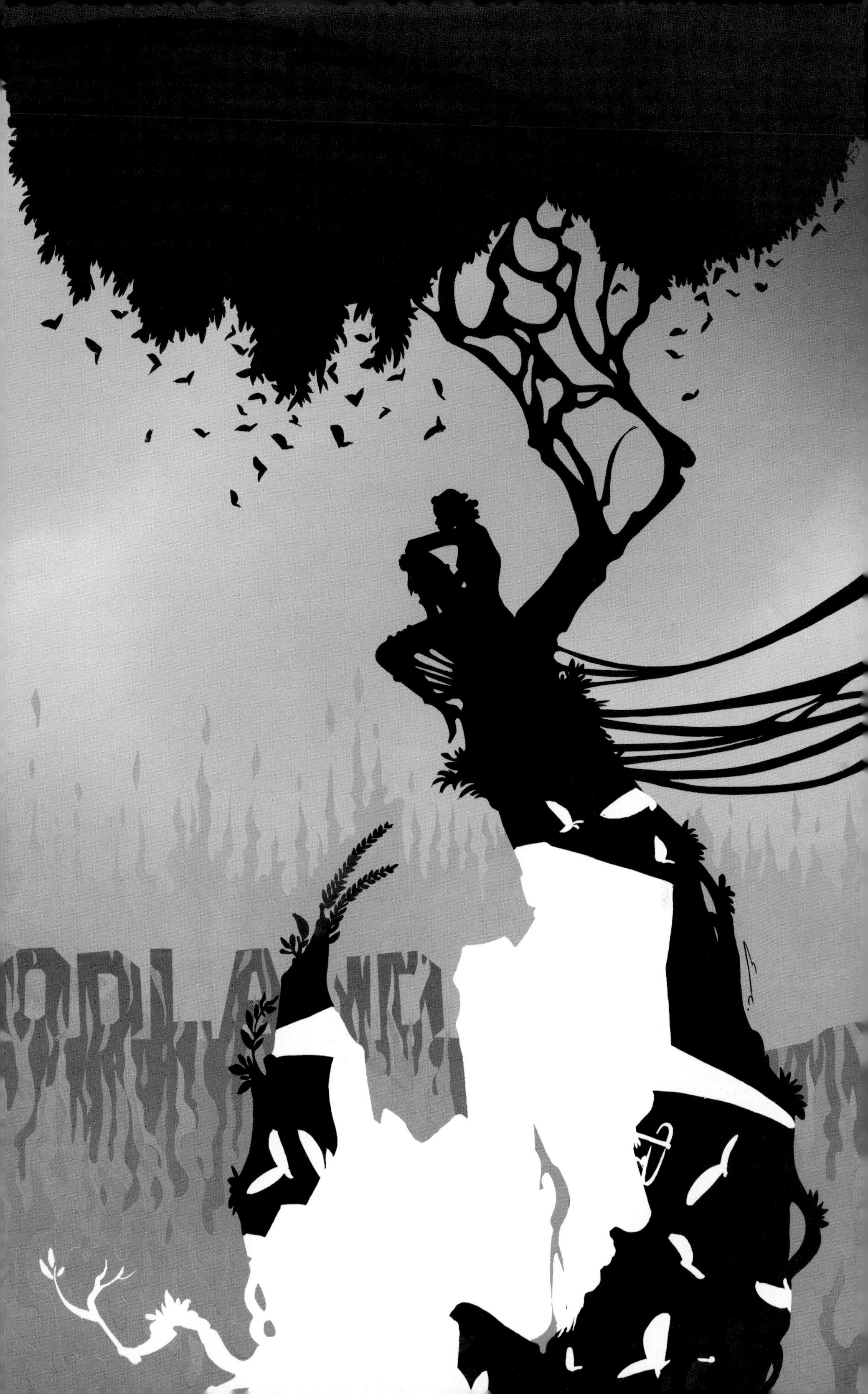

Bones Bunny tells Butterfly the tale.

The Ballad was a history. With Death's daughter Ginny at her side, Sissy, the child of blood and violence raised on love, defeated Old Death in his own domain and took his place in the long-fallow World Garden.

There, her work has only just begun. Having assumed the mantle of Death herself, Sissy must bring the Garden back to life...and seek out the errant Reapers, long left scattered, and return them to the fold.

In the mortal realm, Sarah Fields, mother to many, and the woman who pulled Sissy from the river of blood that bore her, has died...but her children, and their connection to the Reapers, live on. Striking out from their birthplace, Sarah's progeny have found themselves as far-flung as the bloody trenches of France to the arid streets of Hollywoodland...

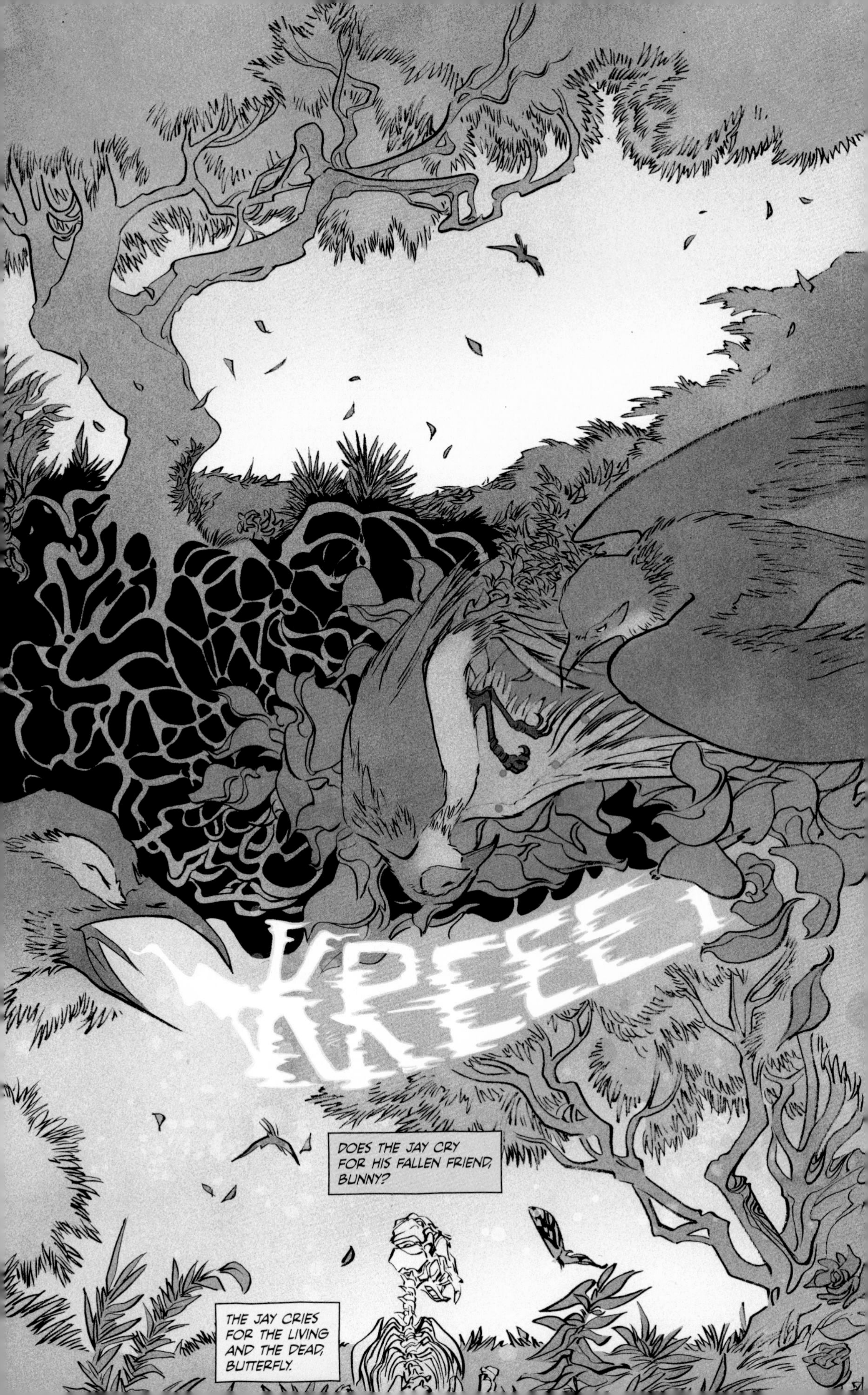
KREEE!
DOES THE JAY CRY FOR HIS FALLEN FRIEND, BUNNY?
THE JAY CRIES FOR THE LIVING AND THE DEAD, BUTTERFLY.

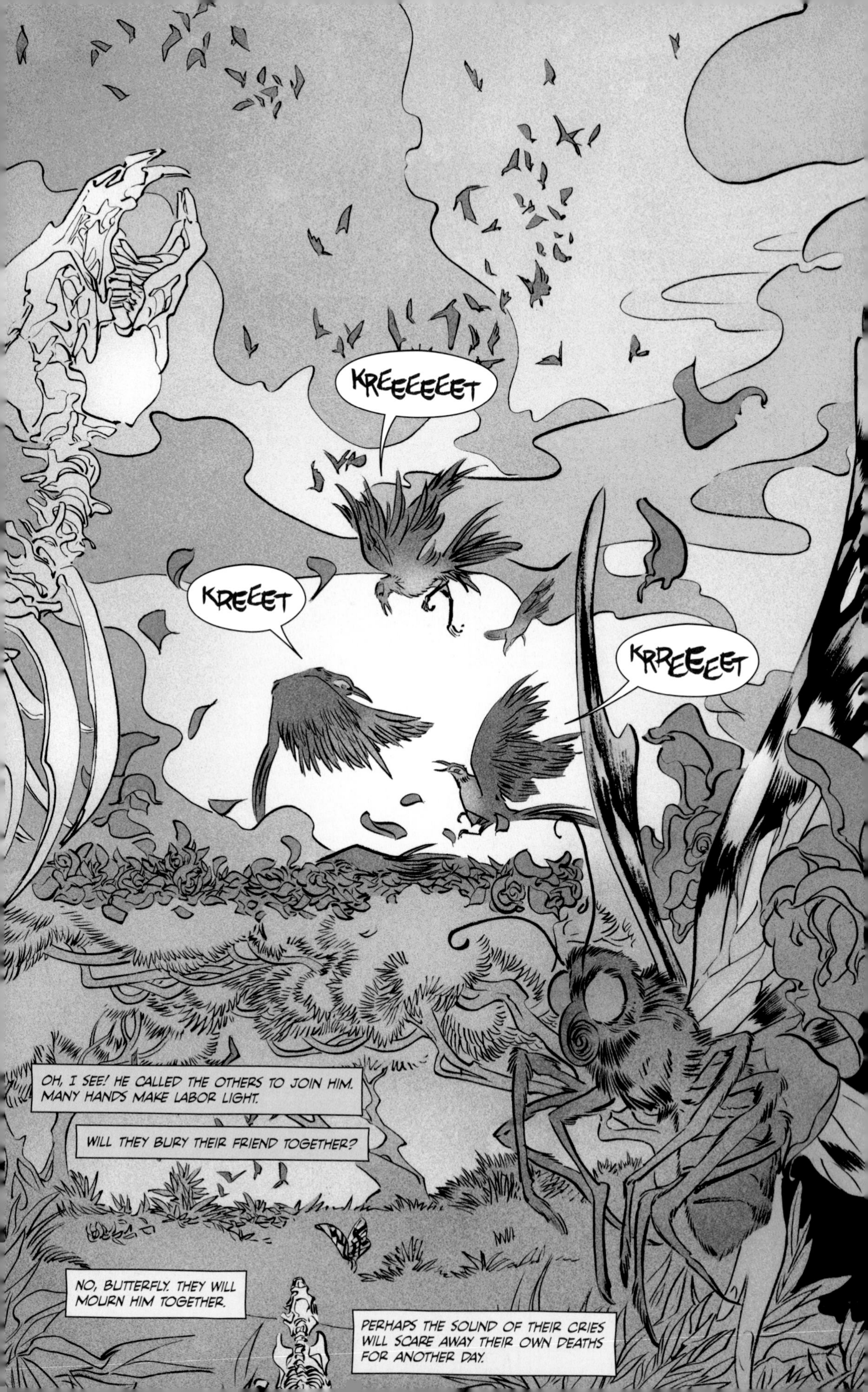
KREEEEEEET
KREEET
KRREEEEET
OH, I SEE! HE CALLED THE OTHERS TO JOIN HIM. MANY HANDS MAKE LABOR LIGHT.
WILL THEY BURY THEIR FRIEND TOGETHER?
NO, BUTTERFLY. THEY WILL MOURN HIM TOGETHER.
PERHAPS THE SOUND OF THEIR CRIES WILL SCARE AWAY THEIR OWN DEATHS FOR ANOTHER DAY.

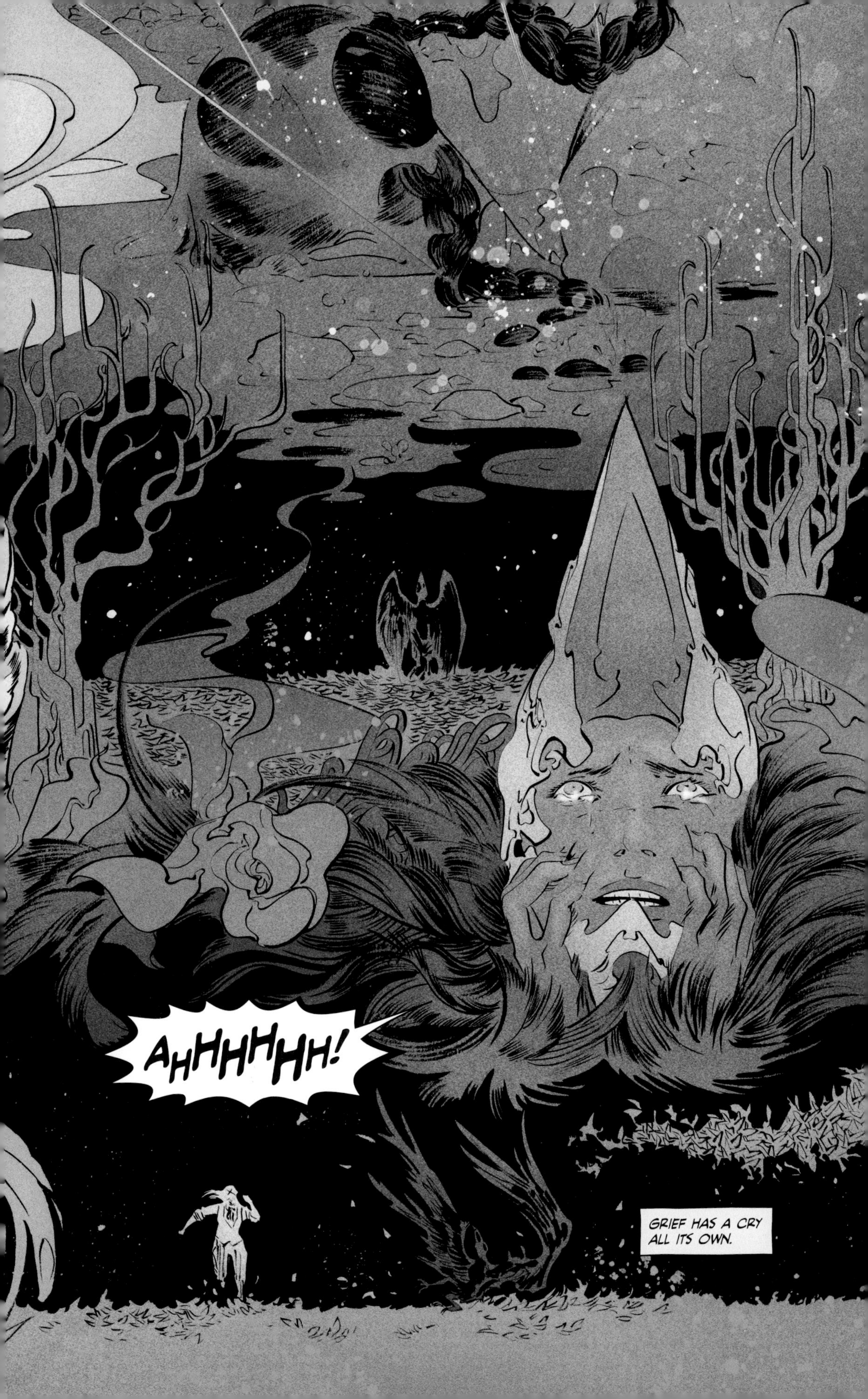
AHHHHHH!
GRIEF HAS A CRY ALL ITS OWN.

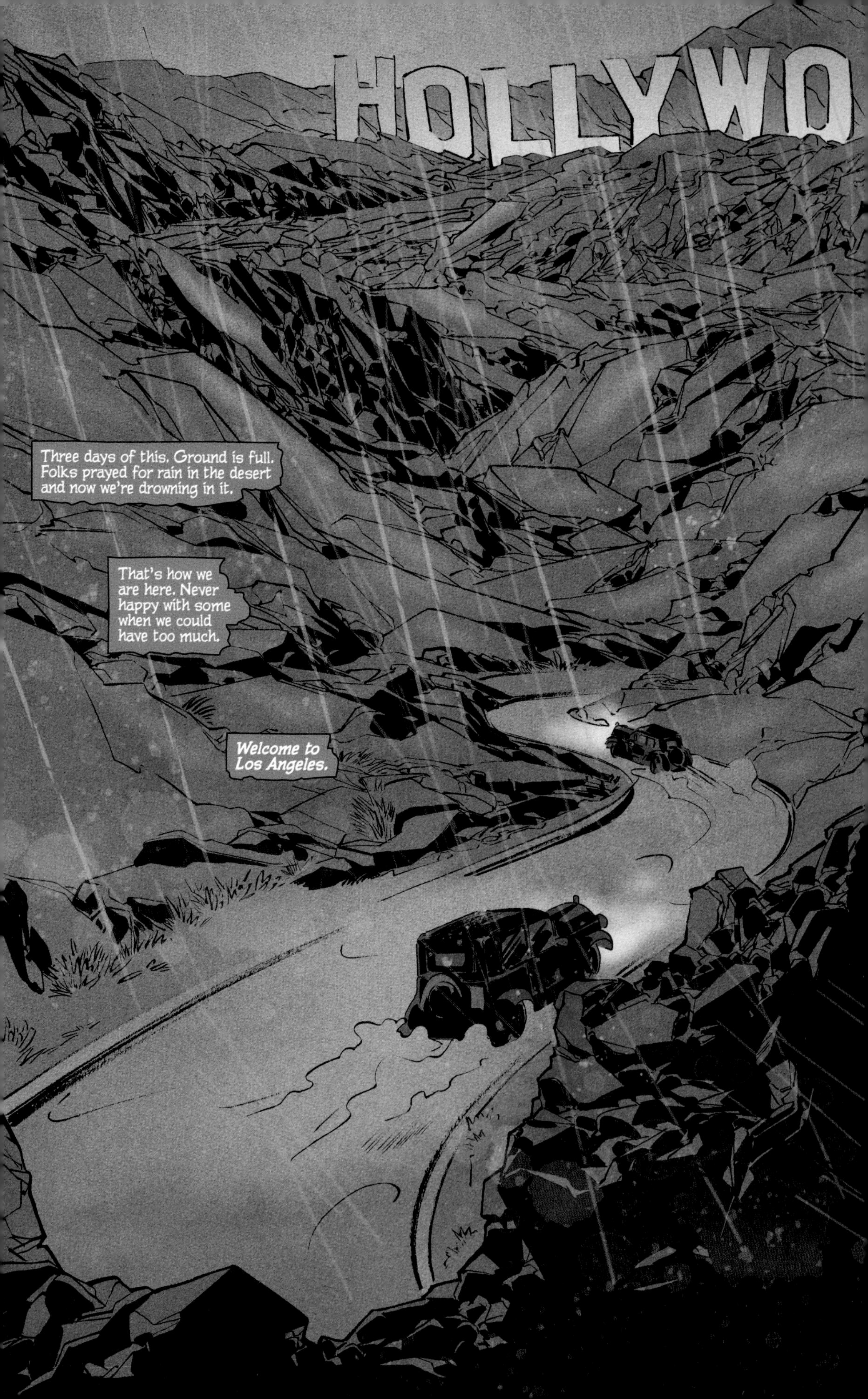
HOLLYWO
Three days of this. Ground is full. Folks prayed for rain in the desert and now we're drowning in it.
That's how we are here. Never happy with some when we could have too much.
Welcome to Los Angeles.

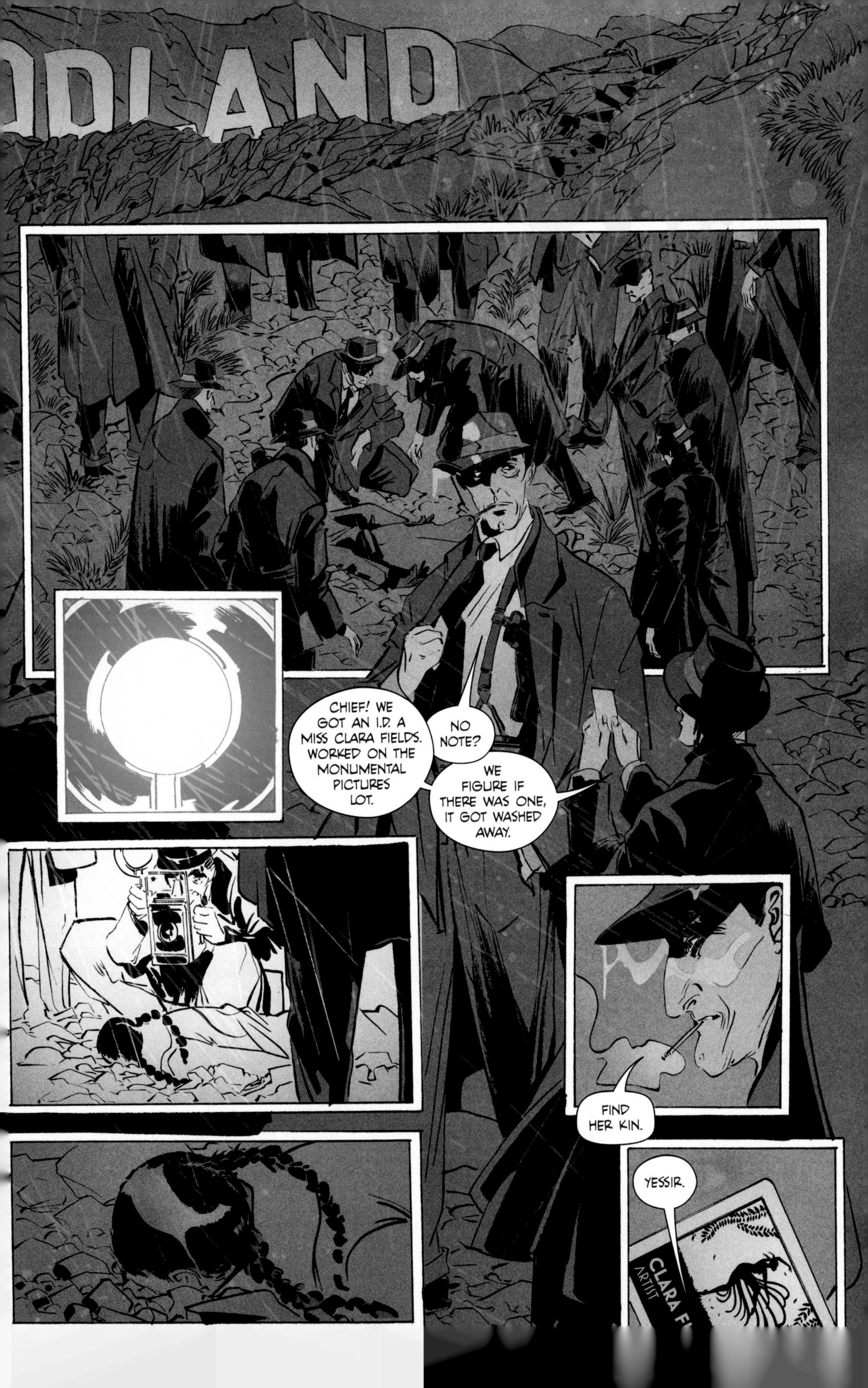
ODLAND
CHIEF! WE GOT AN I.D. A MISS CLARA FIELDS. WORKED ON THE MONUMENTAL PICTURES LOT.
NO NOTE?
WE FIGURE IF THERE WAS ONE, IT GOT WASHED AWAY.
FIND HER KIN.
YESSIR.
CLARA F
ARTIST

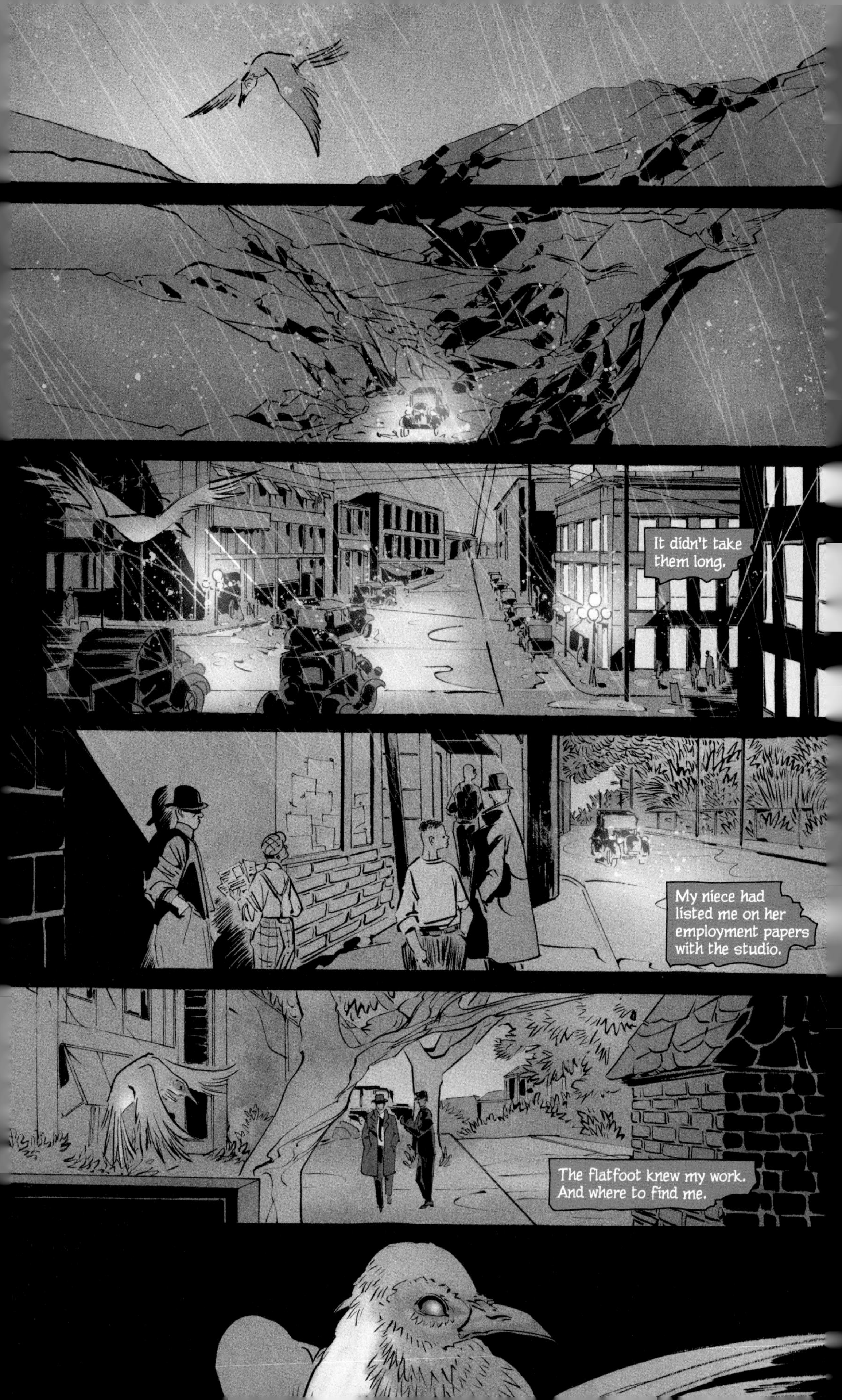
It didn't take them long.
My niece had listed me on her employment papers with the studio.
The flatfoot knew my work. And where to find me.

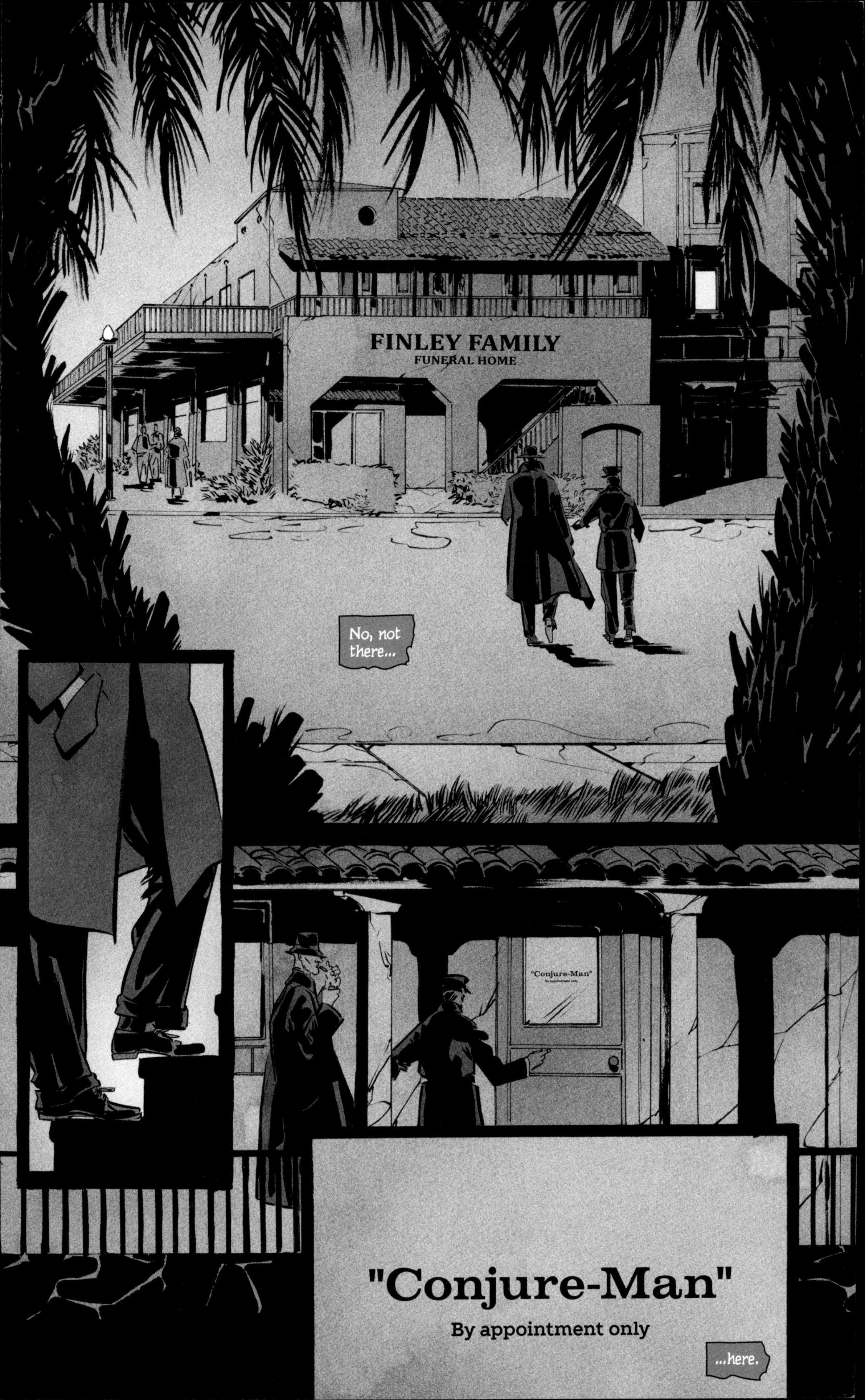
FINLEY FAMILY
FUNERAL HOME
No, not there...
"Conjure-Man"
By appointment only
"Conjure-Man"
By appointment only
...here.

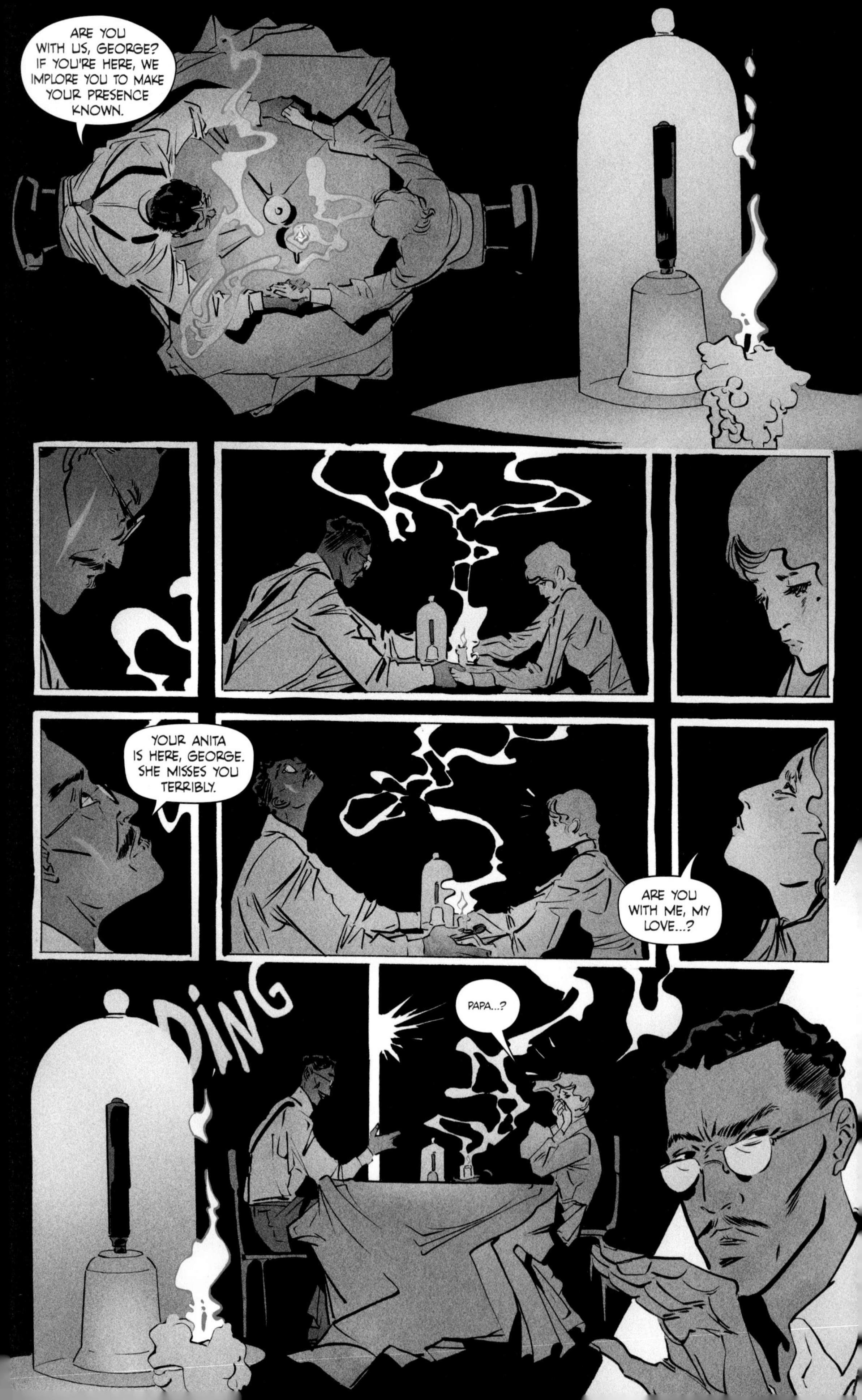
ARE YOU WITH US, GEORGE? IF YOU'RE HERE, WE IMPLORE YOU TO MAKE YOUR PRESENCE KNOWN.
YOUR ANITA IS HERE, GEORGE. SHE MISSES YOU TERRIBLY.
ARE YOU WITH ME, MY LOVE...?
DING
PAPA...?

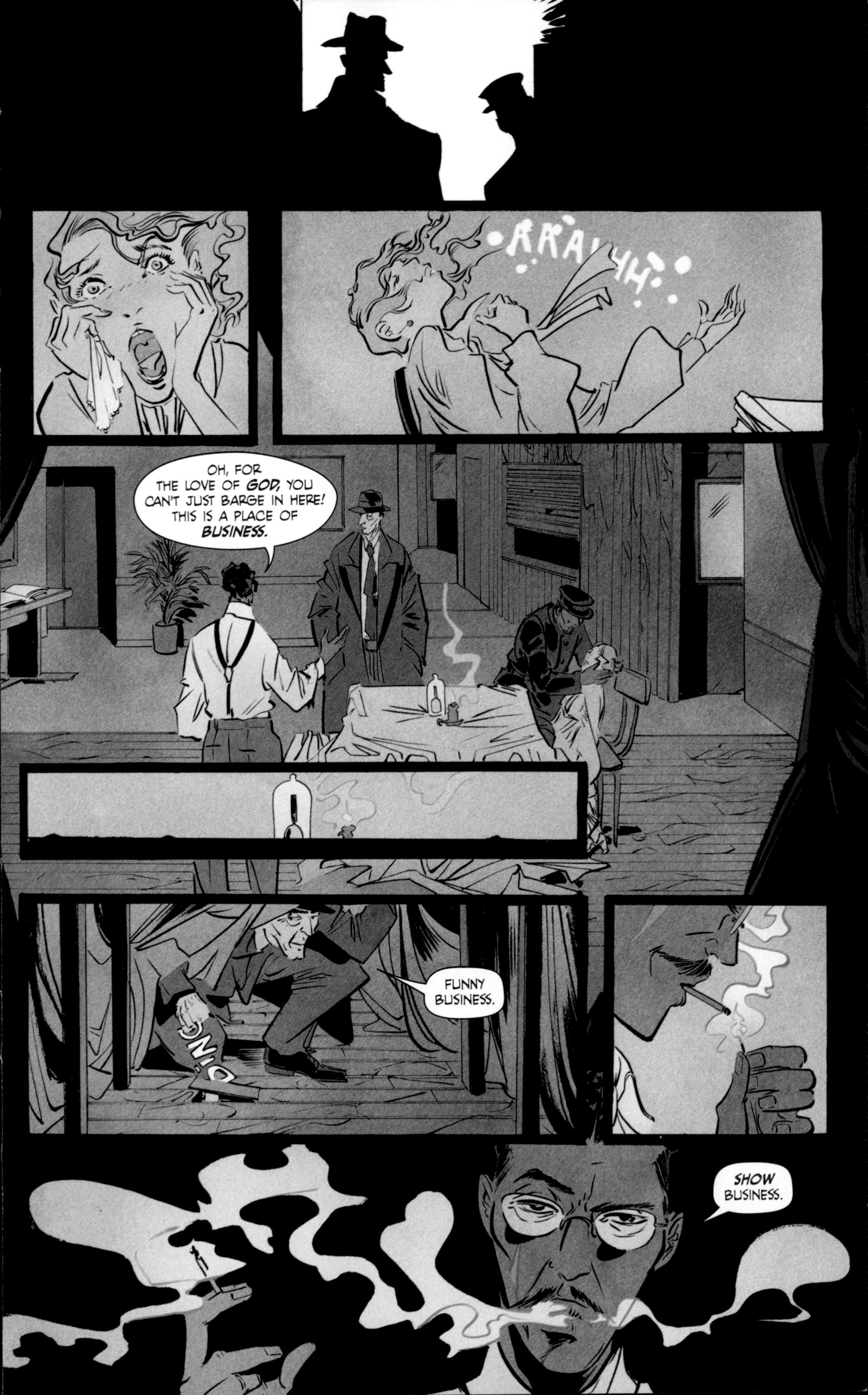
OH, FOR THE LOVE OF GOD, YOU CAN'T JUST BARGE IN HERE! THIS IS A PLACE OF BUSINESS.
FUNNY BUSINESS.
SHOW BUSINESS.

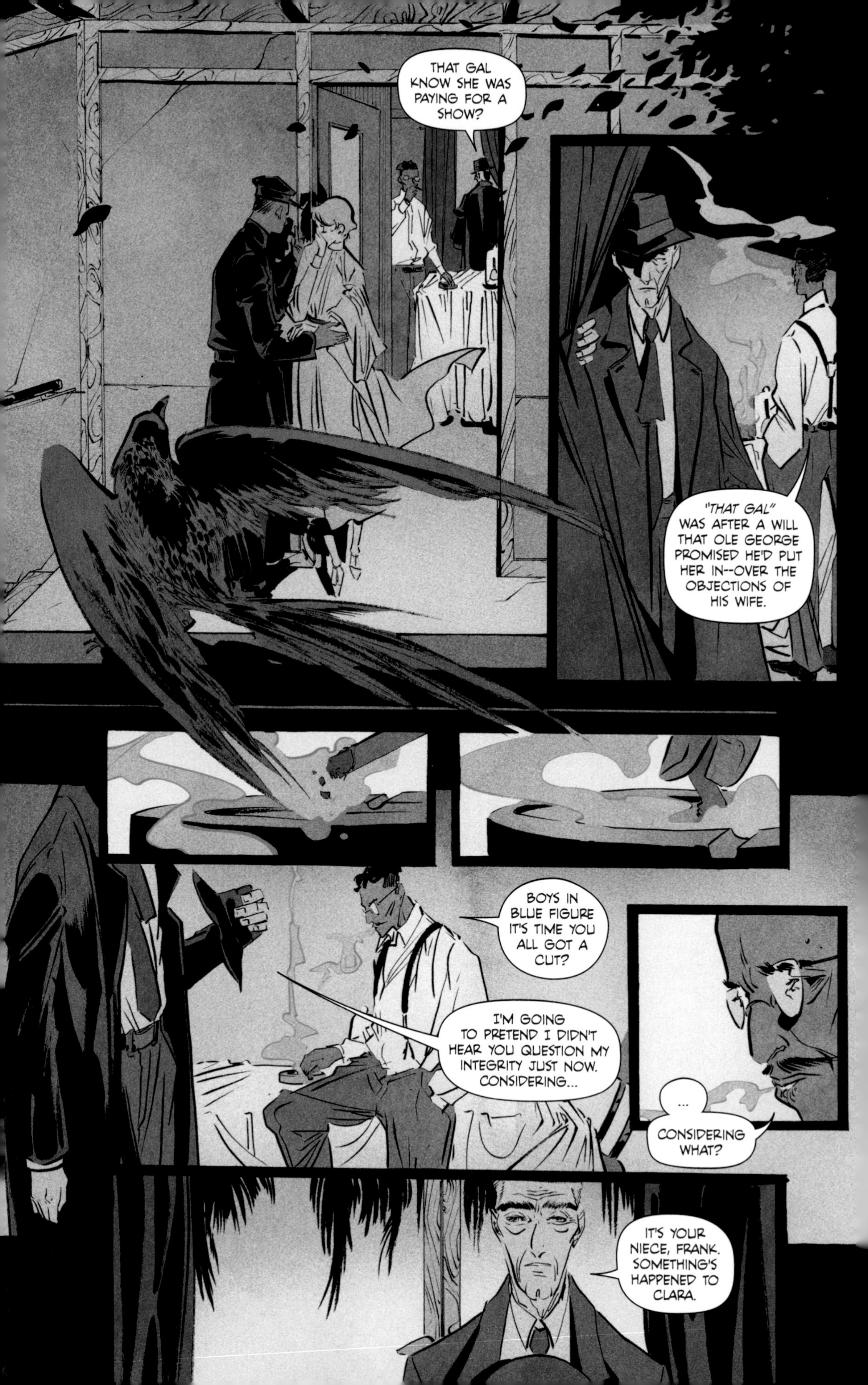
THAT GAL KNOW SHE WAS PAYING FOR A SHOW?
"THAT GAL" WAS AFTER A WILL THAT OLE GEORGE PROMISED HE'D PUT HER IN--OVER THE OBJECTIONS OF HIS WIFE.
BOYS IN BLUE FIGURE IT'S TIME YOU ALL GOT A CUT?
I'M GOING TO PRETEND I DIDN'T HEAR YOU QUESTION MY INTEGRITY JUST NOW. CONSIDERING...
...
CONSIDERING WHAT?
IT'S YOUR NIECE, FRANK. SOMETHING'S HAPPENED TO CLARA.

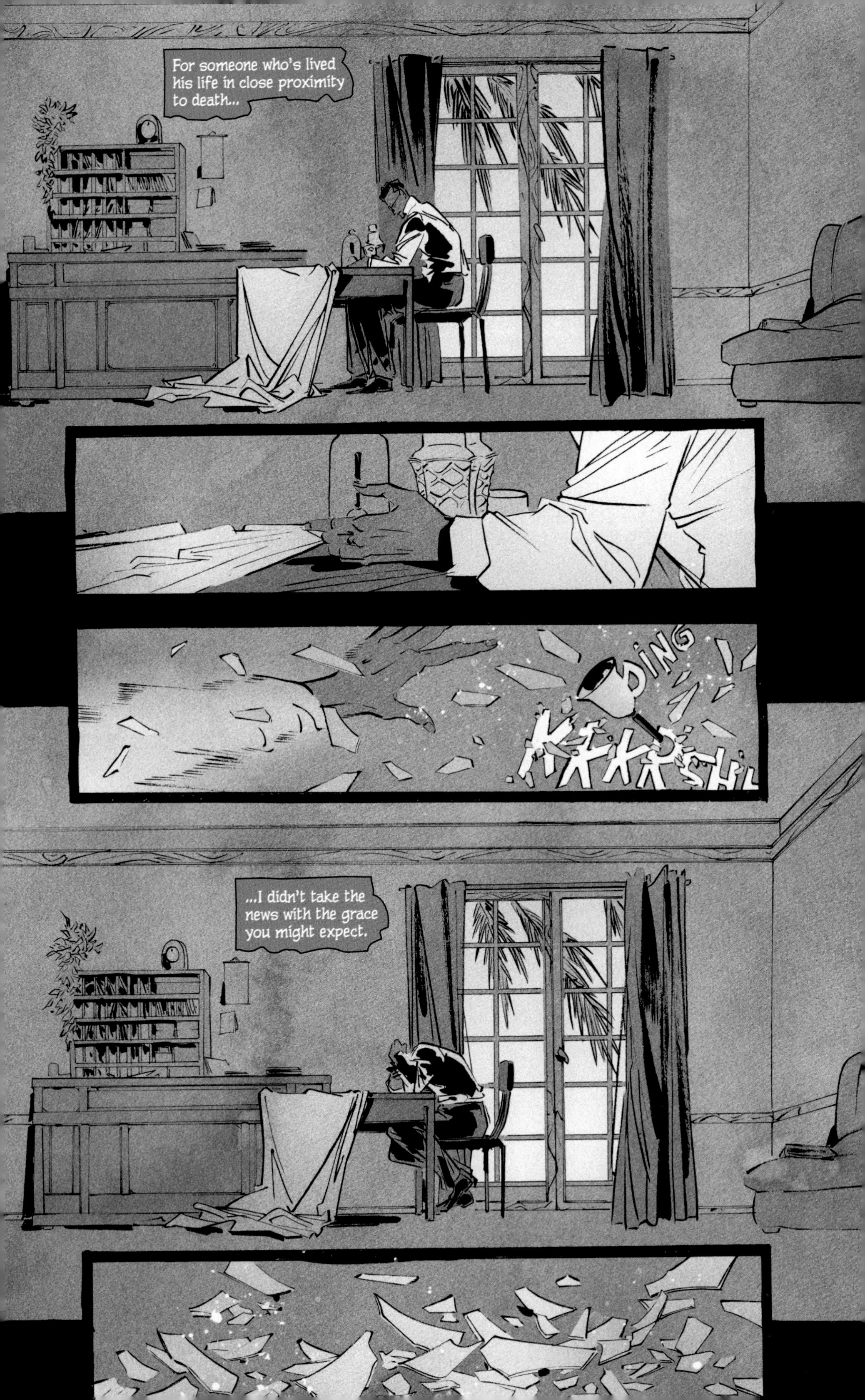
For someone who's lived his life in close proximity to death...
DING
KKKRSH
...I didn't take the news with the grace you might expect.

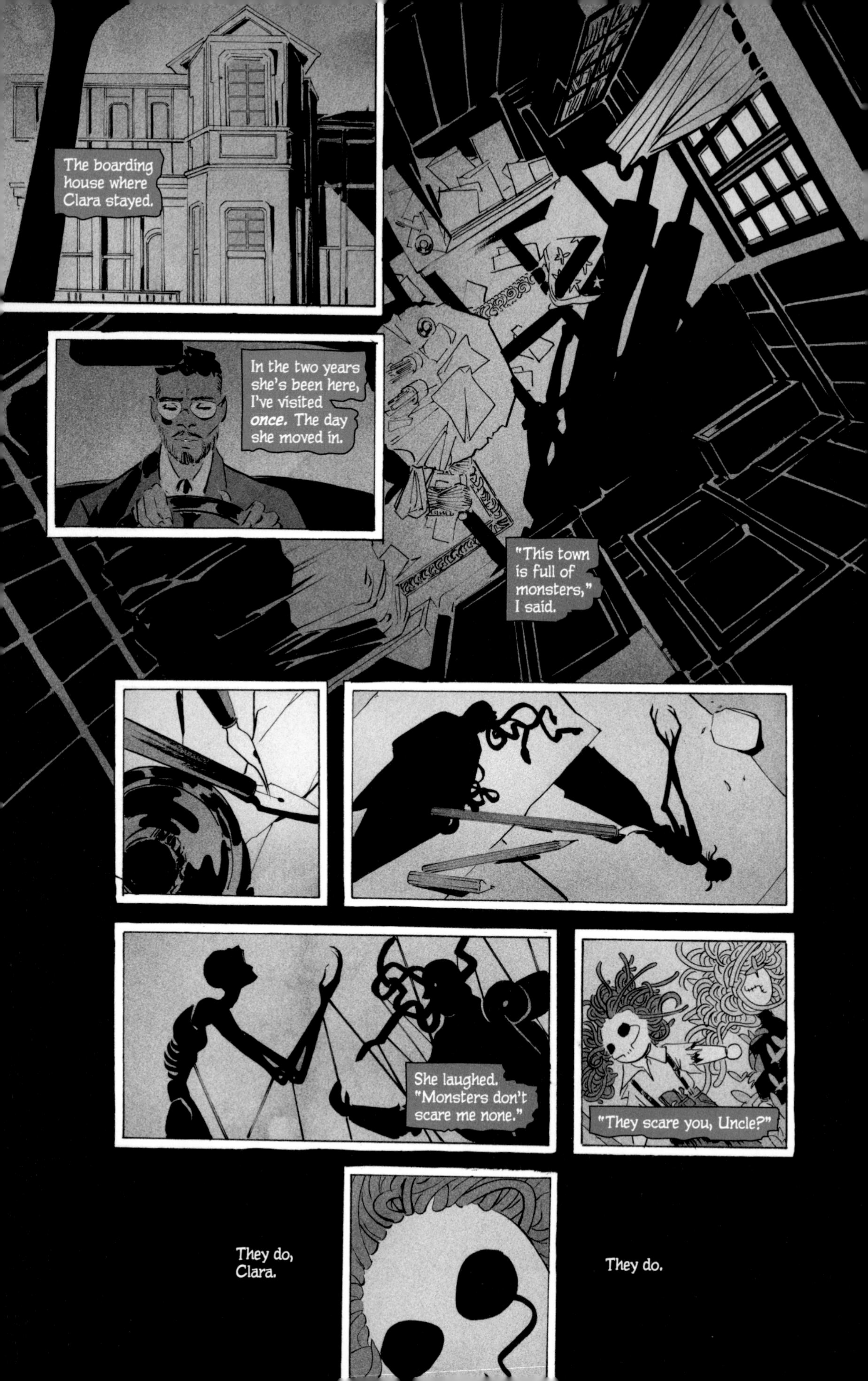
The boarding house where Clara stayed.
In the two years she's been here, I've visited *once.* The day she moved in.
"This town is full of monsters," I said.
She laughed. "Monsters don't scare me none."
"They scare you, Uncle?"
They do, Clara.
They do.

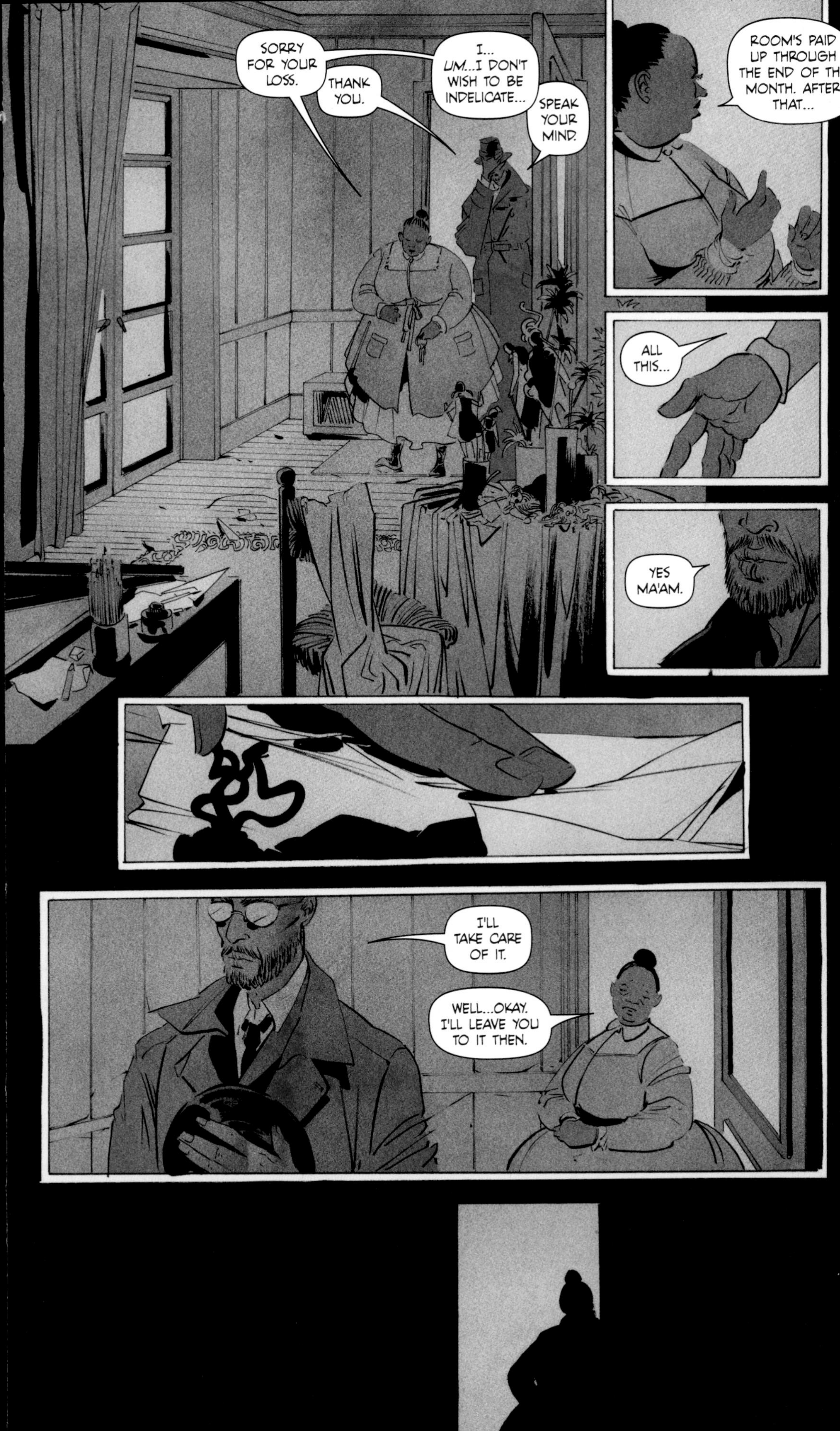
SORRY FOR YOUR LOSS.
THANK YOU.
I... UM...I DON'T WISH TO BE INDELICATE...
SPEAK YOUR MIND.
ROOM'S PAID UP THROUGH THE END OF TH MONTH. AFTER THAT...
ALL THIS...
YES MA'AM.
I'LL TAKE CARE OF IT.
WELL...OKAY. I'LL LEAVE YOU TO IT THEN.

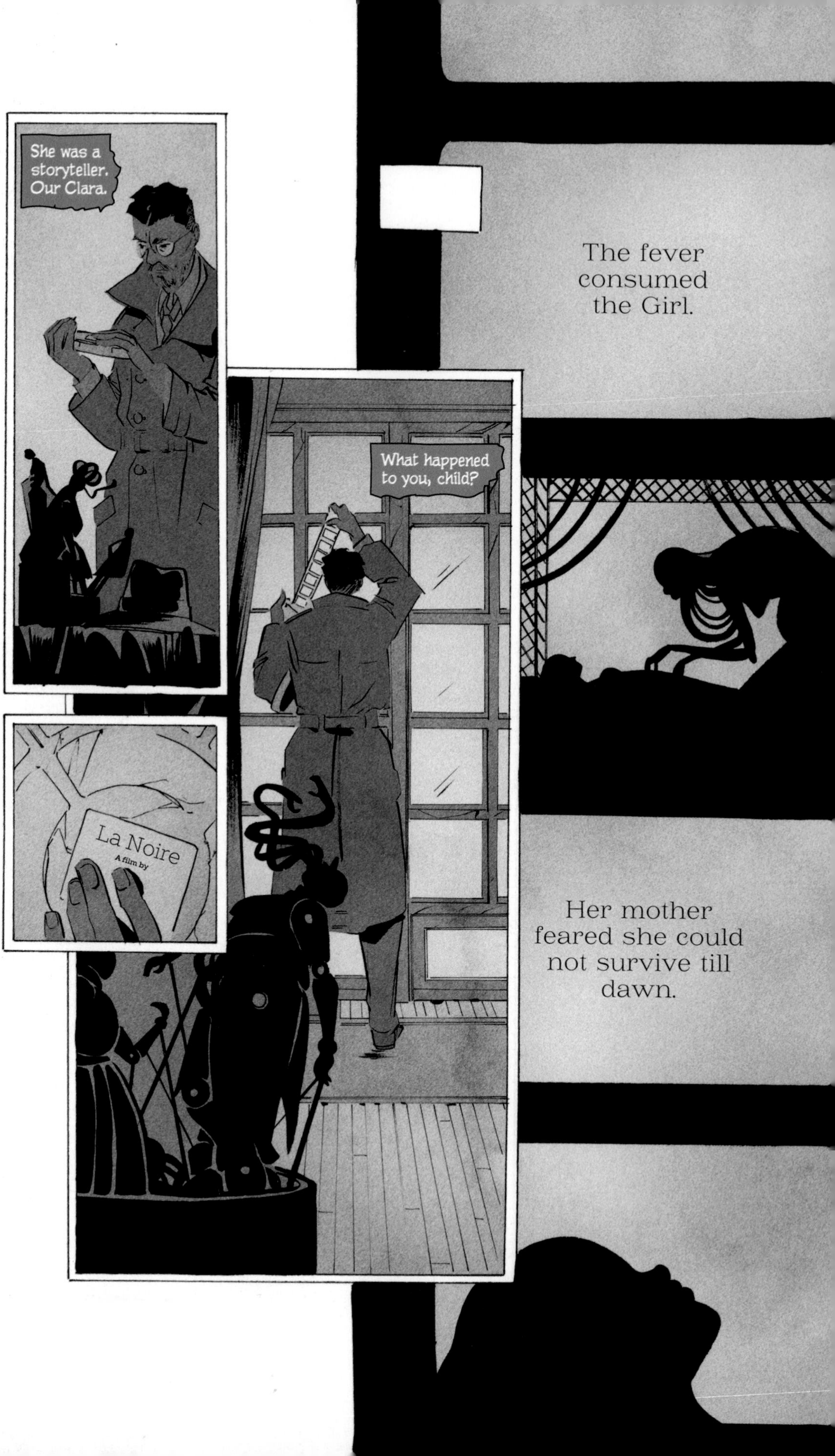
She was a storyteller. Our Clara.
What happened to you, child?
La Noire
A film by
The fever consumed the Girl.
Her mother feared she could not survive till dawn.

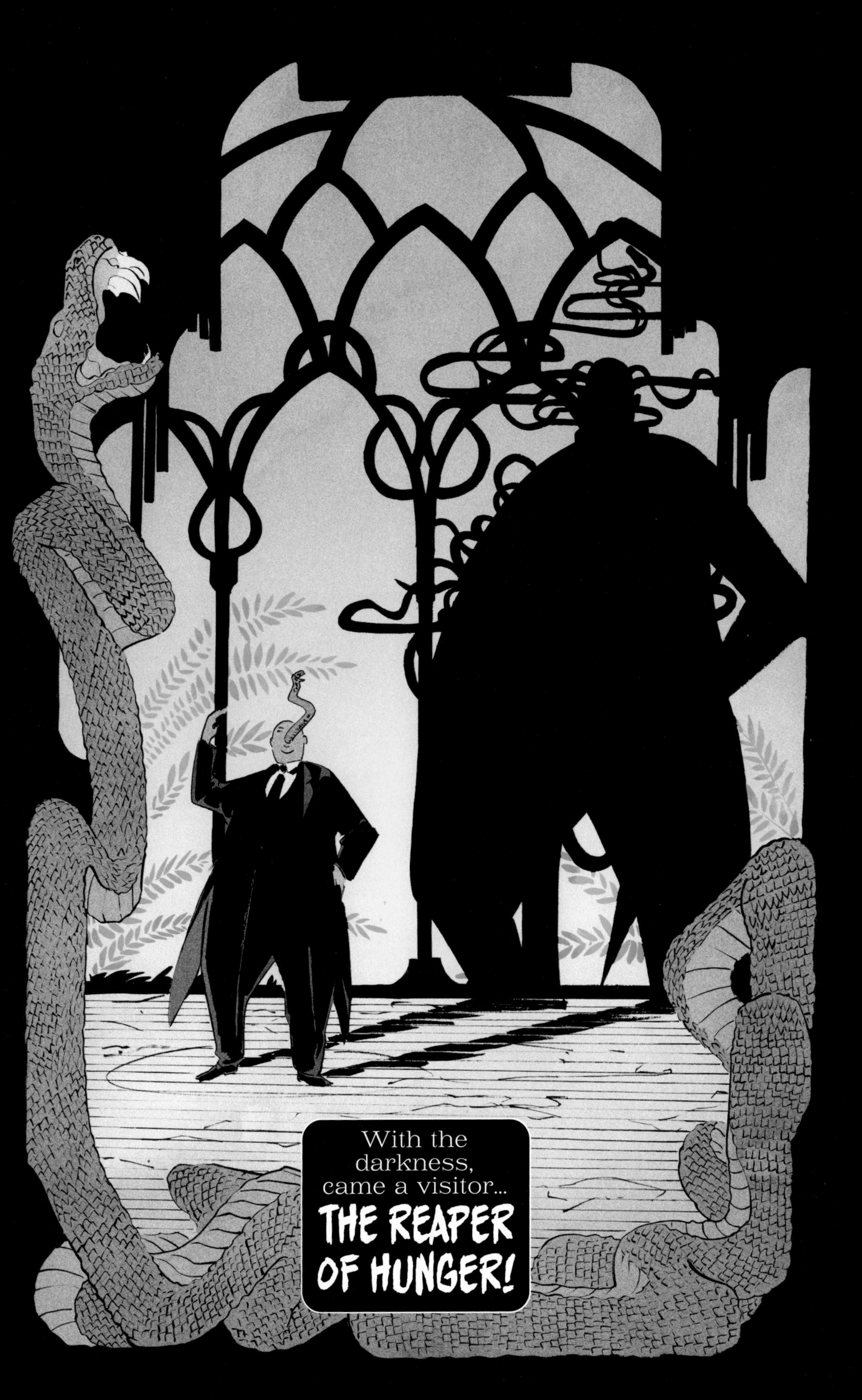
With the darkness, came a visitor...
THE REAPER OF HUNGER!

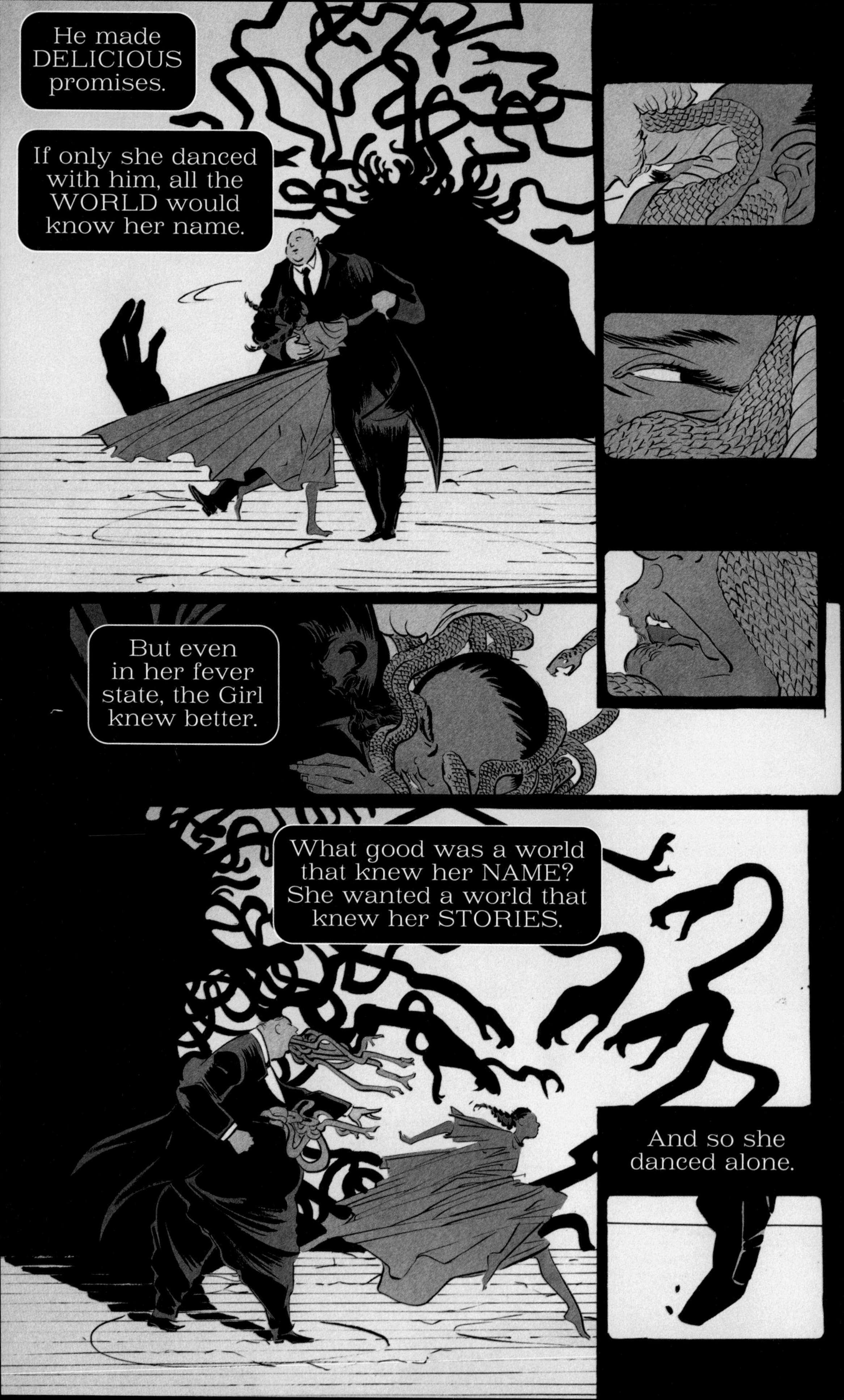
He made DELICIOUS promises.
If only she danced with him, all the WORLD would know her name.
But even in her fever state, the Girl knew better.
What good was a world that knew her NAME? She wanted a world that knew her STORIES.
And so she danced alone.

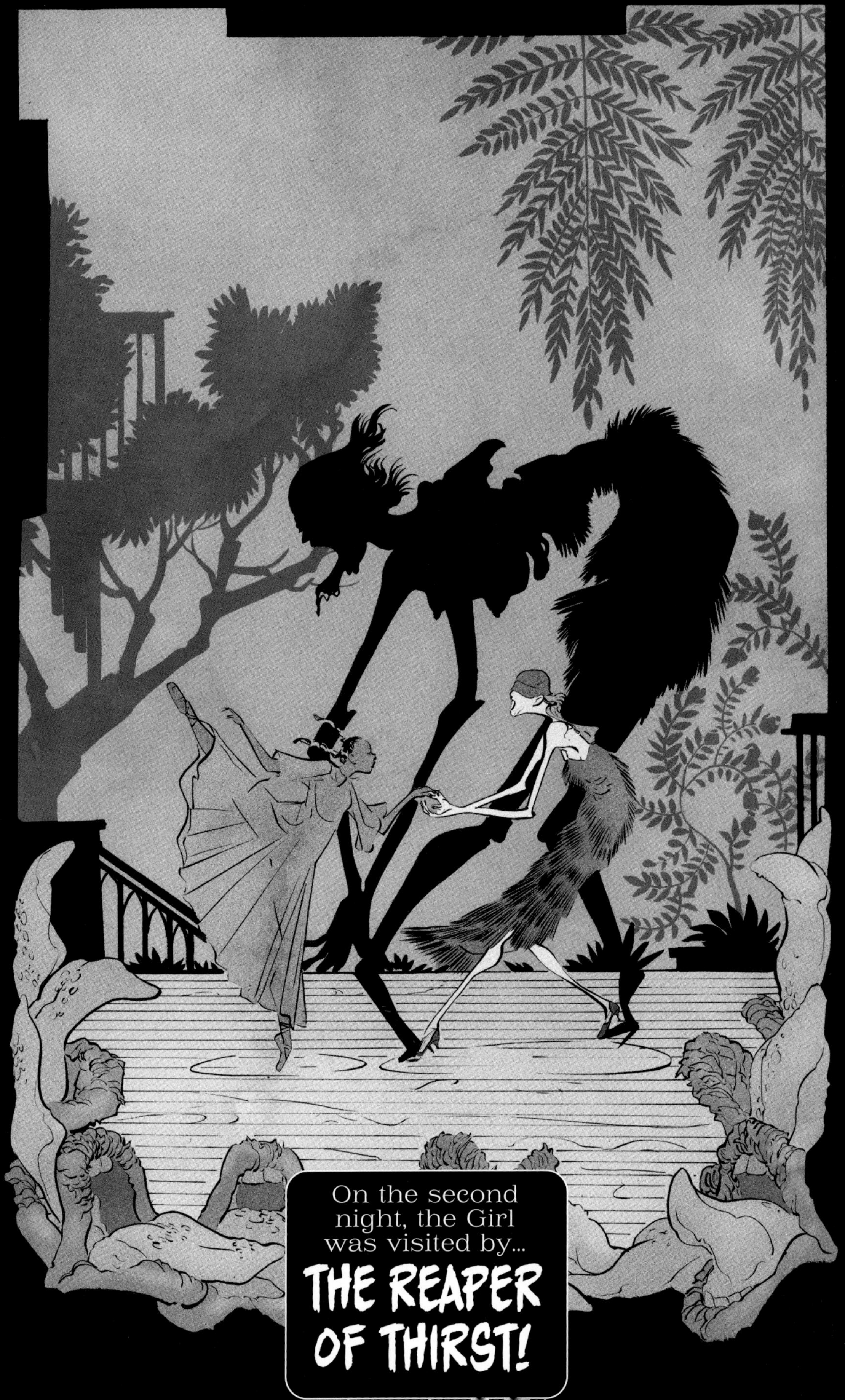
On the second night, the Girl was visited by...
THE REAPER OF THIRST!

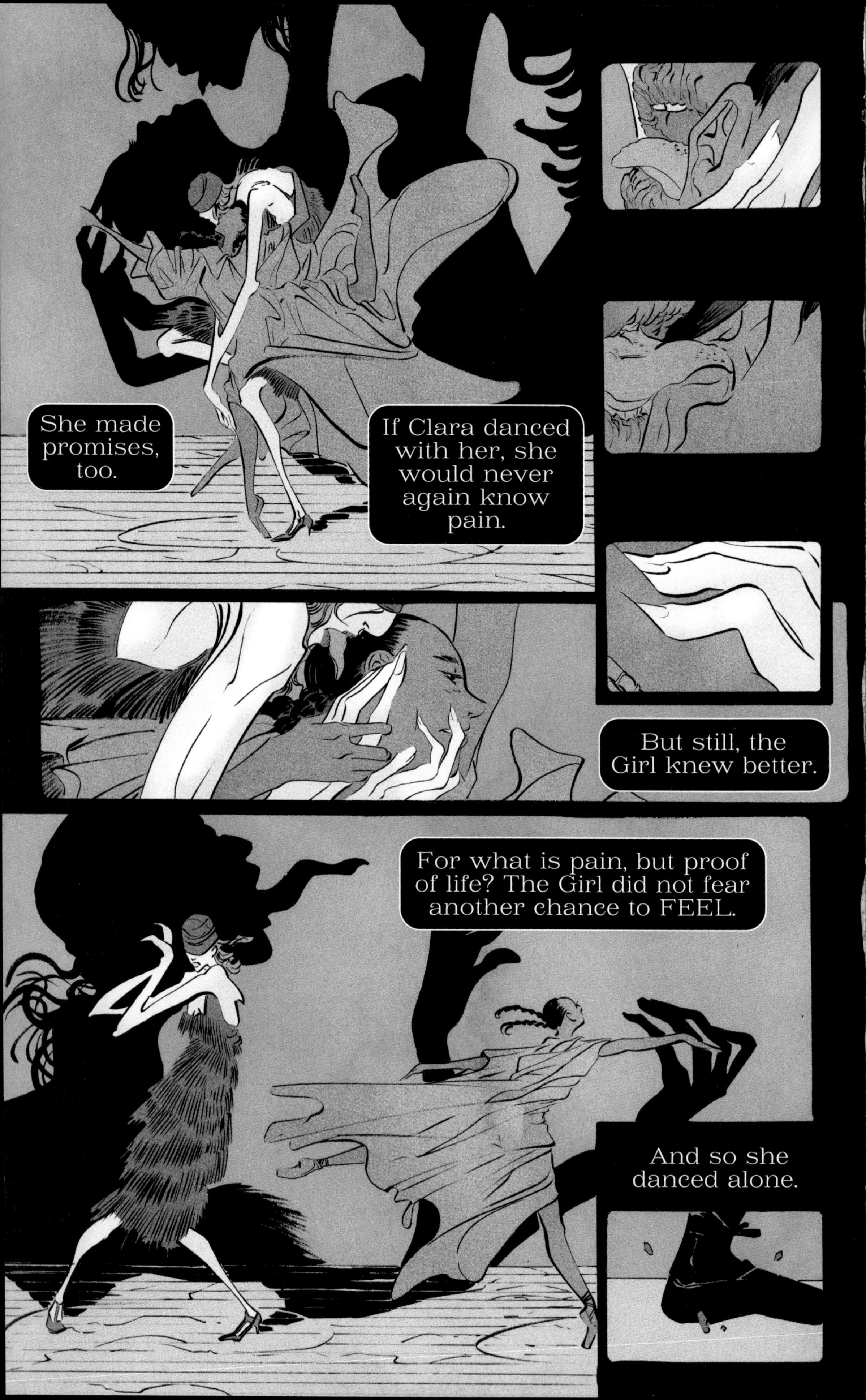
She made promises, too.
If Clara danced with her, she would never again know pain.
But still, the Girl knew better.
For what is pain, but proof of life? The Girl did not fear another chance to FEEL.
And so she danced alone.

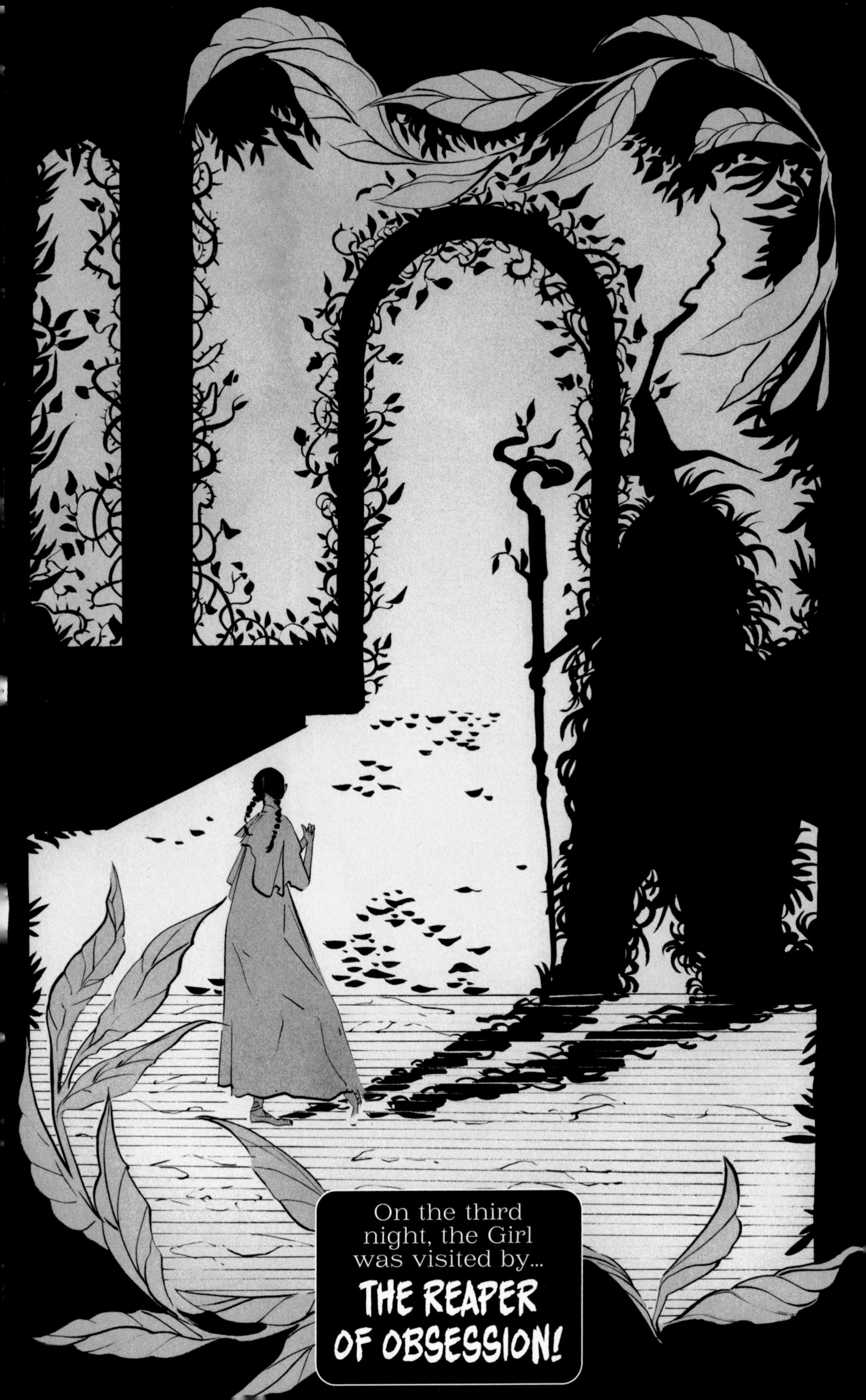
On the third night, the Girl was visited by...
THE REAPER OF OBSESSION!

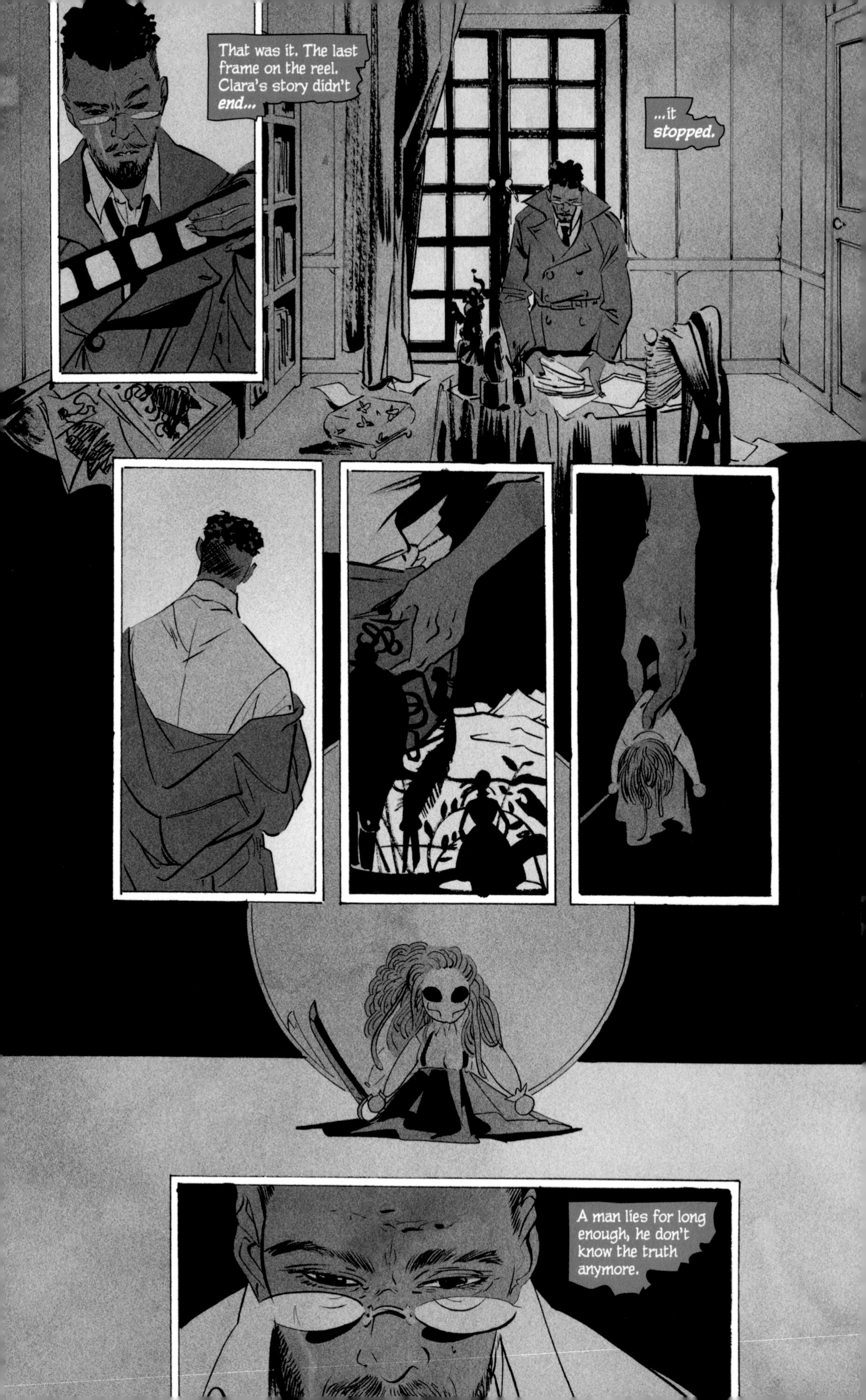
That was it. The last frame on the reel. Clara's story didn't *end...*
...it *stopped.*
A man lies for long enough, he don't know the truth anymore.

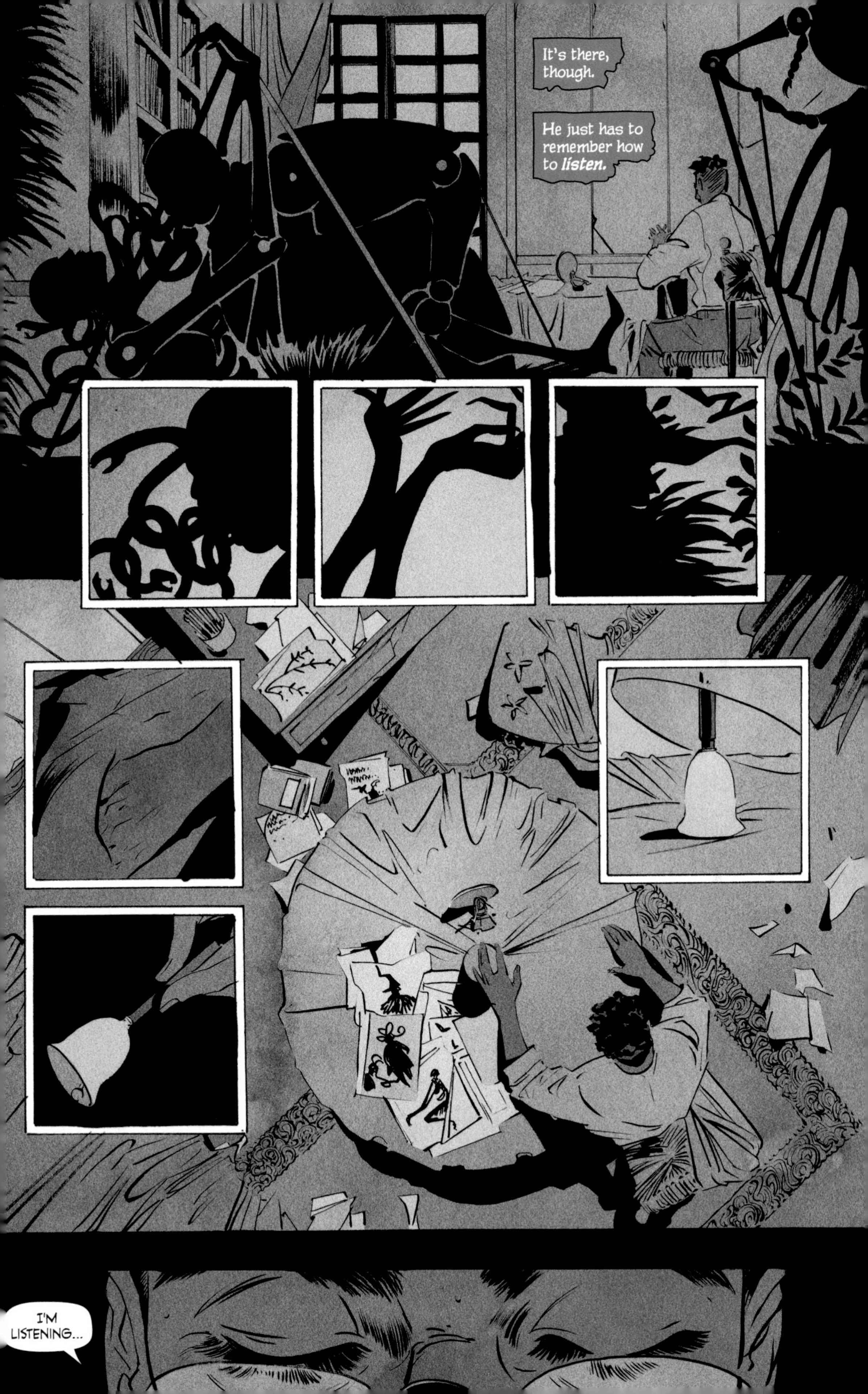
It's there, though.
He just has to remember how to *listen.*
I'M LISTENING...

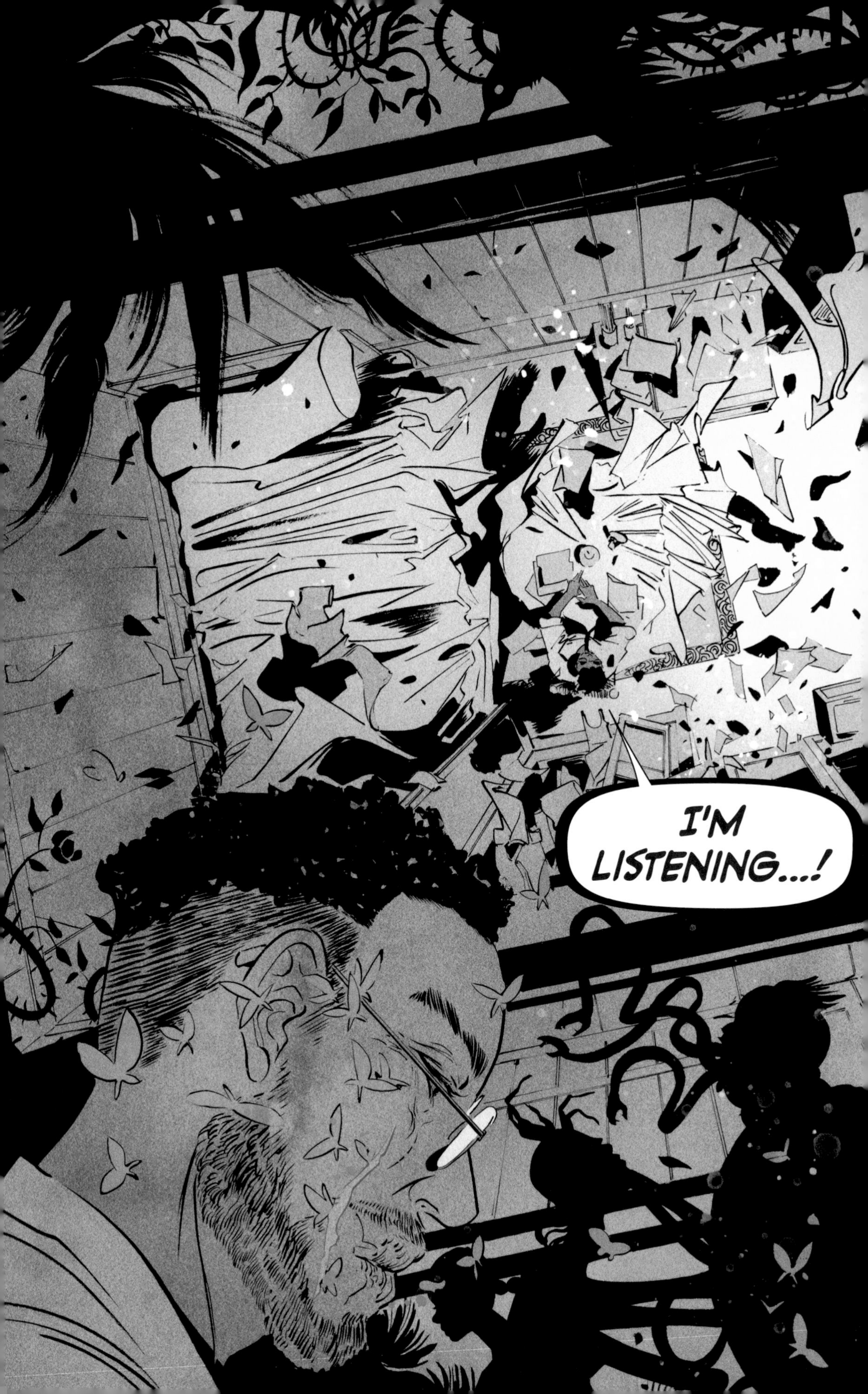
I'M LISTENING...!

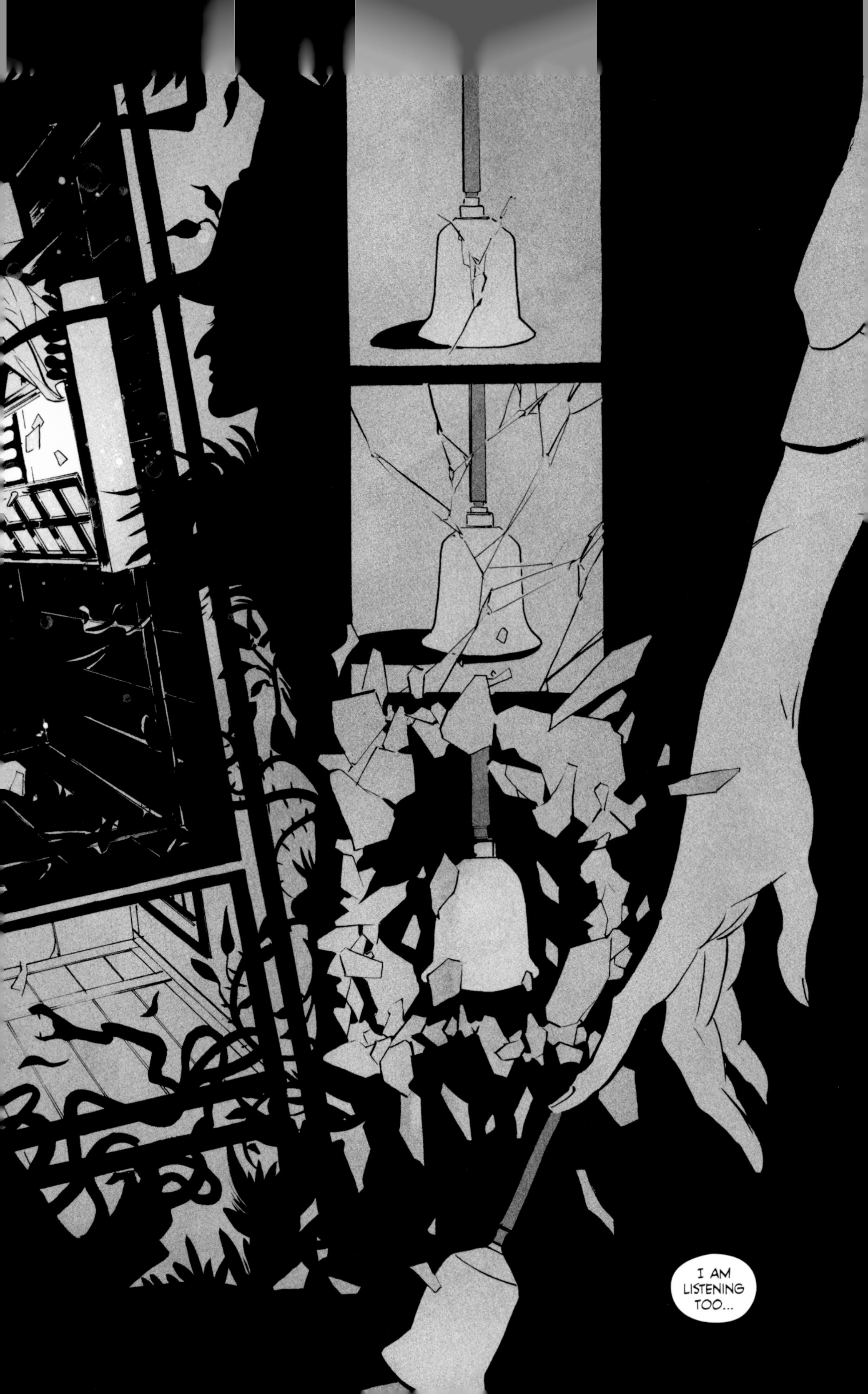
I AM LISTENING TOO...

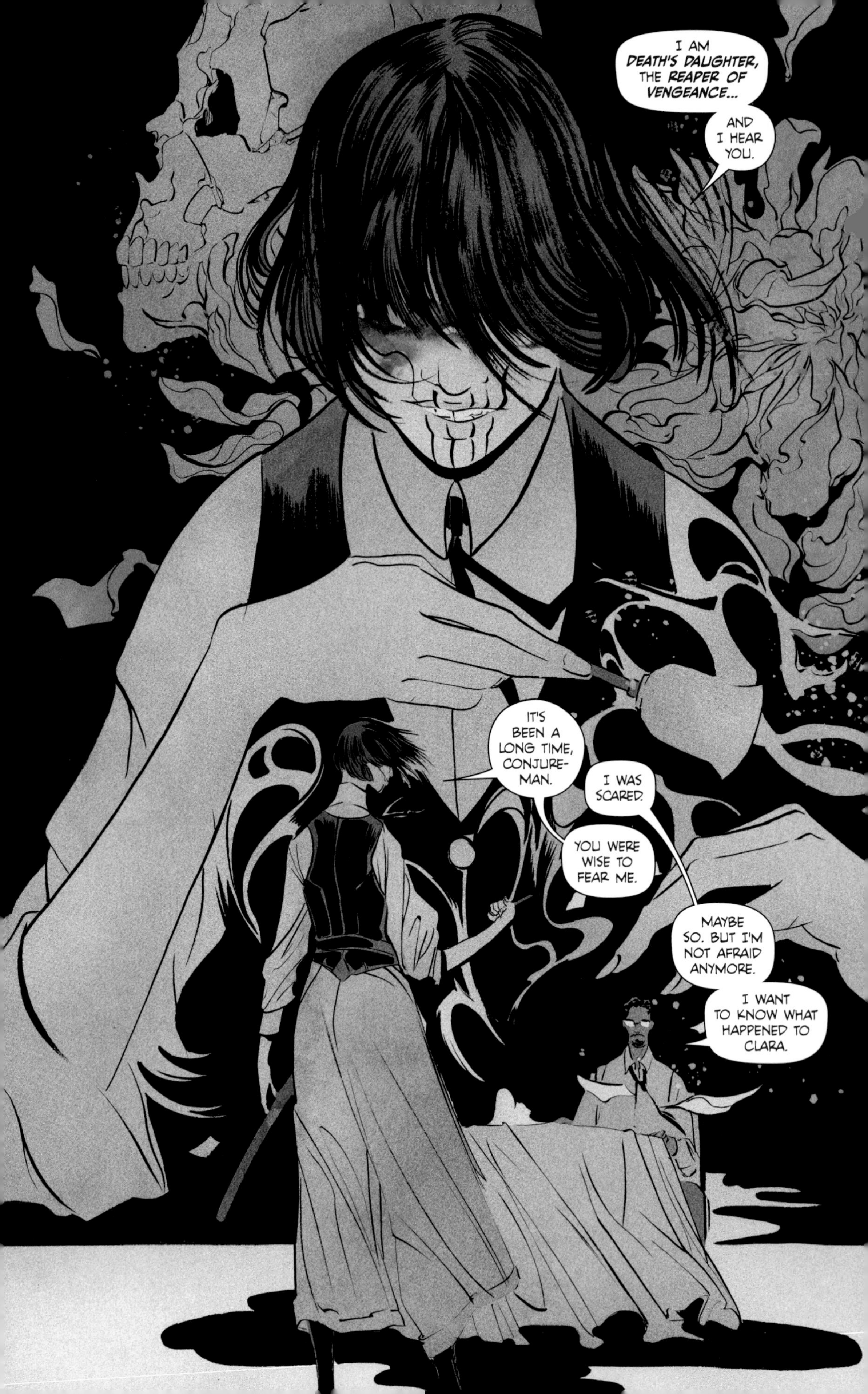
I AM DEATH'S DAUGHTER, THE REAPER OF VENGEANCE...
AND I HEAR YOU.
IT'S BEEN A LONG TIME, CONJURE-MAN.
I WAS SCARED.
YOU WERE WISE TO FEAR ME.
MAYBE SO. BUT I'M NOT AFRAID ANYMORE.
I WANT TO KNOW WHAT HAPPENED TO CLARA.

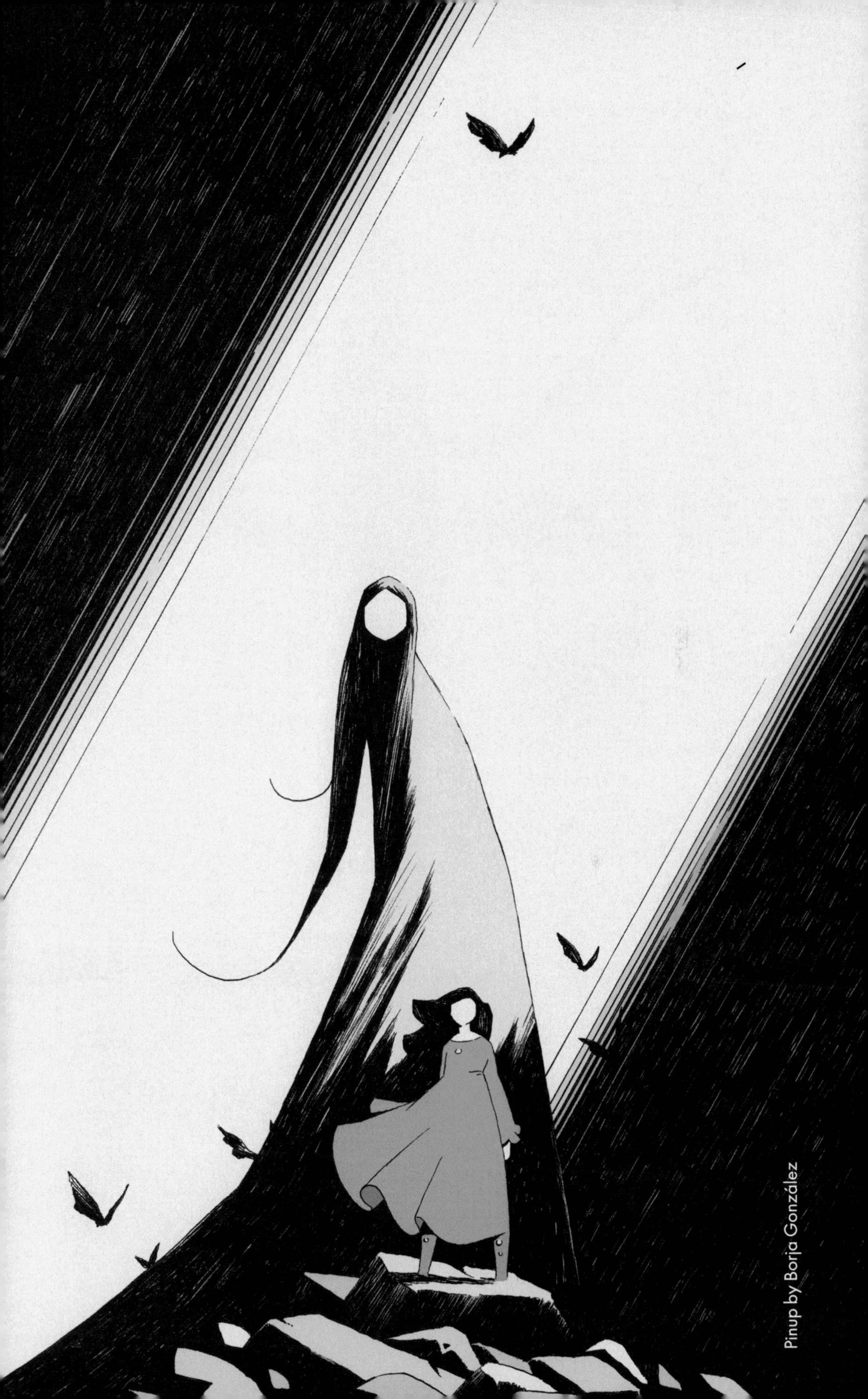
Pinup by Borja González

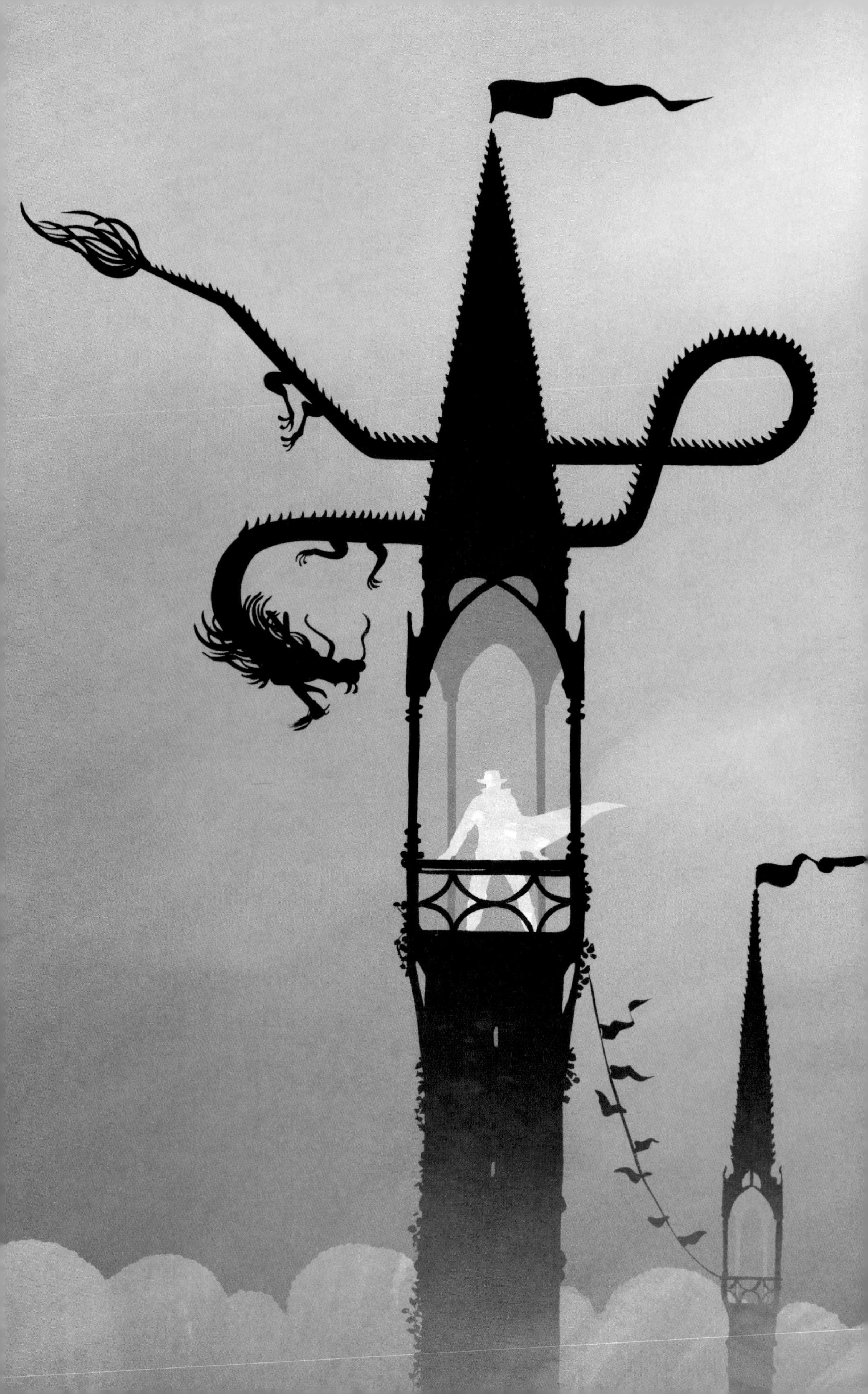

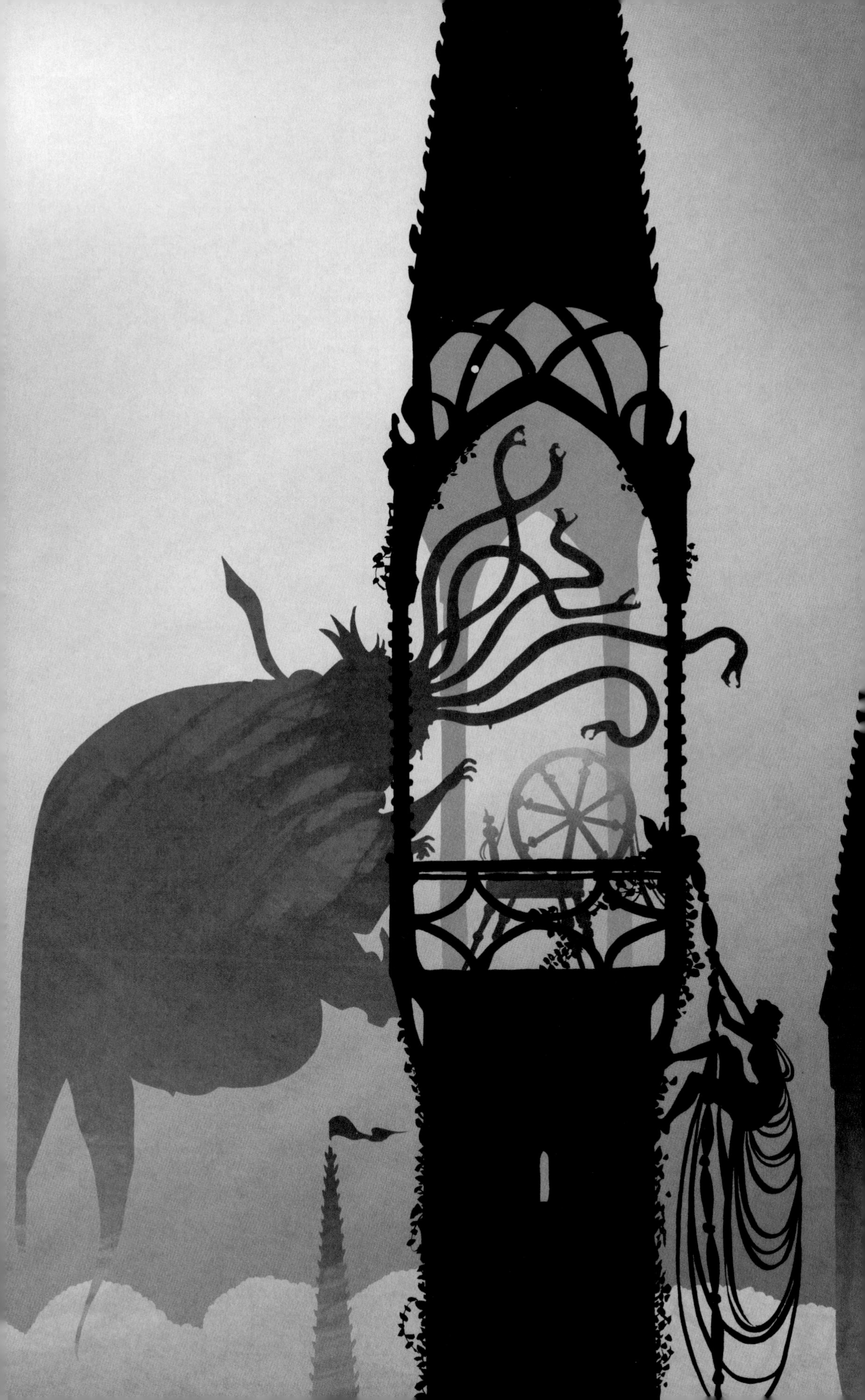

Bones Bunny tells Butterfly the tale.

The Ballad was a history. With Death's daughter Ginny at her side, Sissy, the child of blood and violence raised on love, defeated Old Death in his own domain and took his place in the long-fallow World Garden.

There, her work has only just begun. Having assumed the mantle of Death herself, Sissy must bring the Garden back to life...and seek out the errant Reapers, long left scattered, and return them to the fold.

In the mortal realm, Sarah Fields, mother to many, and the woman who pulled Sissy from the river of blood that bore her, has died...but her children, and their connection to the Reapers, live on. Striking out from their birthplace, Sarah's progeny have found themselves as far-flung as the bloody trenches of France to the arid streets of Hollywoodland.

But tragedy strikes the family. In between the glitz, the glamour, and the bright lights, Clara Fields is found dead. Wrecked with grief, Clara's uncle Frank, the Conjure-Man, sets out to solve the mystery of her death. As he desperately listens for a sign, Ginny, the Reaper of Vengeance, comes calling...

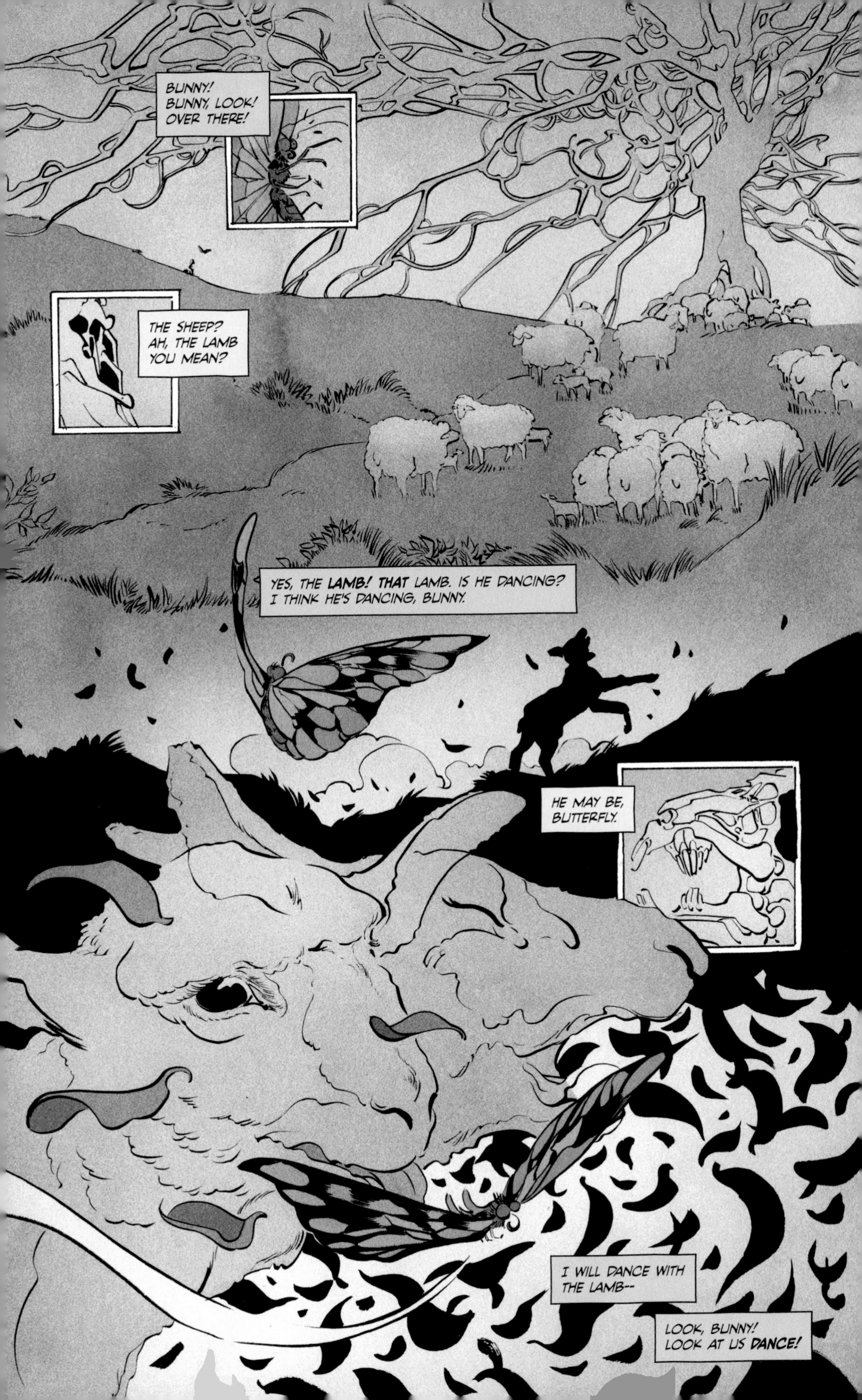
BUNNY! BUNNY, LOOK! OVER THERE!
THE SHEEP? AH, THE LAMB YOU MEAN?
YES, THE LAMB! THAT LAMB. IS HE DANCING? I THINK HE'S DANCING, BUNNY.
HE MAY BE, BUTTERFLY.
I WILL DANCE WITH THE LAMB--
LOOK, BUNNY! LOOK AT US DANCE!

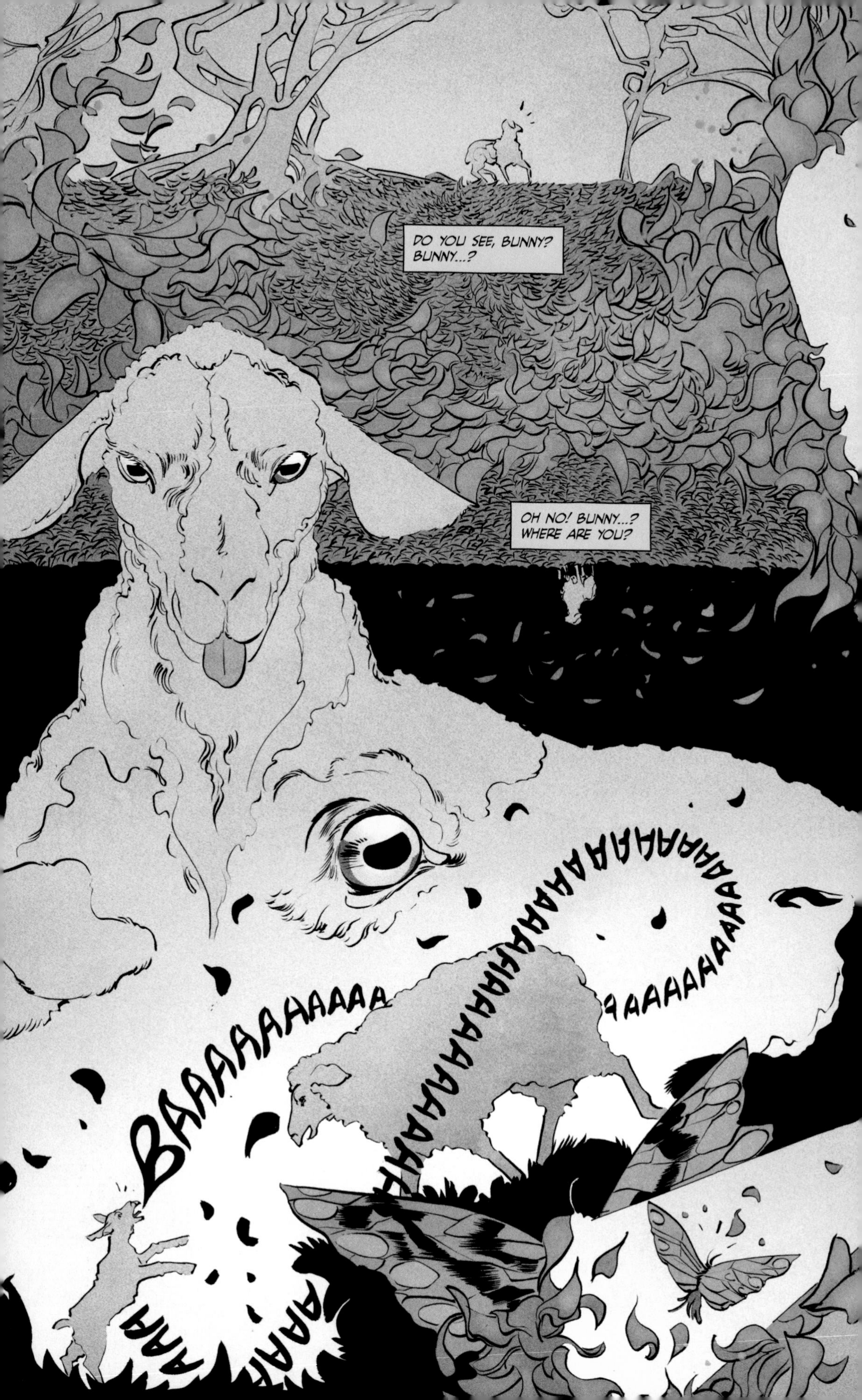

DO YOU SEE, BUNNY? BUNNY...?
OH NO! BUNNY...? WHERE ARE YOU?
BAAAAAAAAAAA

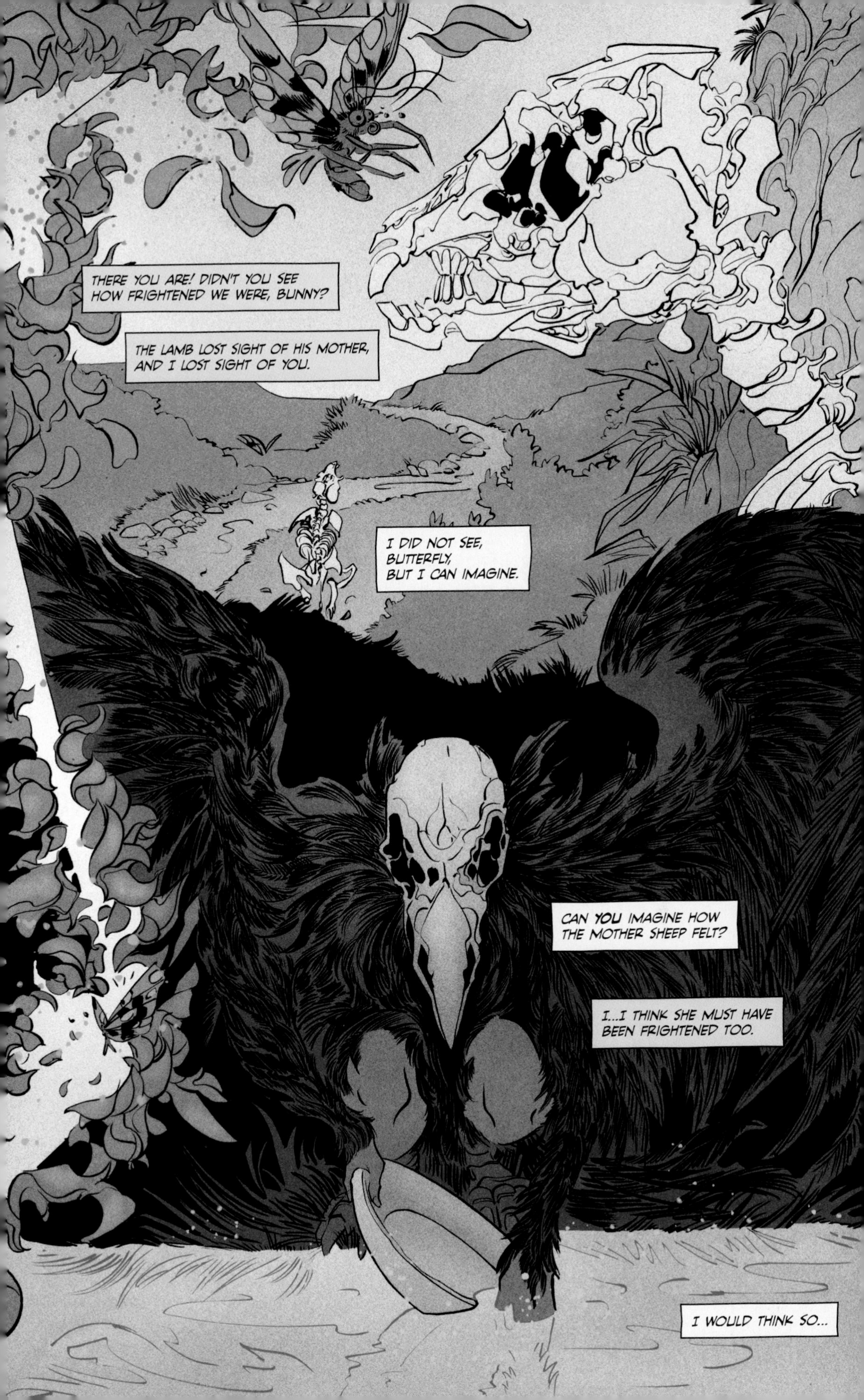
THERE YOU ARE! DIDN'T YOU SEE HOW FRIGHTENED WE WERE, BUNNY?
THE LAMB LOST SIGHT OF HIS MOTHER, AND I LOST SIGHT OF YOU.
I DID NOT SEE, BUTTERFLY, BUT I CAN IMAGINE.
CAN **YOU** IMAGINE HOW THE MOTHER SHEEP FELT?
I...I THINK SHE MUST HAVE BEEN FRIGHTENED TOO.
I WOULD THINK SO...

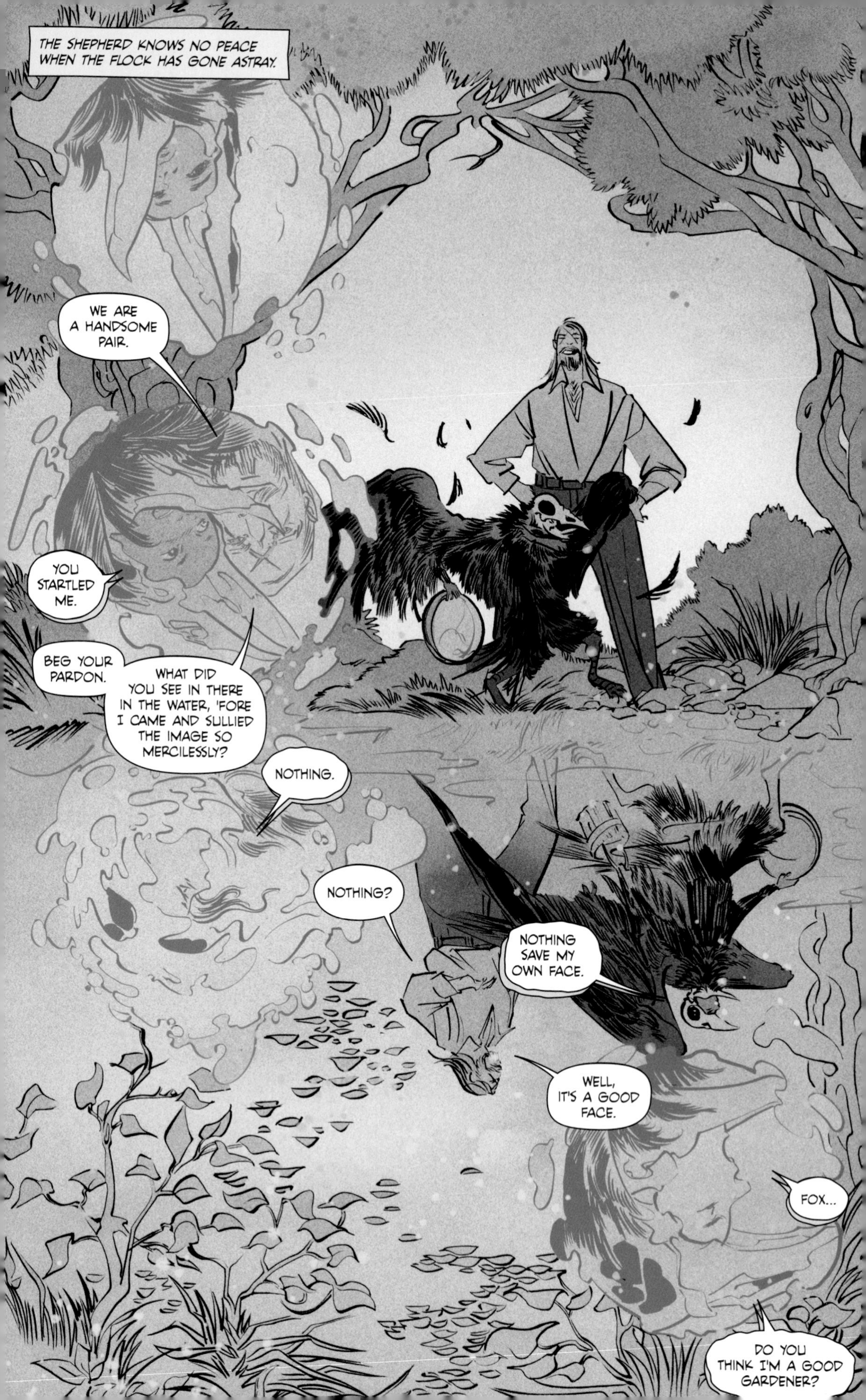
THE SHEPHERD KNOWS NO PEACE WHEN THE FLOCK HAS GONE ASTRAY.
WE ARE A HANDSOME PAIR.
YOU STARTLED ME.
BEG YOUR PARDON.
WHAT DID YOU SEE IN THERE IN THE WATER, 'FORE I CAME AND SULLIED THE IMAGE SO MERCILESSLY?
NOTHING.
NOTHING?
NOTHING SAVE MY OWN FACE.
WELL, IT'S A GOOD FACE.
FOX...
DO YOU THINK I'M A GOOD GARDENER?

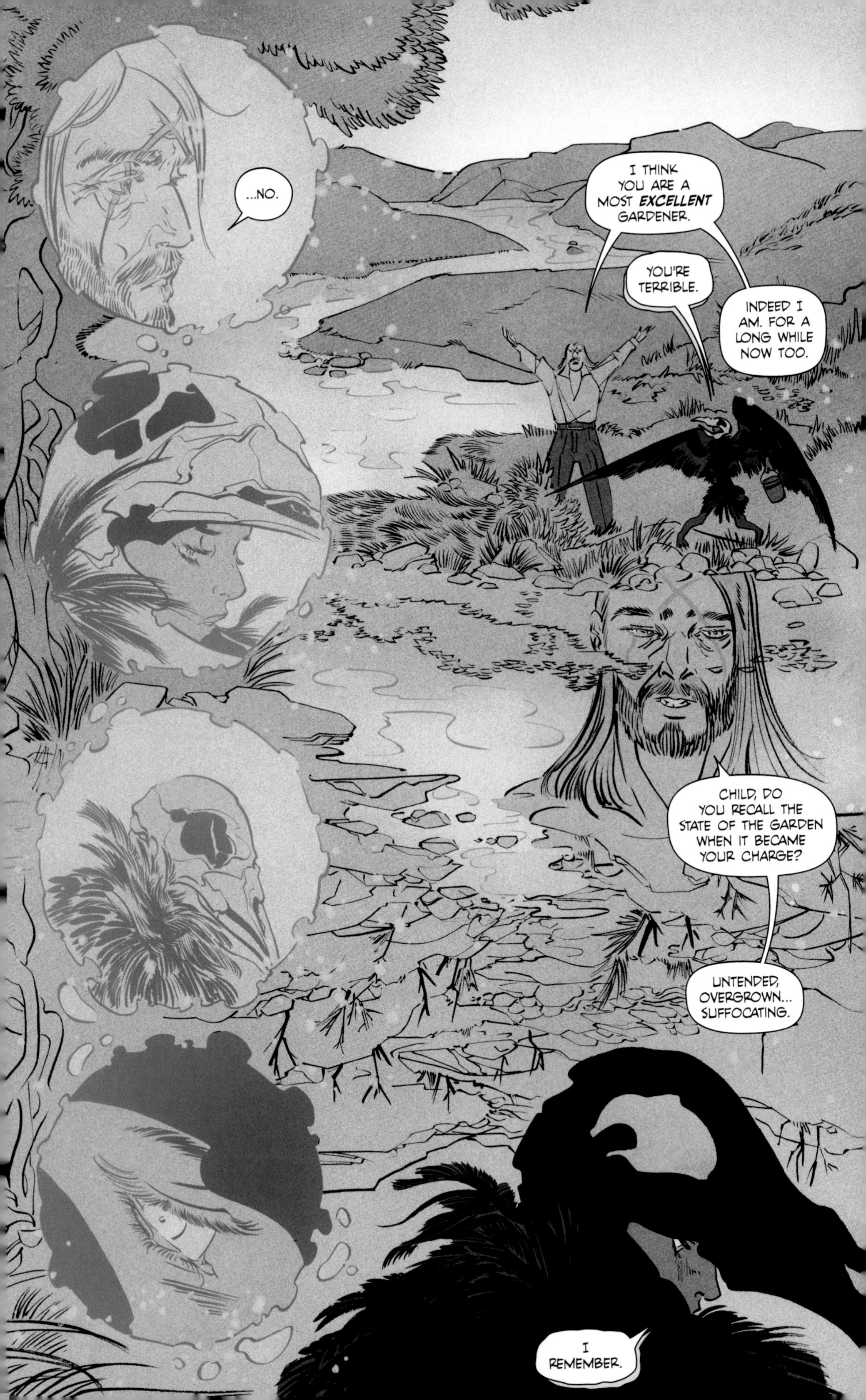
...NO.
I THINK YOU ARE A MOST ***EXCELLENT*** GARDENER.
YOU'RE TERRIBLE.
INDEED I AM. FOR A LONG WHILE NOW TOO.
CHILD, DO YOU RECALL THE STATE OF THE GARDEN WHEN IT BECAME YOUR CHARGE?
UNTENDED, OVERGROWN... SUFFOCATING.
I REMEMBER.

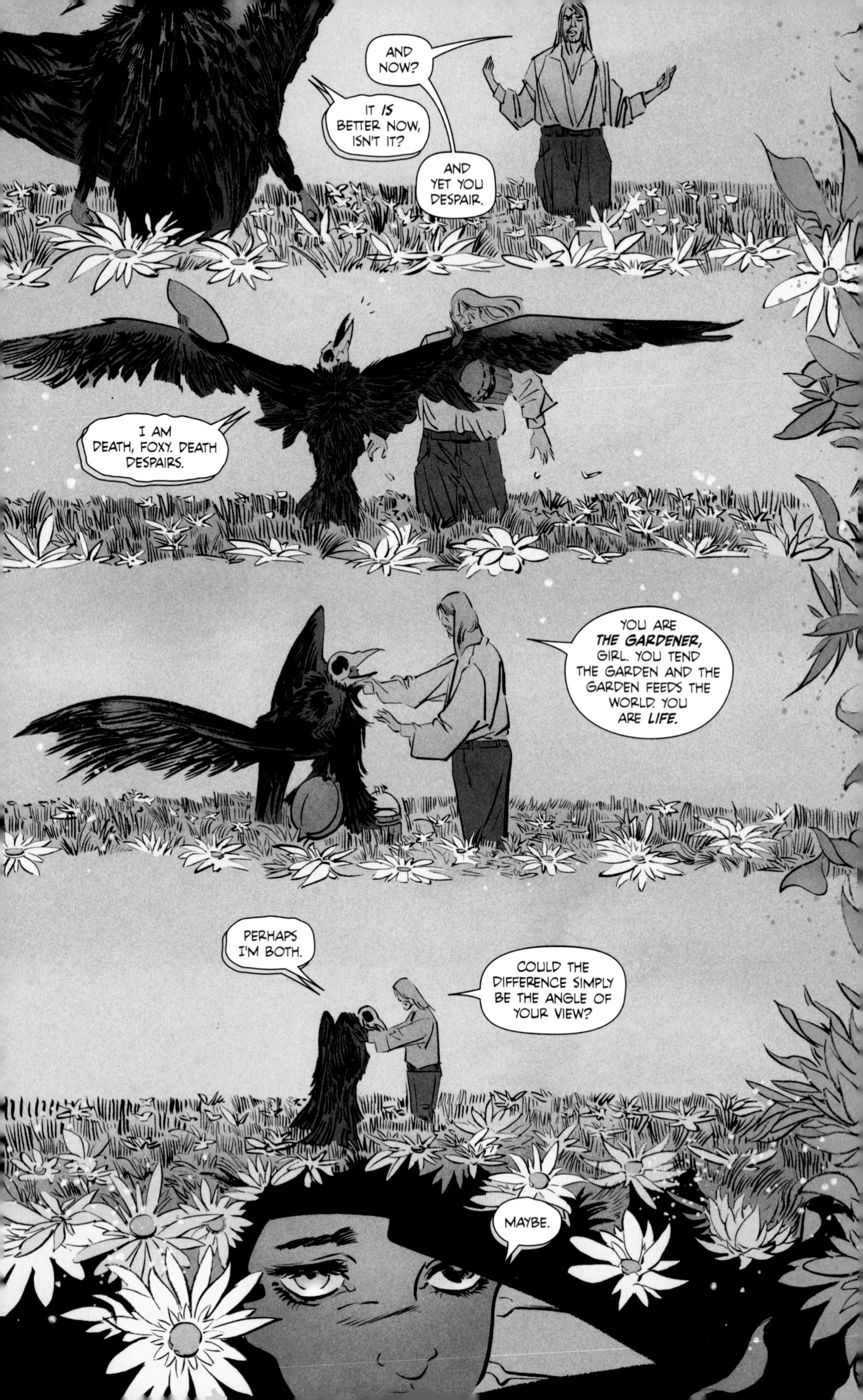
AND NOW?
IT IS BETTER NOW, ISN'T IT?
AND YET YOU DESPAIR.
I AM DEATH, FOXY. DEATH DESPAIRS.
YOU ARE THE GARDENER, GIRL. YOU TEND THE GARDEN AND THE GARDEN FEEDS THE WORLD. YOU ARE LIFE.
PERHAPS I'M BOTH.
COULD THE DIFFERENCE SIMPLY BE THE ANGLE OF YOUR VIEW?
MAYBE.

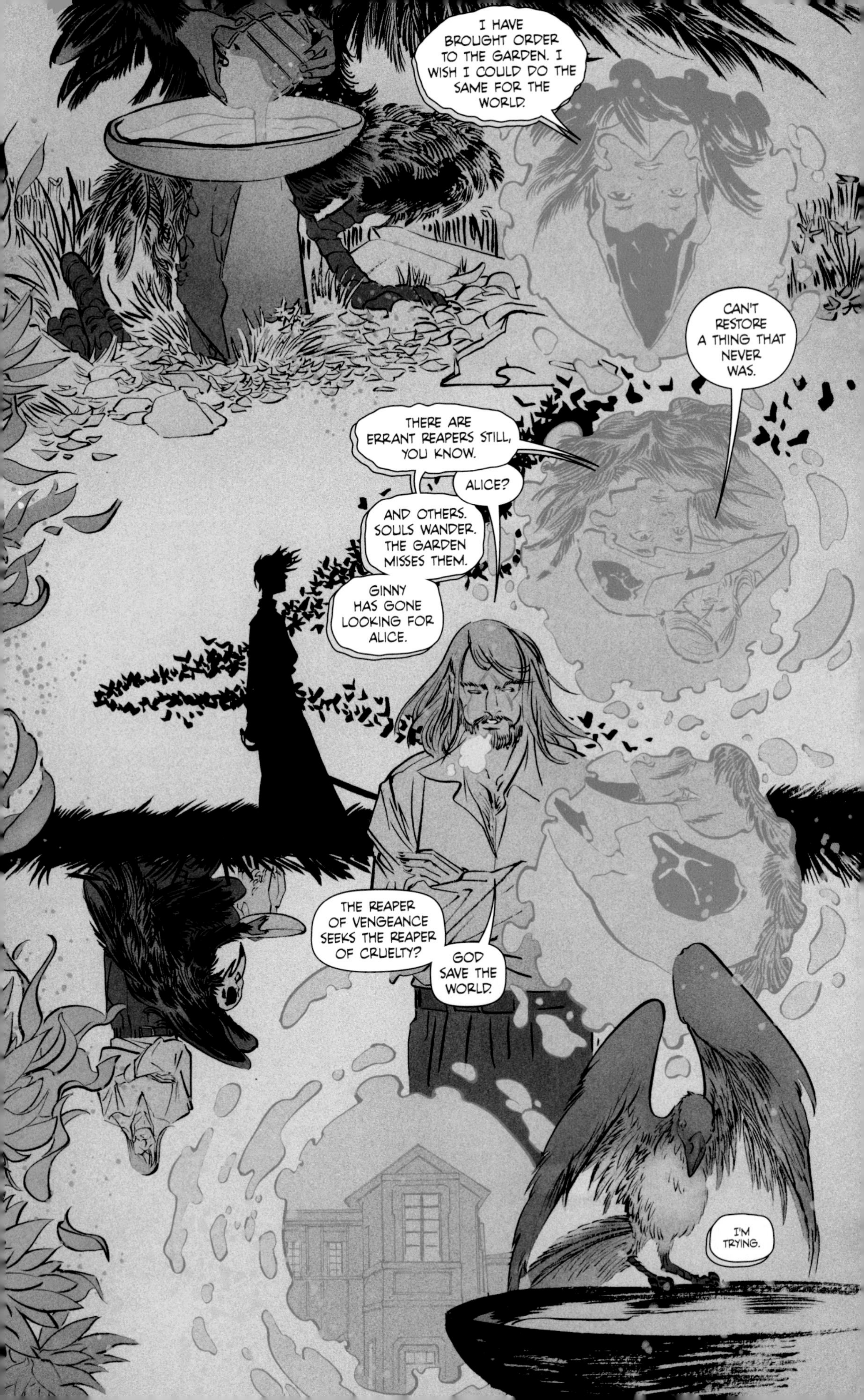
I HAVE BROUGHT ORDER TO THE GARDEN. I WISH I COULD DO THE SAME FOR THE WORLD.
CAN'T RESTORE A THING THAT NEVER WAS.
THERE ARE ERRANT REAPERS STILL, YOU KNOW.
ALICE?
AND OTHERS. SOULS WANDER. THE GARDEN MISSES THEM.
GINNY HAS GONE LOOKING FOR ALICE.
THE REAPER OF VENGEANCE SEEKS THE REAPER OF CRUELTY?
GOD SAVE THE WORLD.
I'M TRYING.

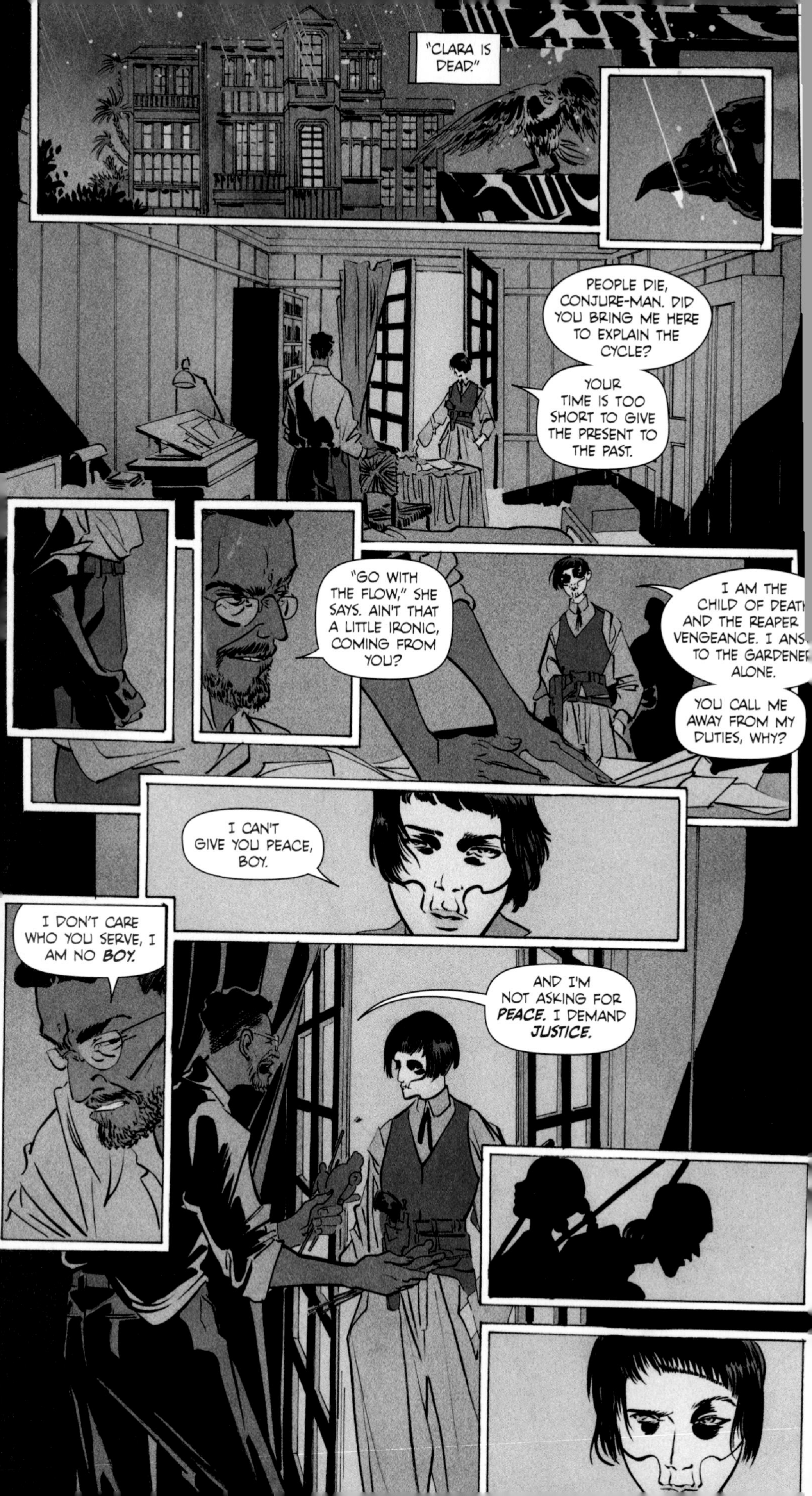
"CLARA IS DEAD."
PEOPLE DIE, CONJURE-MAN. DID YOU BRING ME HERE TO EXPLAIN THE CYCLE?
YOUR TIME IS TOO SHORT TO GIVE THE PRESENT TO THE PAST.
"GO WITH THE FLOW," SHE SAYS. AIN'T THAT A LITTLE IRONIC, COMING FROM YOU?
I AM THE CHILD OF DEAT AND THE REAPER VENGEANCE. I ANS TO THE GARDENE ALONE.
YOU CALL ME AWAY FROM MY DUTIES, WHY?
I CAN'T GIVE YOU PEACE, BOY.
I DON'T CARE WHO YOU SERVE, I AM NO *BOY.*
AND I'M NOT ASKING FOR *PEACE.* I DEMAND *JUSTICE.*

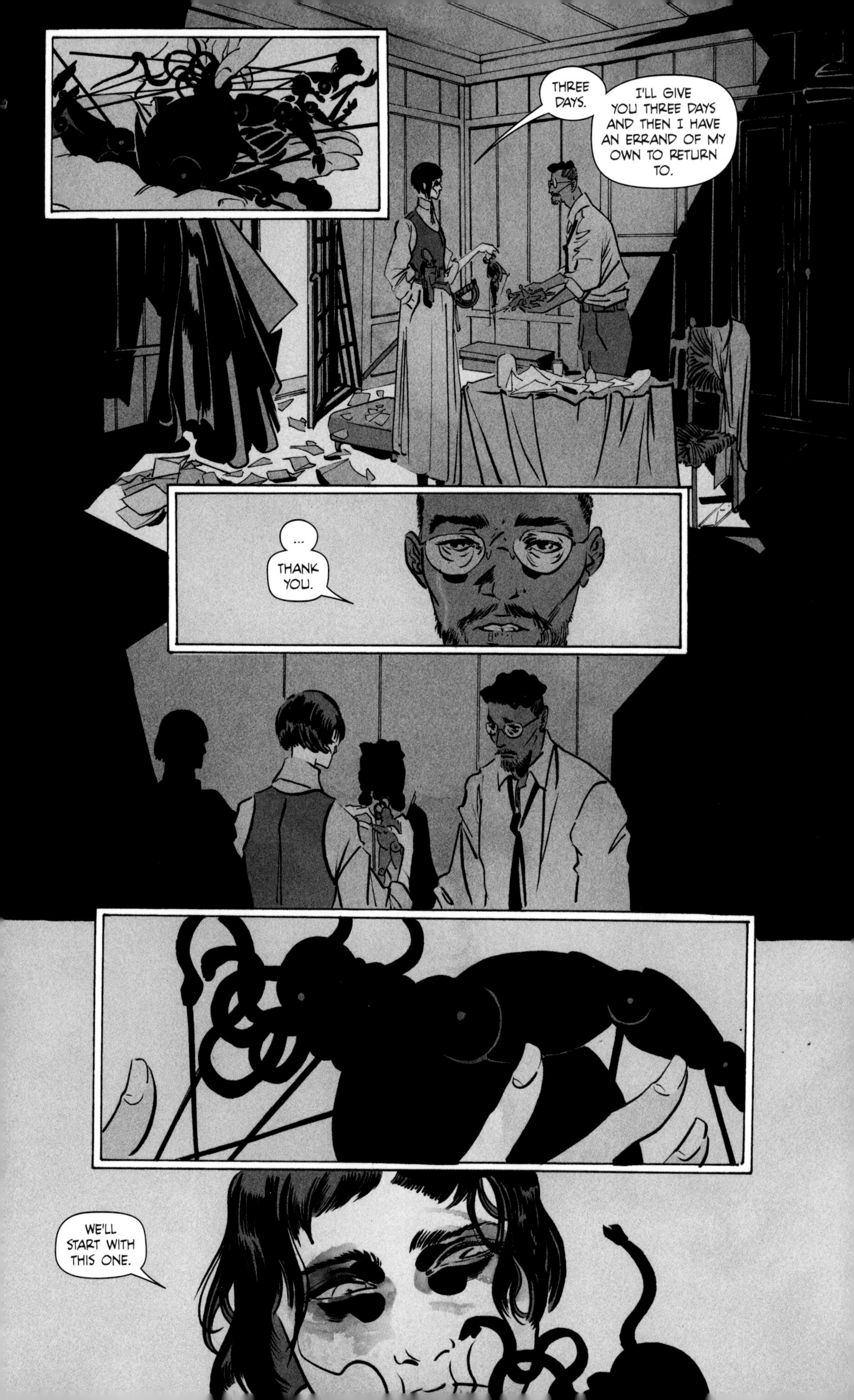
THREE DAYS.
I'LL GIVE YOU THREE DAYS AND THEN I HAVE AN ERRAND OF MY OWN TO RETURN TO.
...
THANK YOU.
WE'LL START WITH THIS ONE.

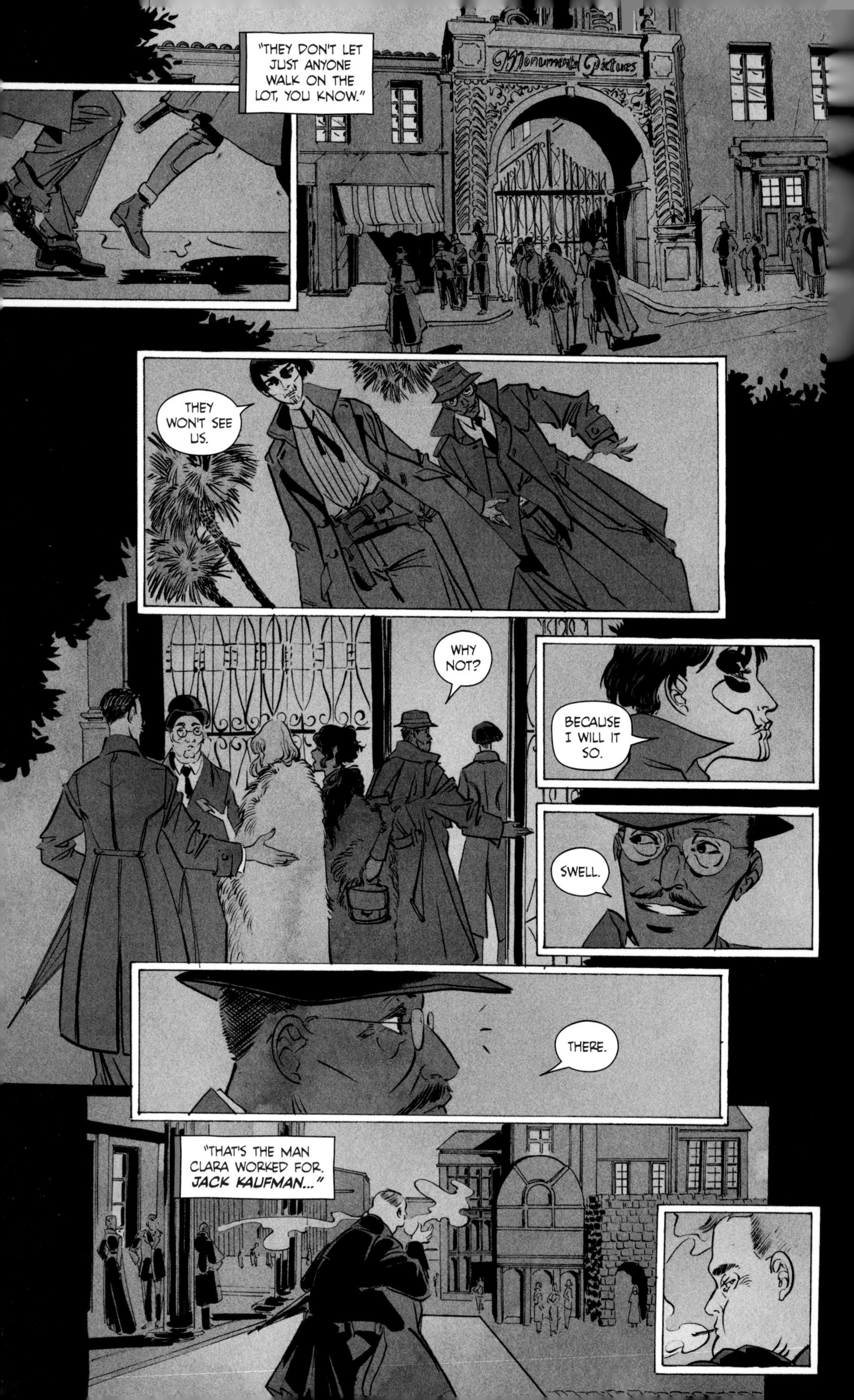
Monumental Pictures
"THEY DON'T LET JUST ANYONE WALK ON THE LOT, YOU KNOW."
THEY WON'T SEE US.
WHY NOT?
BECAUSE I WILL IT SO.
SWELL.
THERE.
"THAT'S THE MAN CLARA WORKED FOR. JACK KAUFMAN..."

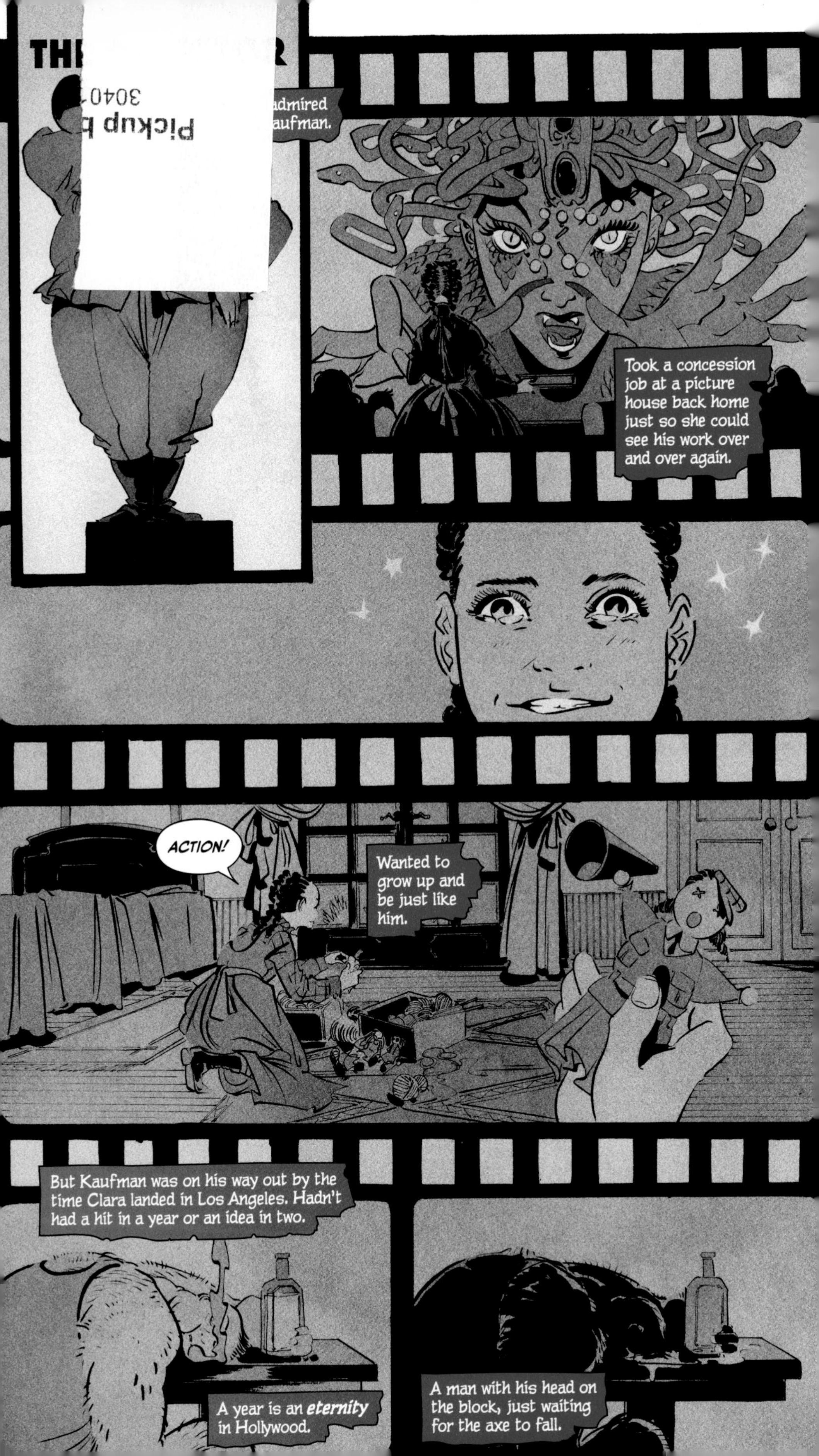
admired
aufman.
Took a concession job at a picture house back home just so she could see his work over and over again.
ACTION!
Wanted to grow up and be just like him.
But Kaufman was on his way out by the time Clara landed in Los Angeles. Hadn't had a hit in a year or an idea in two.
A year is an *eternity* in Hollywood.
A man with his head on the block, just waiting for the axe to fall.

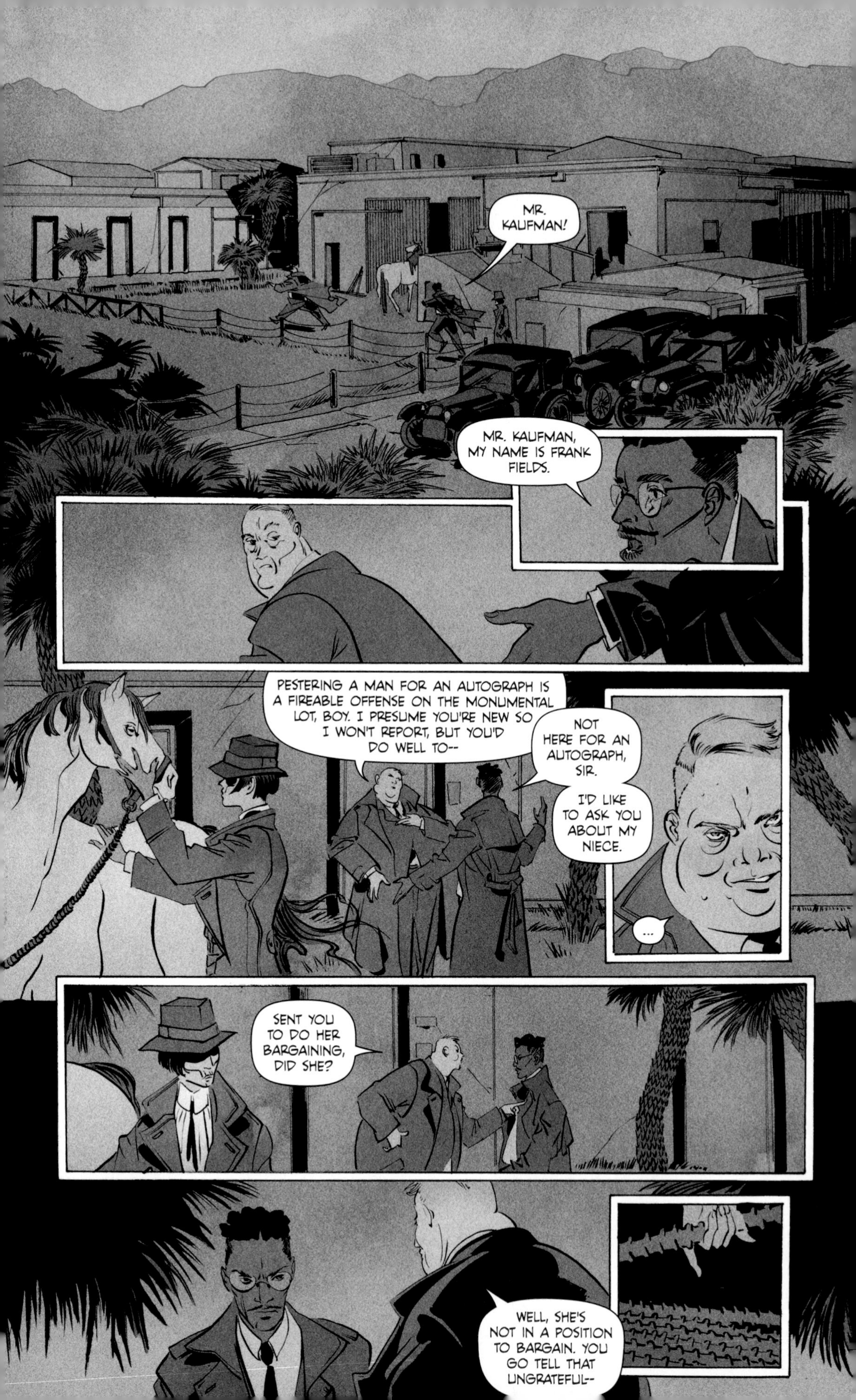
MR. KAUFMAN!
MR. KAUFMAN, MY NAME IS FRANK FIELDS.
PESTERING A MAN FOR AN AUTOGRAPH IS A FIREABLE OFFENSE ON THE MONUMENTAL LOT, BOY. I PRESUME YOU'RE NEW SO I WON'T REPORT, BUT YOU'D DO WELL TO--
NOT HERE FOR AN AUTOGRAPH, SIR.
I'D LIKE TO ASK YOU ABOUT MY NIECE.
...
SENT YOU TO DO HER BARGAINING, DID SHE?
WELL, SHE'S NOT IN A POSITION TO BARGAIN. YOU GO TELL THAT UNGRATEFUL--

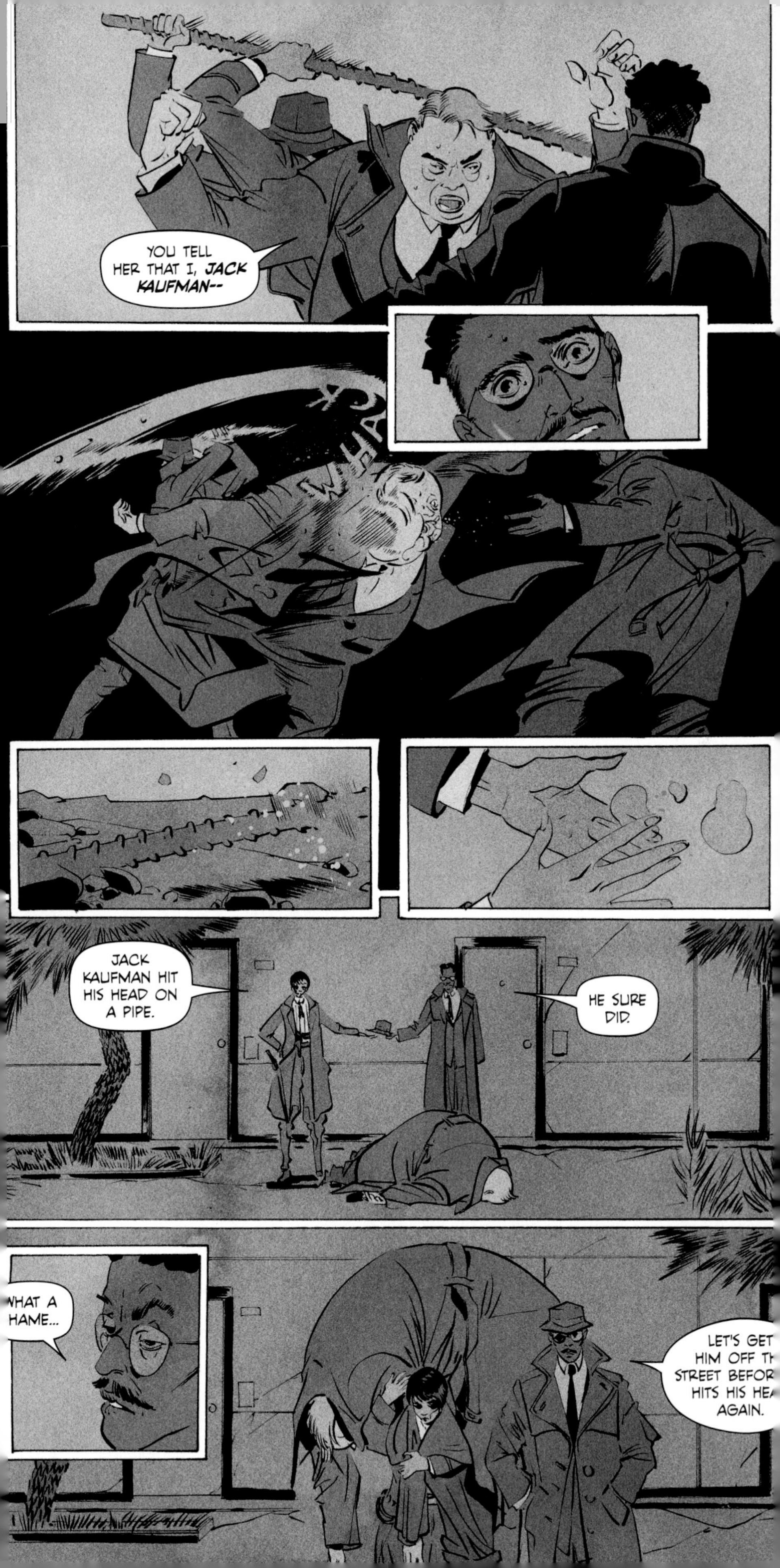
YOU TELL HER THAT I, JACK KAUFMAN--
JACK KAUFMAN HIT HIS HEAD ON A PIPE.
HE SURE DID.
WHAT A HAME...
LET'S GET HIM OFF T STREET BEFOR HITS HIS HE AGAIN.

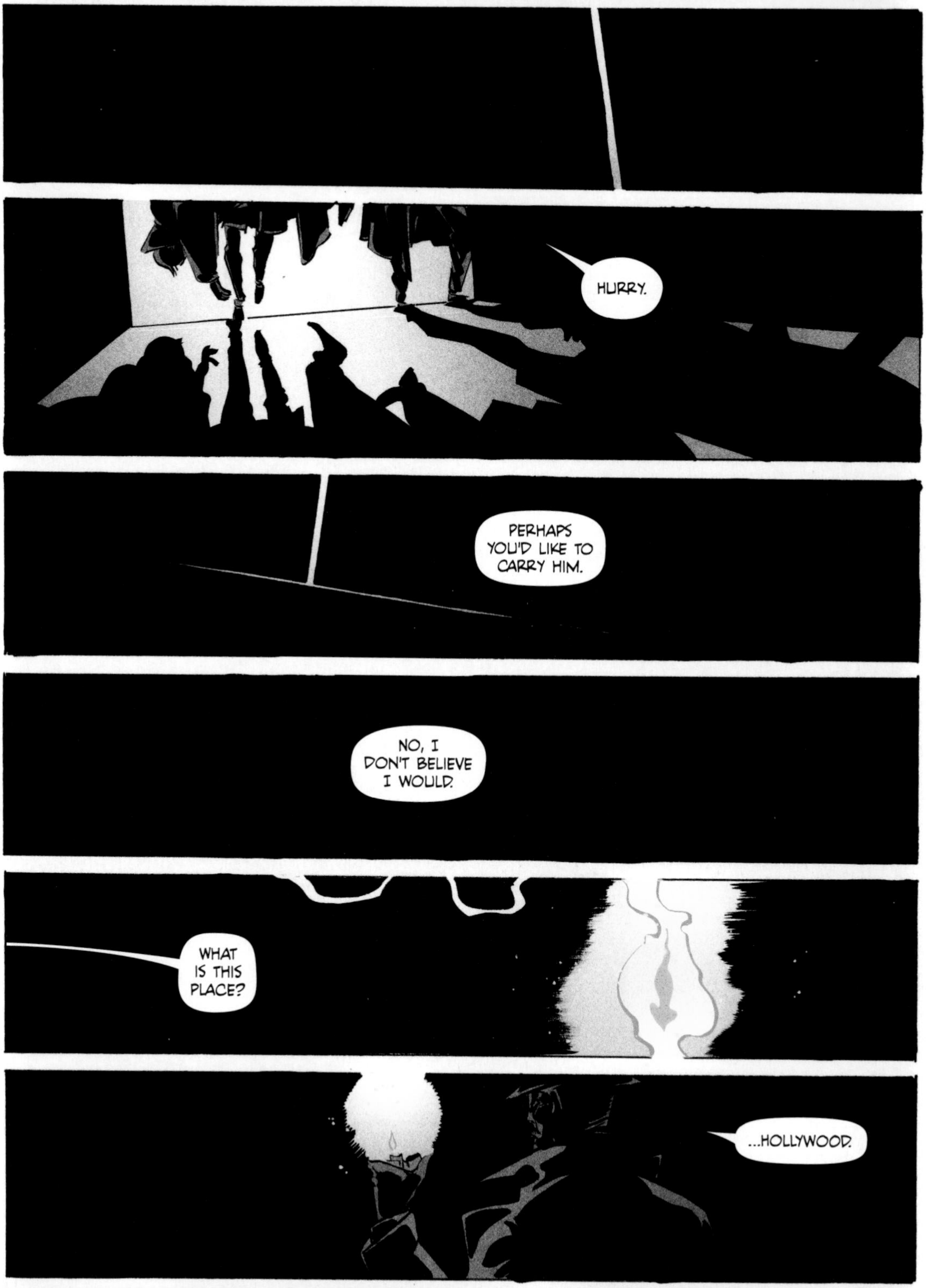
HURRY.
PERHAPS YOU'D LIKE TO CARRY HIM.
NO, I DON'T BELIEVE I WOULD.
WHAT IS THIS PLACE?
...HOLLYWOOD.

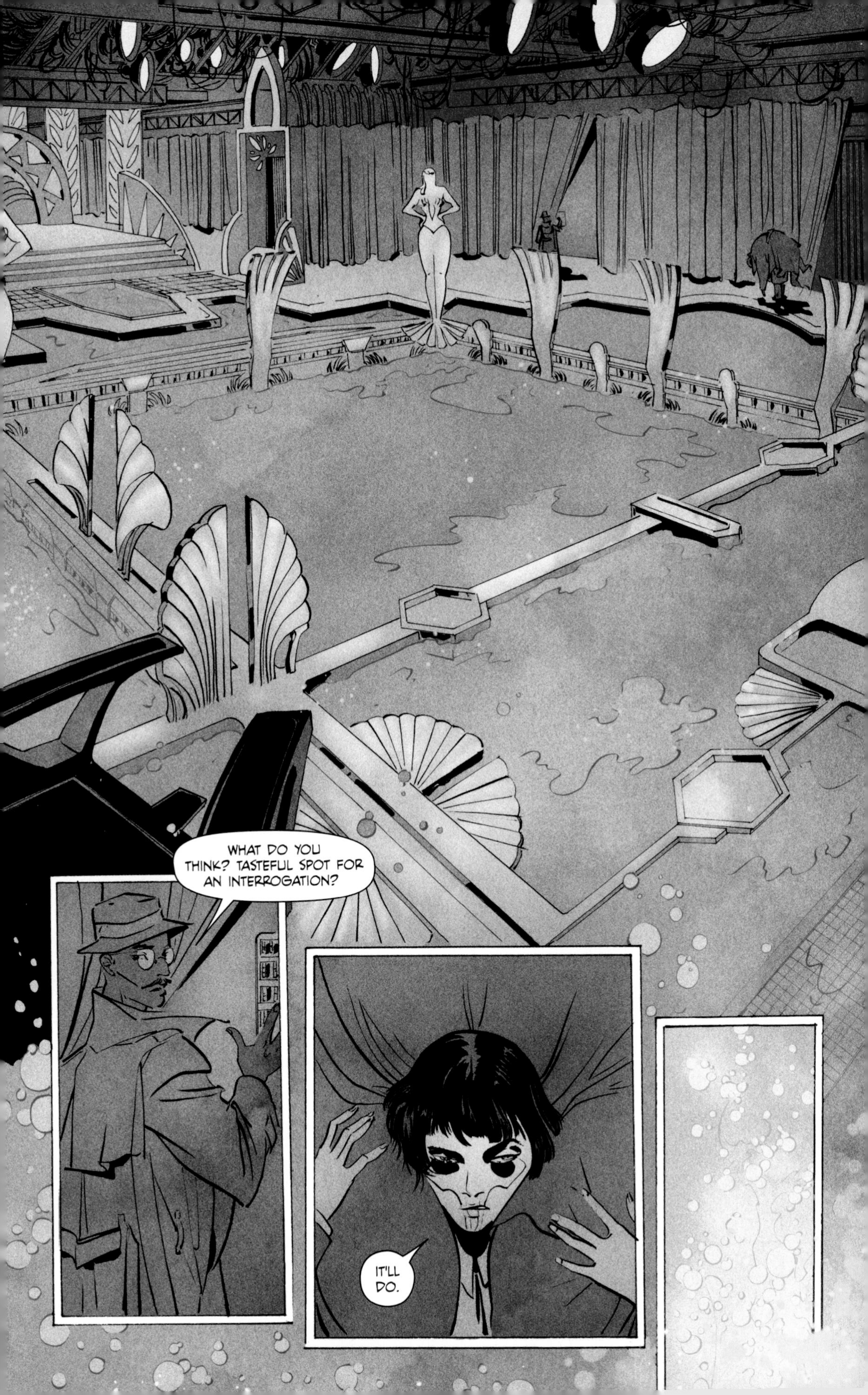
WHAT DO YOU THINK? TASTEFUL SPOT FOR AN INTERROGATION?
IT'LL DO.

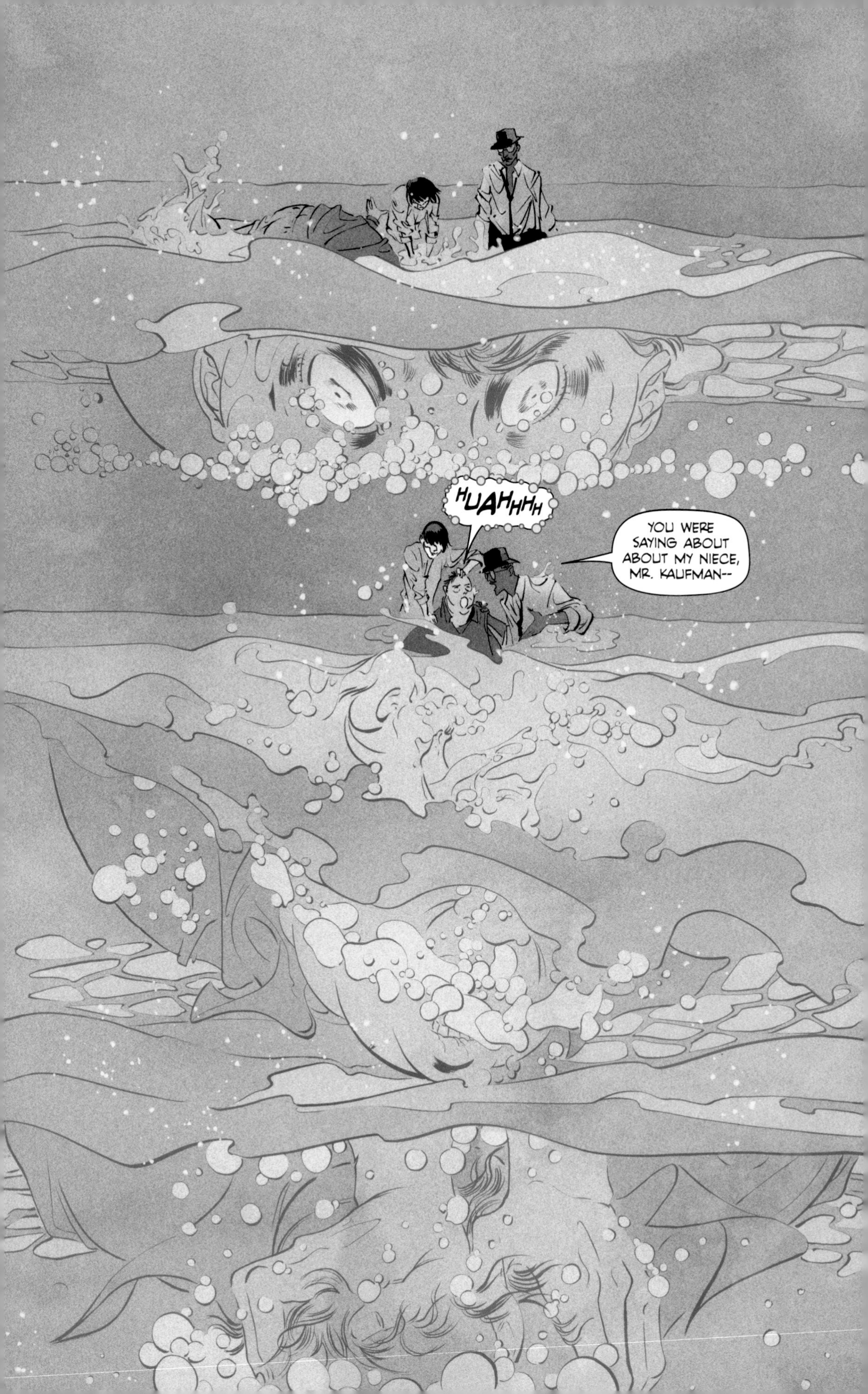
HUAHHHH
YOU WERE SAYING ABOUT ABOUT MY NIECE, MR. KAUFMAN--

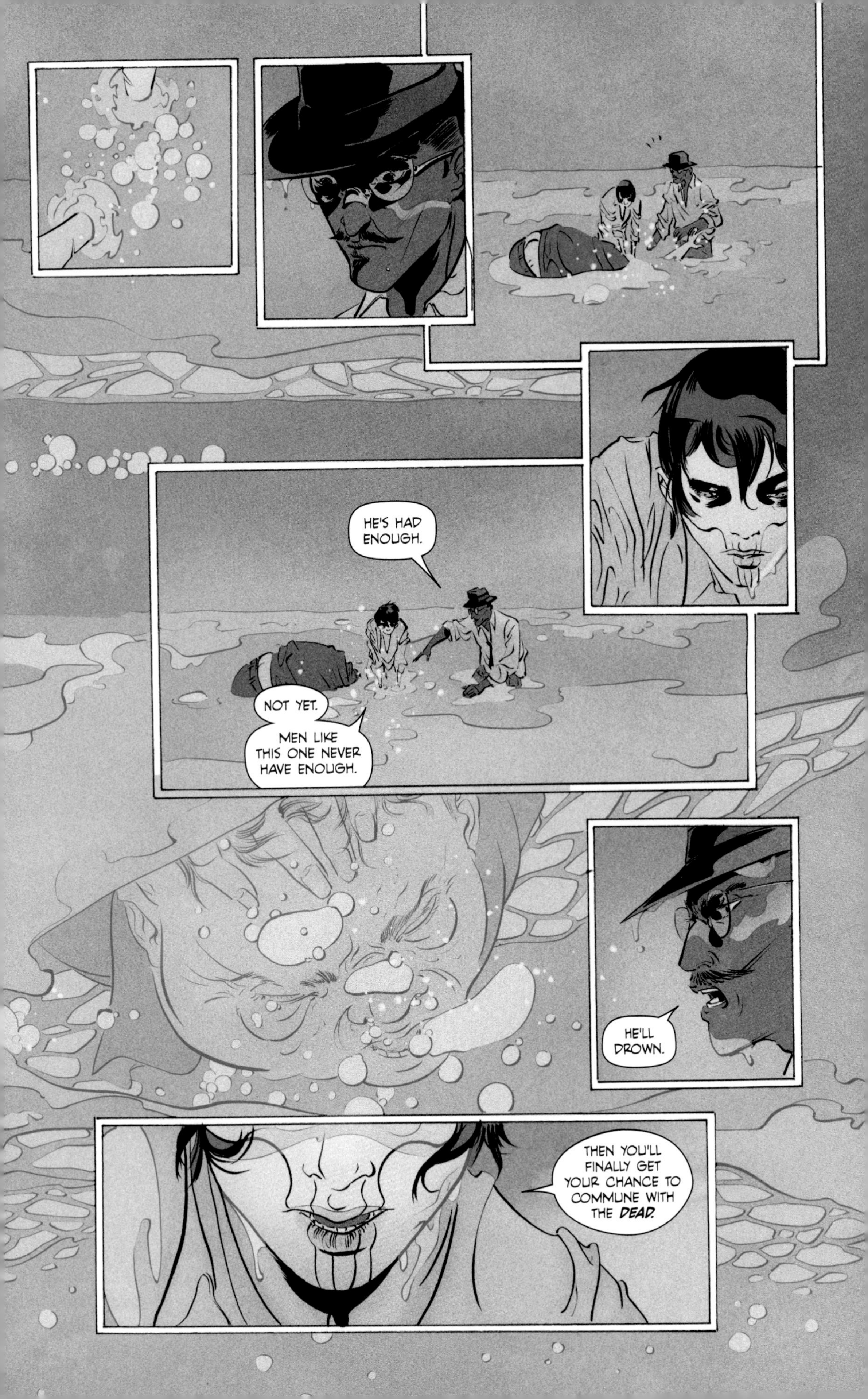
HE'S HAD ENOUGH.
NOT YET.
MEN LIKE THIS ONE NEVER HAVE ENOUGH.
HE'LL DROWN.
THEN YOU'LL FINALLY GET YOUR CHANCE TO COMMUNE WITH THE *DEAD.*

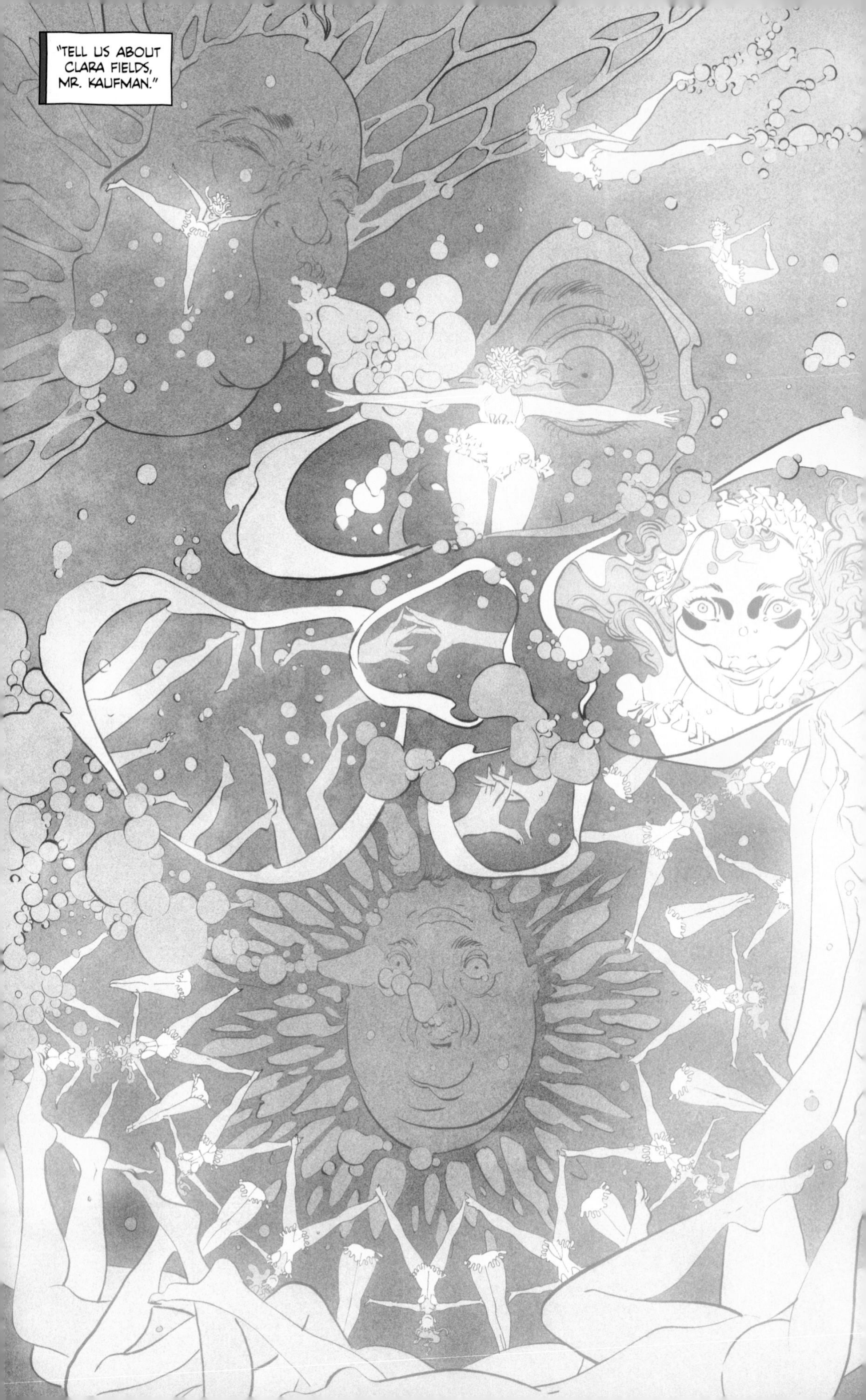
"TELL US ABOUT CLARA FIELDS, MR. KAUFMAN."

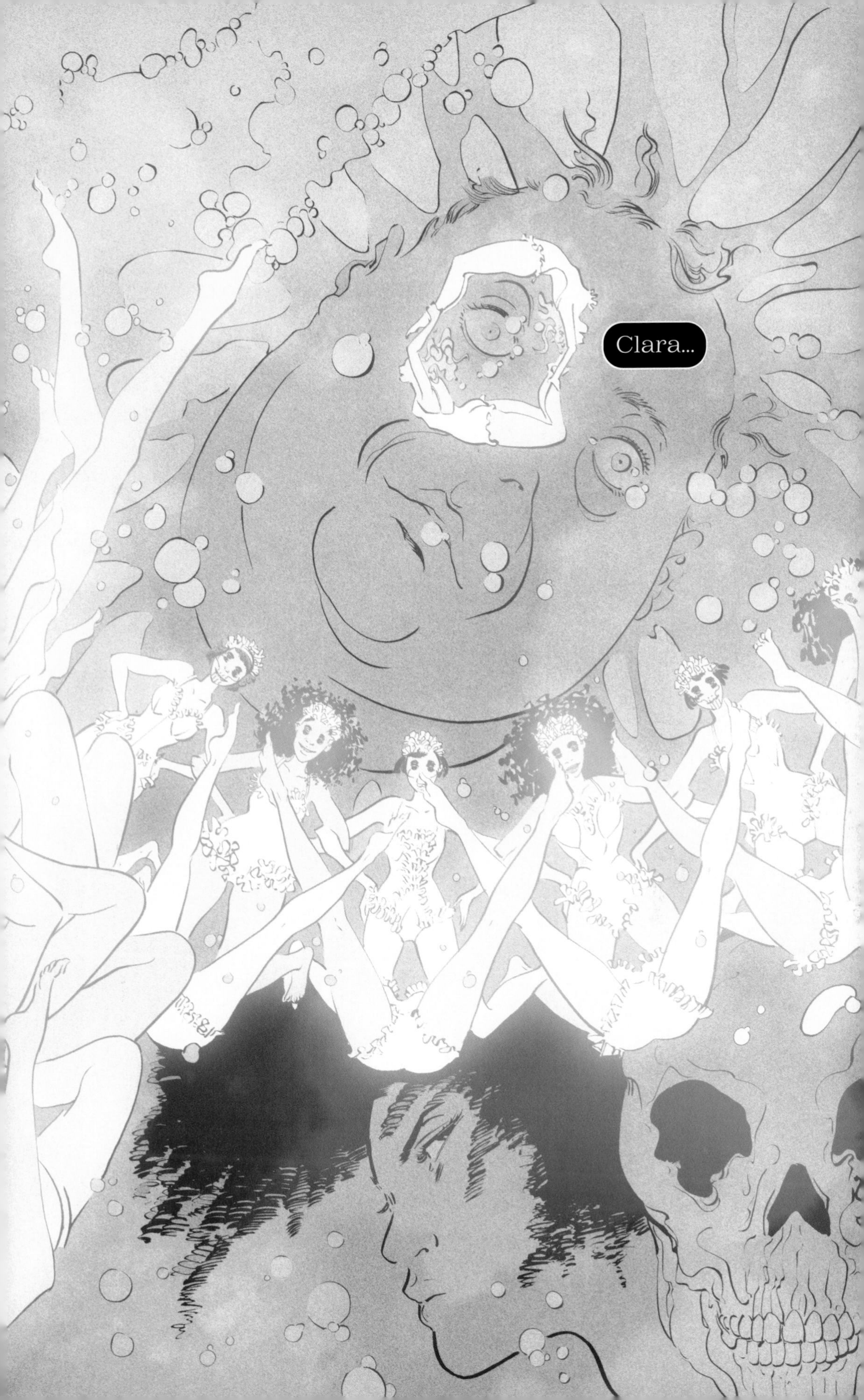
Clara...

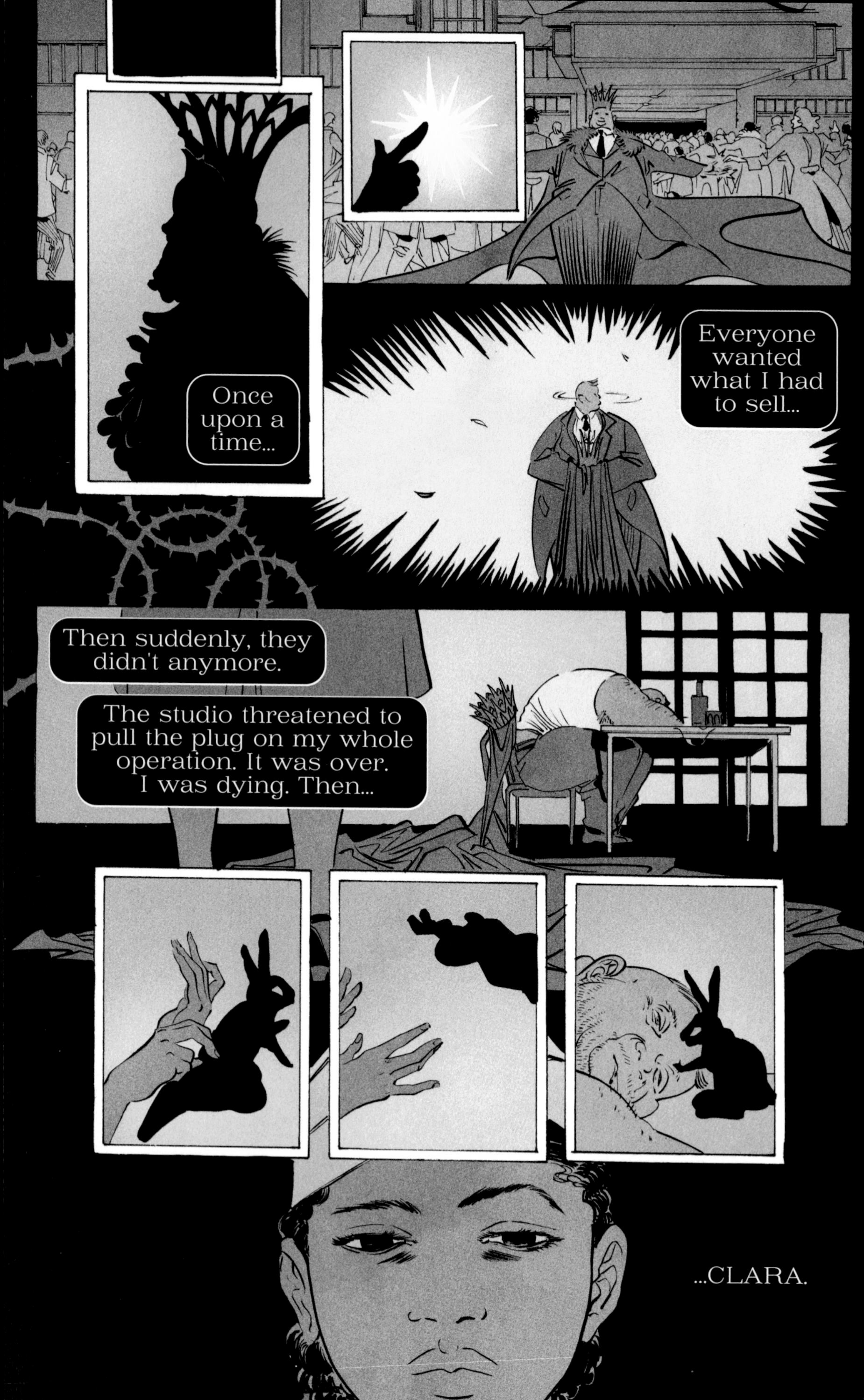
Once upon a time...
Everyone wanted what I had to sell...
Then suddenly, they didn't anymore.
The studio threatened to pull the plug on my whole operation. It was over. I was dying. Then...
...CLARA.

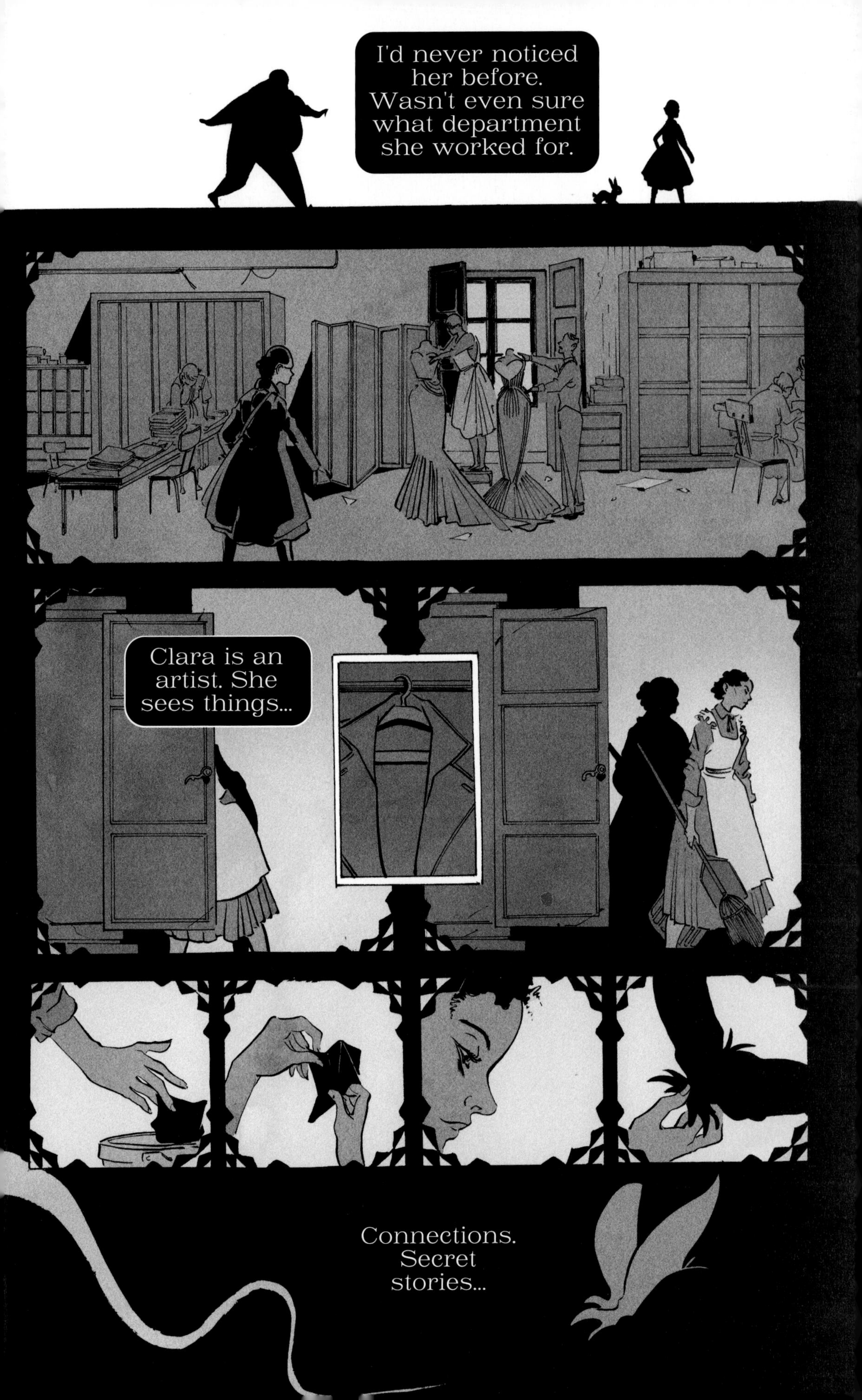
I'd never noticed her before. Wasn't even sure what department she worked for.
Clara is an artist. She sees things...
Connections. Secret stories...

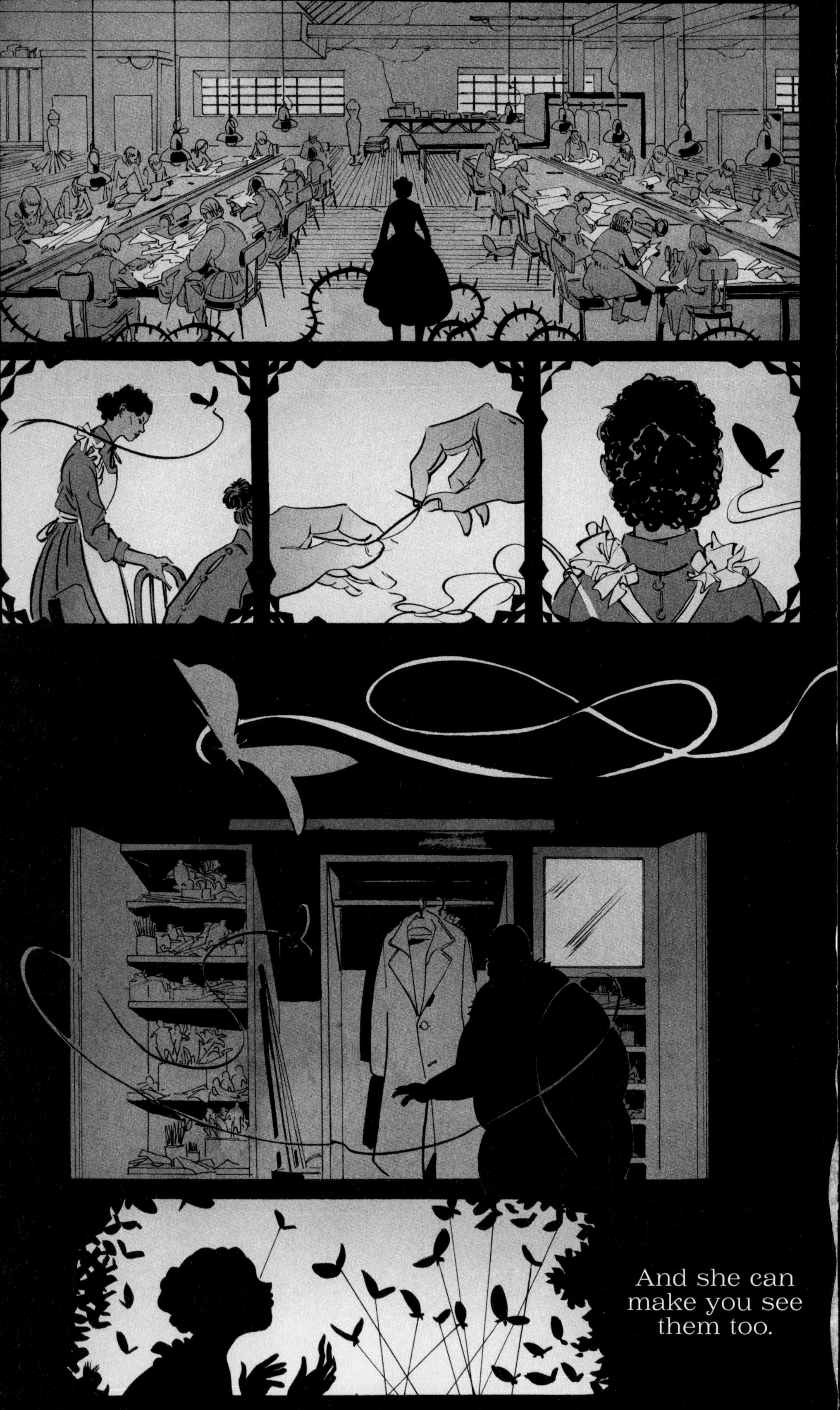
And she can make you see them too.

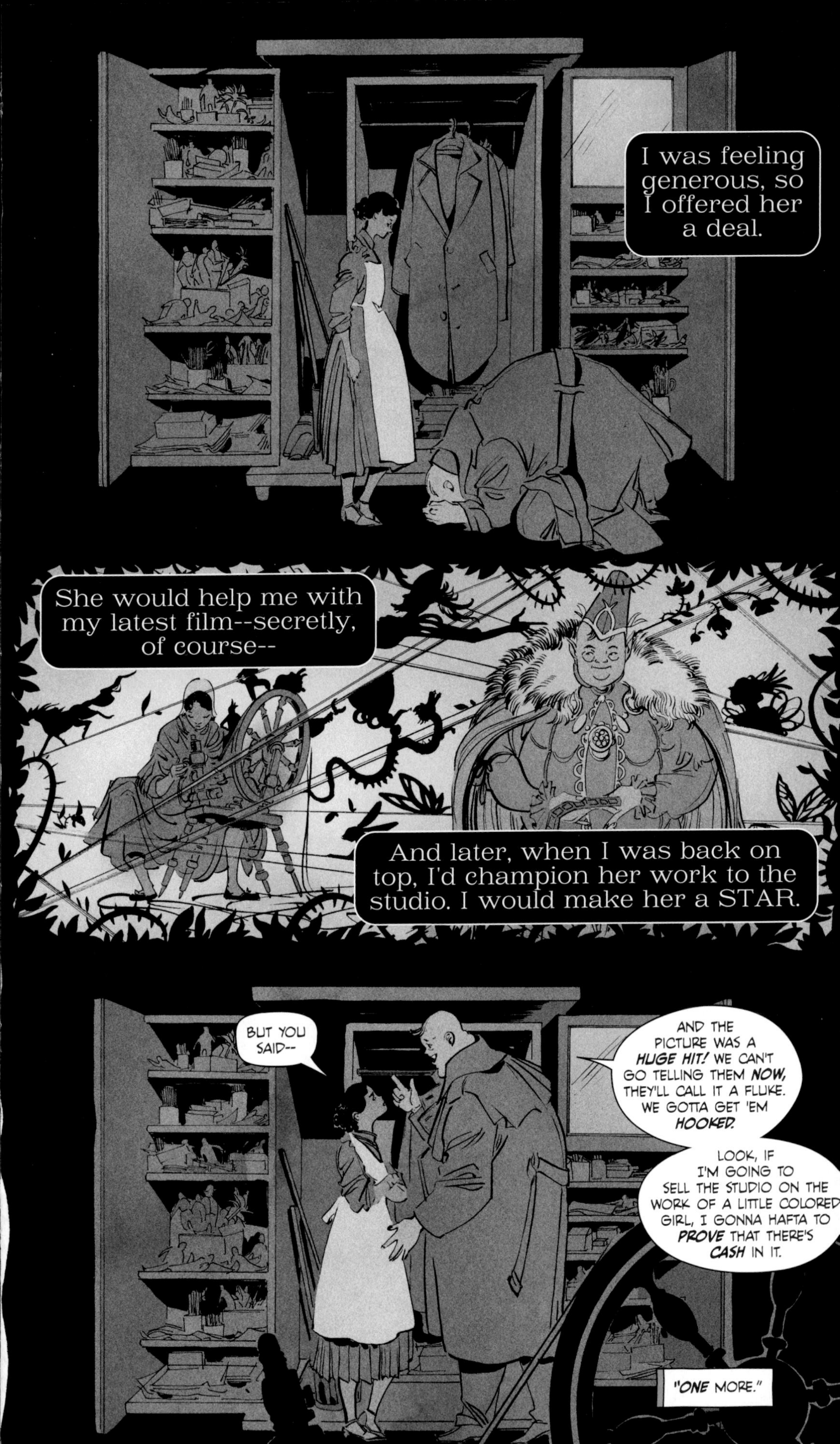
I was feeling generous, so I offered her a deal.
She would help me with my latest film--secretly, of course--
And later, when I was back on top, I'd champion her work to the studio. I would make her a STAR.
BUT YOU SAID--
AND THE PICTURE WAS A HUGE HIT! WE CAN'T GO TELLING THEM NOW, THEY'LL CALL IT A FLUKE. WE GOTTA GET 'EM HOOKED.
LOOK, IF I'M GOING TO SELL THE STUDIO ON THE WORK OF A LITTLE COLORED GIRL, I GONNA HAFTA TO PROVE THAT THERE'S CASH IN IT.
"ONE MORE."

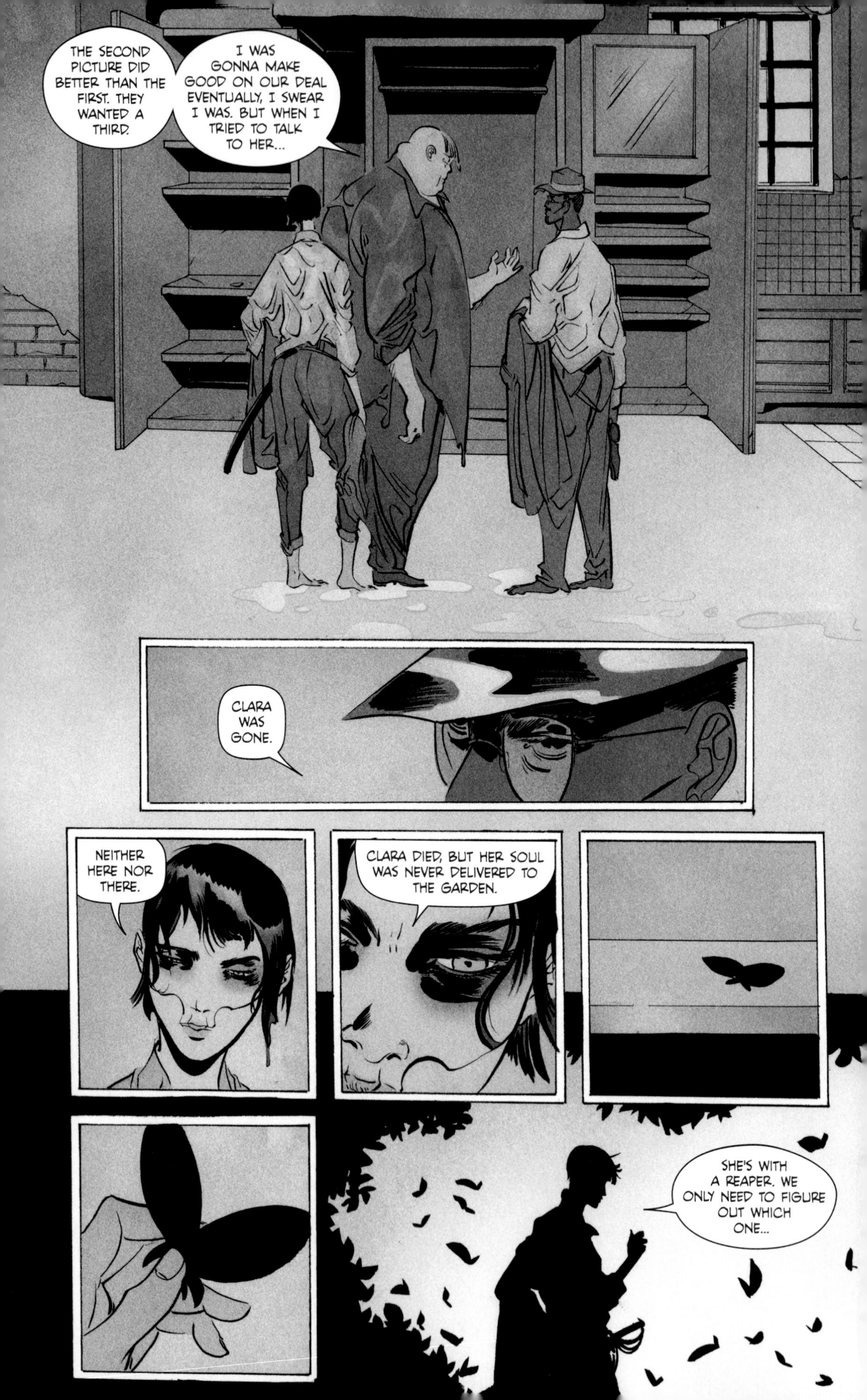
THE SECOND PICTURE DID BETTER THAN THE FIRST. THEY WANTED A THIRD.
I WAS GONNA MAKE GOOD ON OUR DEAL EVENTUALLY, I SWEAR I WAS. BUT WHEN I TRIED TO TALK TO HER...
CLARA WAS GONE.
NEITHER HERE NOR THERE.
CLARA DIED, BUT HER SOUL WAS NEVER DELIVERED TO THE GARDEN.
SHE'S WITH A REAPER. WE ONLY NEED TO FIGURE OUT WHICH ONE...

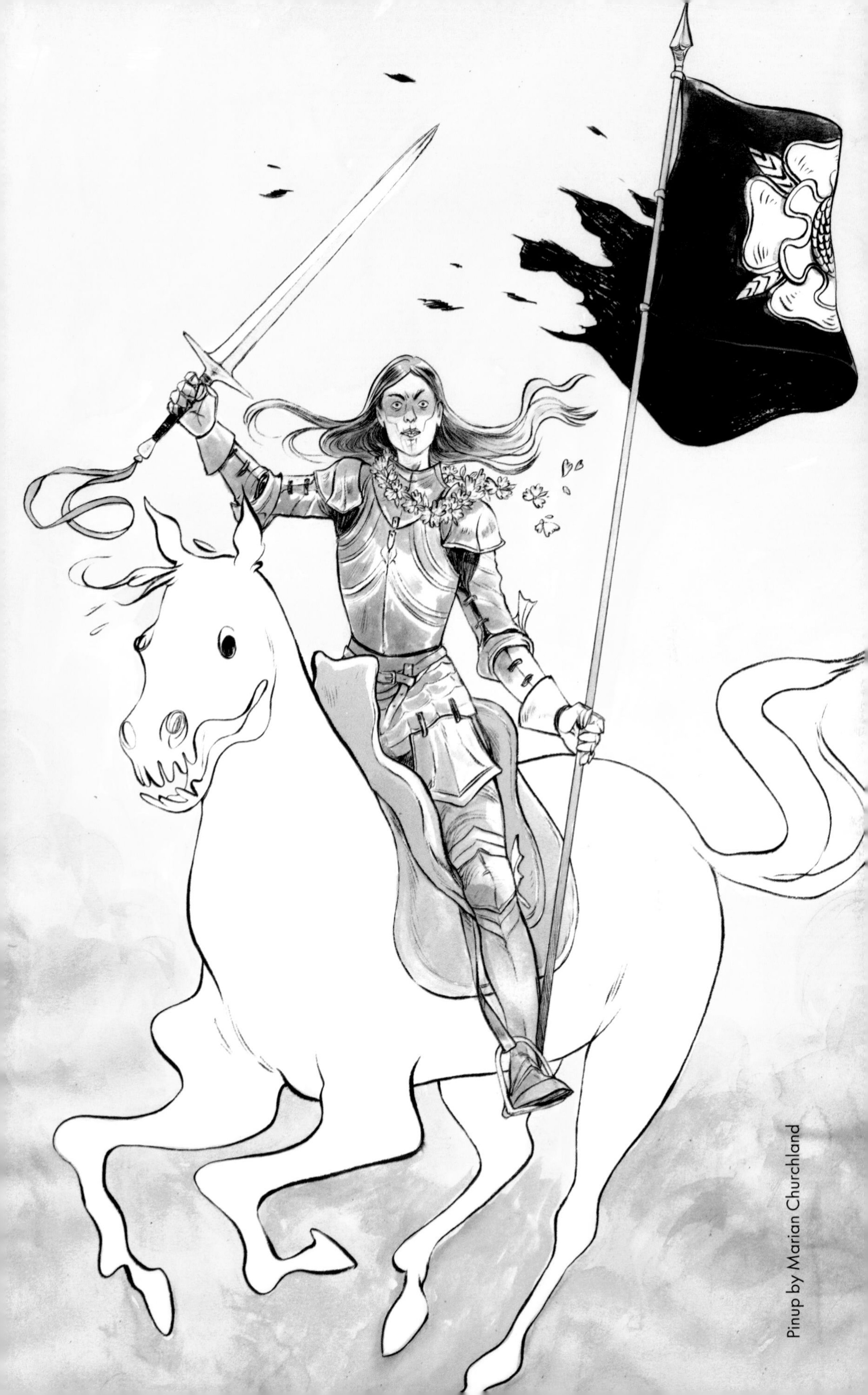

Pinup by Marian Churchland

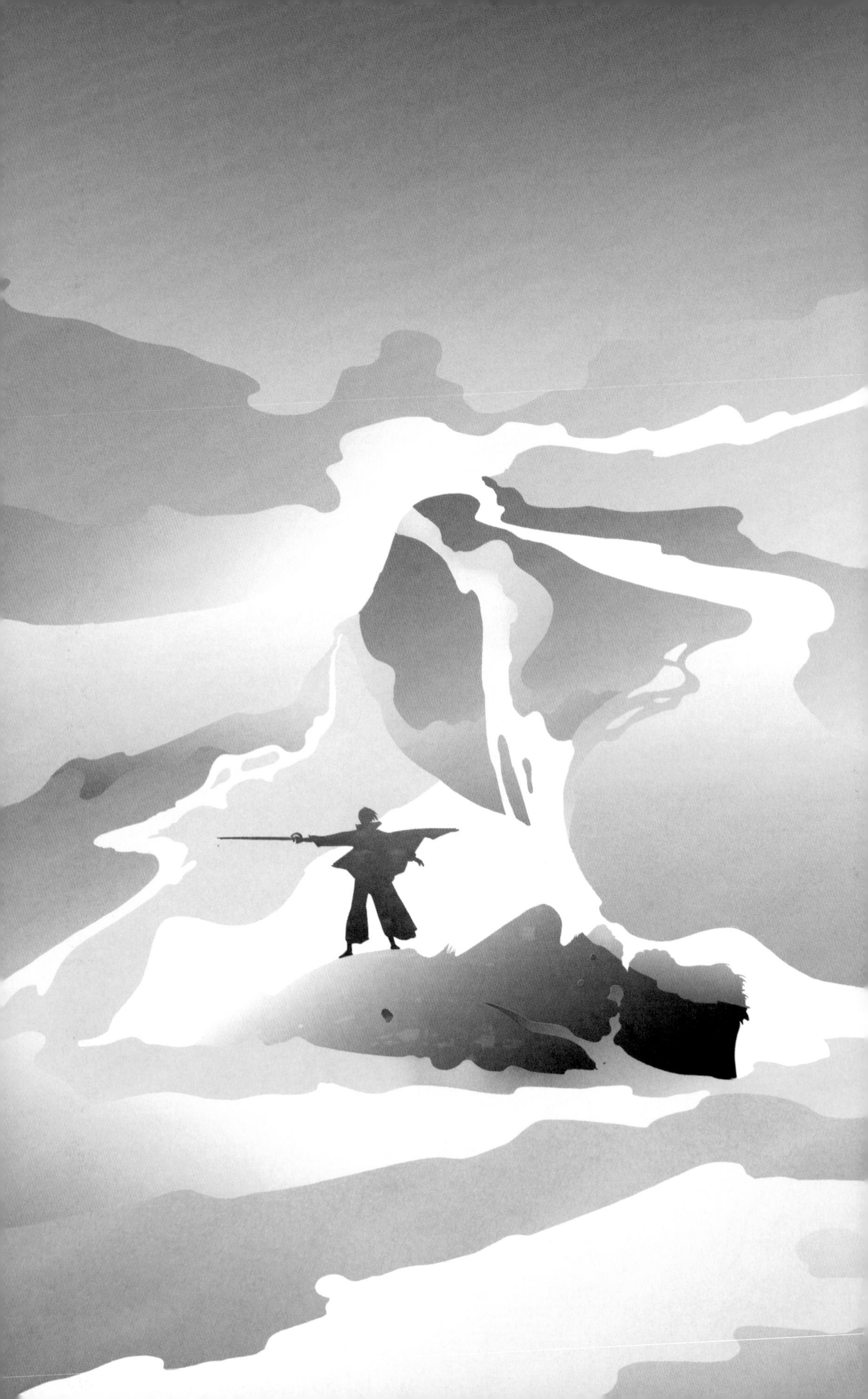

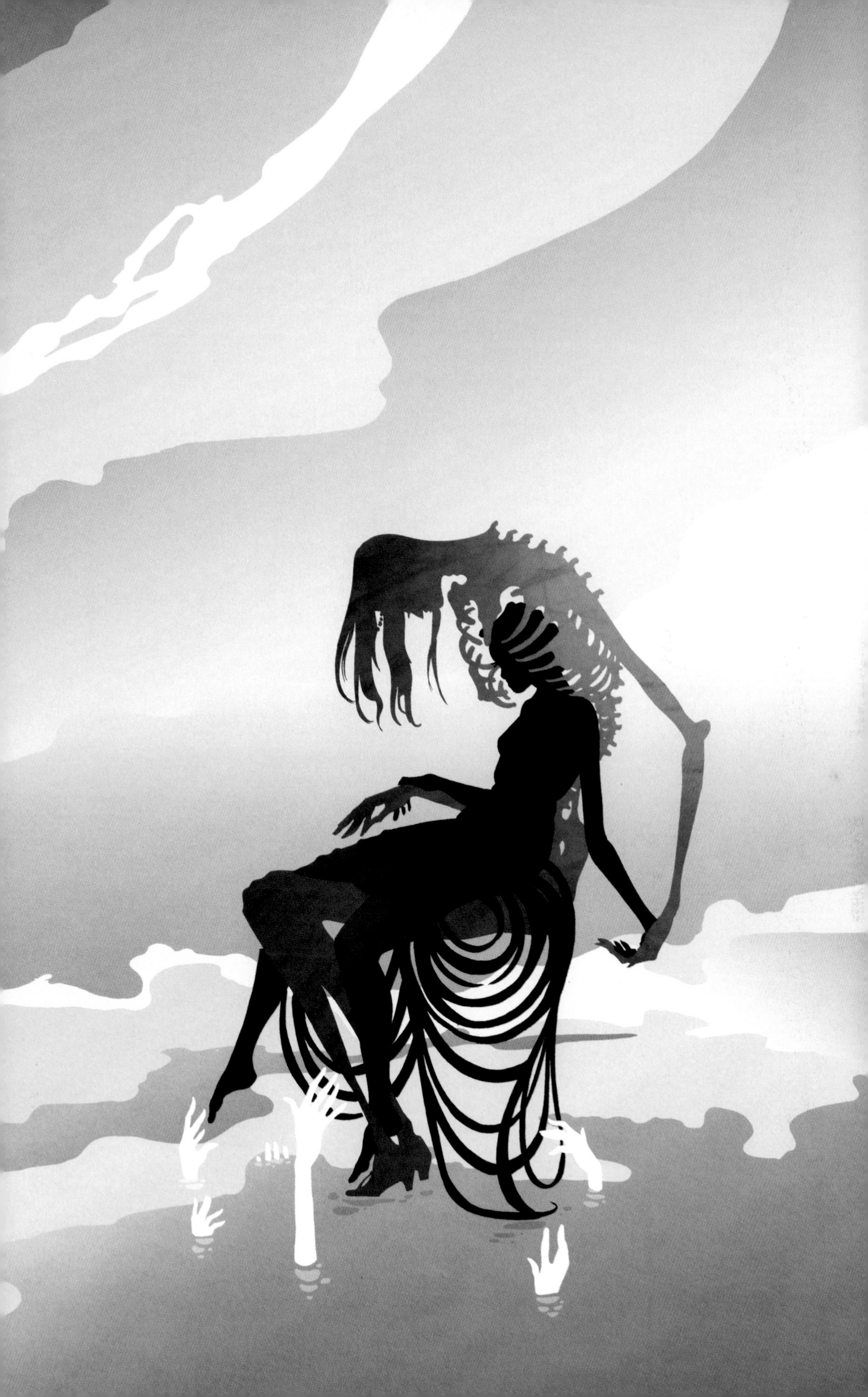

Bones Bunny tells Butterfly the tale.

The Ballad was a history. With Death's daughter Ginny at her side, Sissy, the child of blood and violence raised on love, defeated Old Death in his own domain and took his place in the long-fallow World Garden. Having assumed the mantle of Death, Sissy must bring the Garden back to life and seek out the errant Reapers, and return them to the fold.

In the mortal realm, Sarah Fields, the woman who pulled Sissy from the river of blood that bore her, died. Her children, and their connection to the Reapers, live on. Striking out from their birthplace, Sarah's progeny have found themselves as far-flung as the bloody trenches of France to the arid streets of Hollywoodland.

In between the glitz, the glamour, and the bright lights, Clara Fields is found dead. Her uncle Frank, the Conjure-Man, sets out to solve the mystery of her death. As he desperately searches for answers, Ginny, the Reaper of Vengeance, sets aside her duties, granting him three days of assistance in his quest. Their search starts with Director Jack Kaufman, a man with insatiable hunger. He took advantage of Clara's talent for a time, but then she disappeared. Clara passed, but her soul never arrived in the Garden. Only a Reaper could be responsible. The questions is which one...?

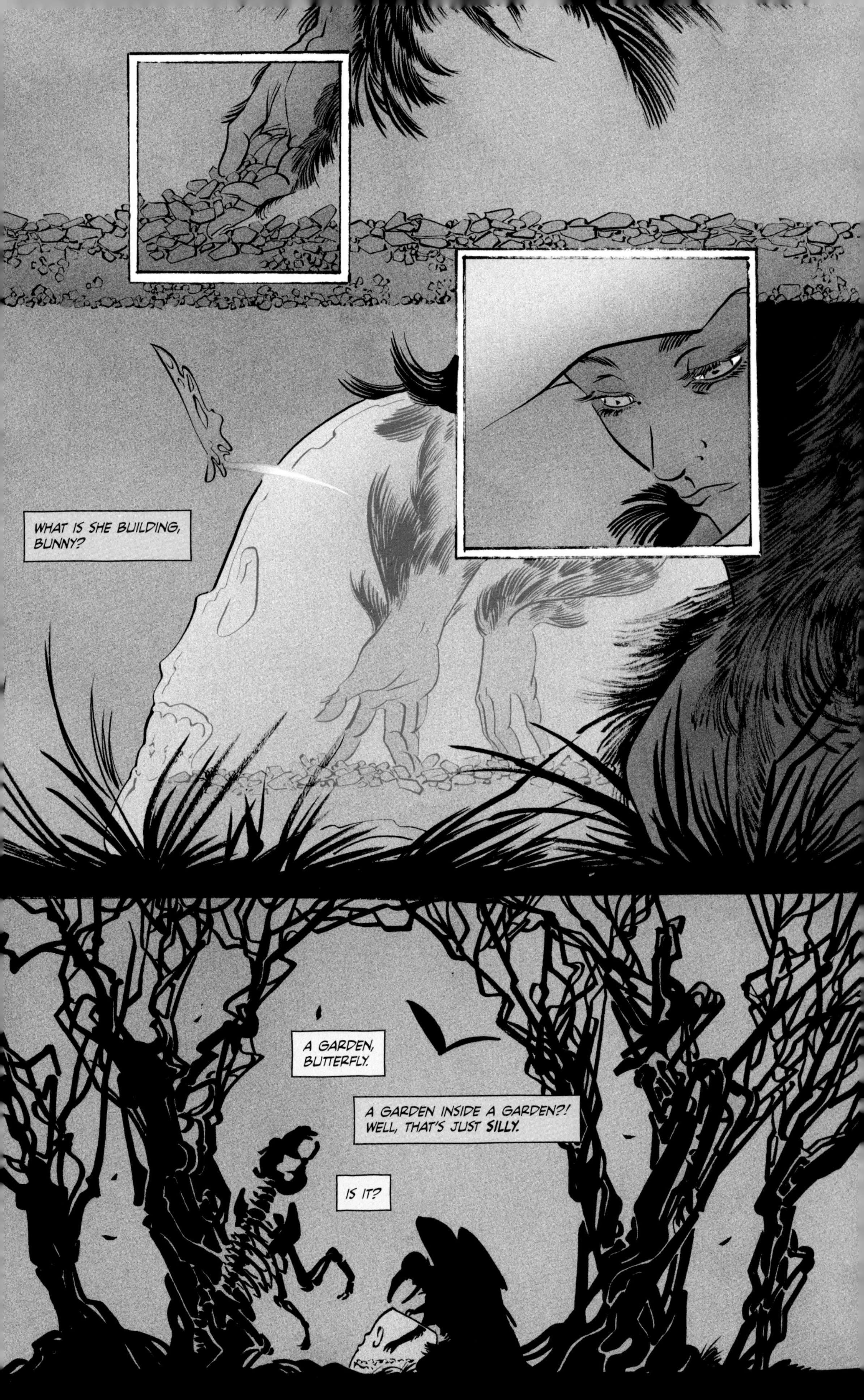
WHAT IS SHE BUILDING, BUNNY?
A GARDEN, BUTTERFLY.
A GARDEN INSIDE A GARDEN?! WELL, THAT'S JUST SILLY.
IS IT?

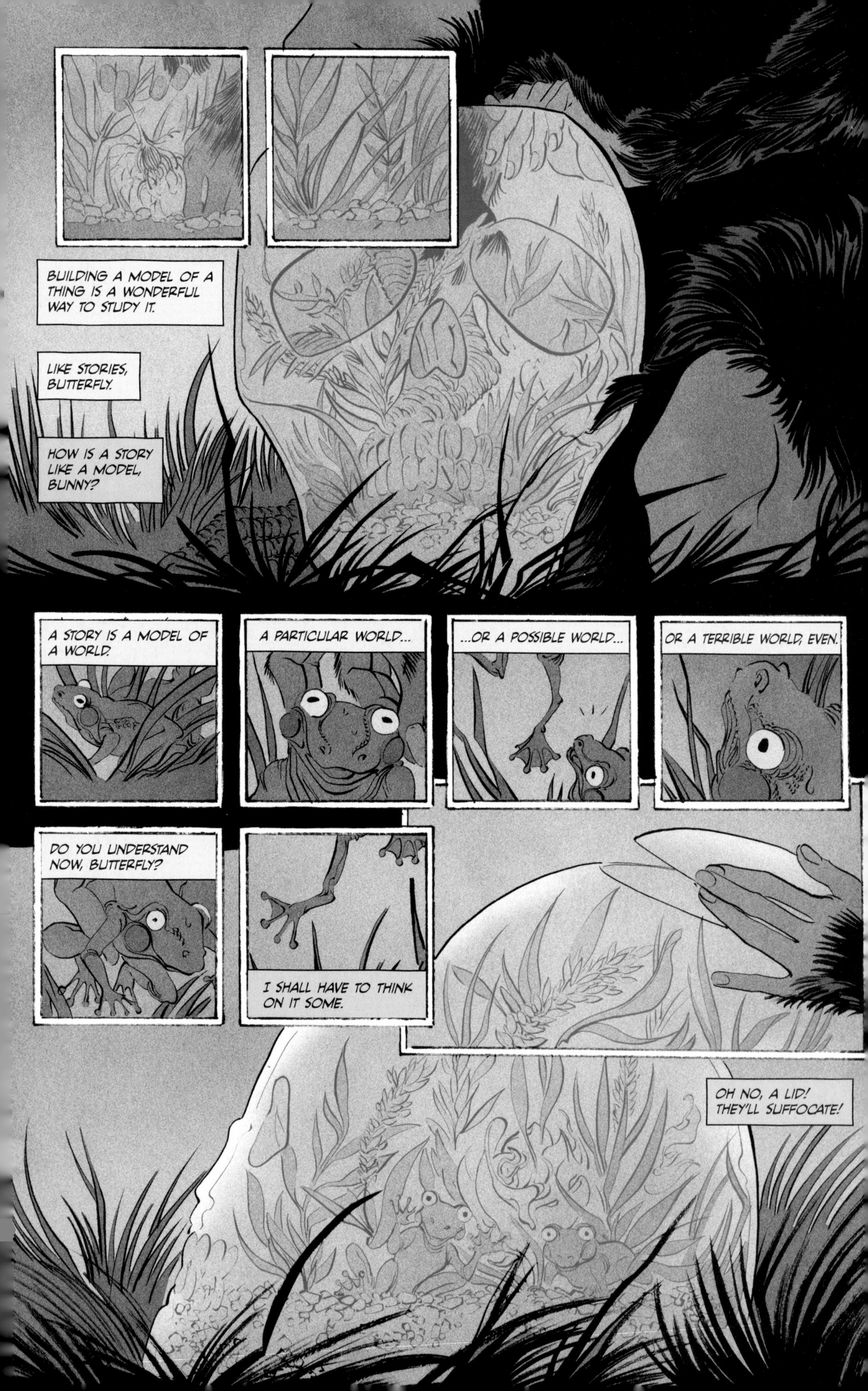
BUILDING A MODEL OF A THING IS A WONDERFUL WAY TO STUDY IT.
LIKE STORIES, BUTTERFLY.
HOW IS A STORY LIKE A MODEL, BUNNY?
A STORY IS A MODEL OF A WORLD.
A PARTICULAR WORLD...
...OR A POSSIBLE WORLD...
OR A TERRIBLE WORLD, EVEN.
DO YOU UNDERSTAND NOW, BUTTERFLY?
I SHALL HAVE TO THINK ON IT SOME.
OH NO, A LID! THEY'LL SUFFOCATE!

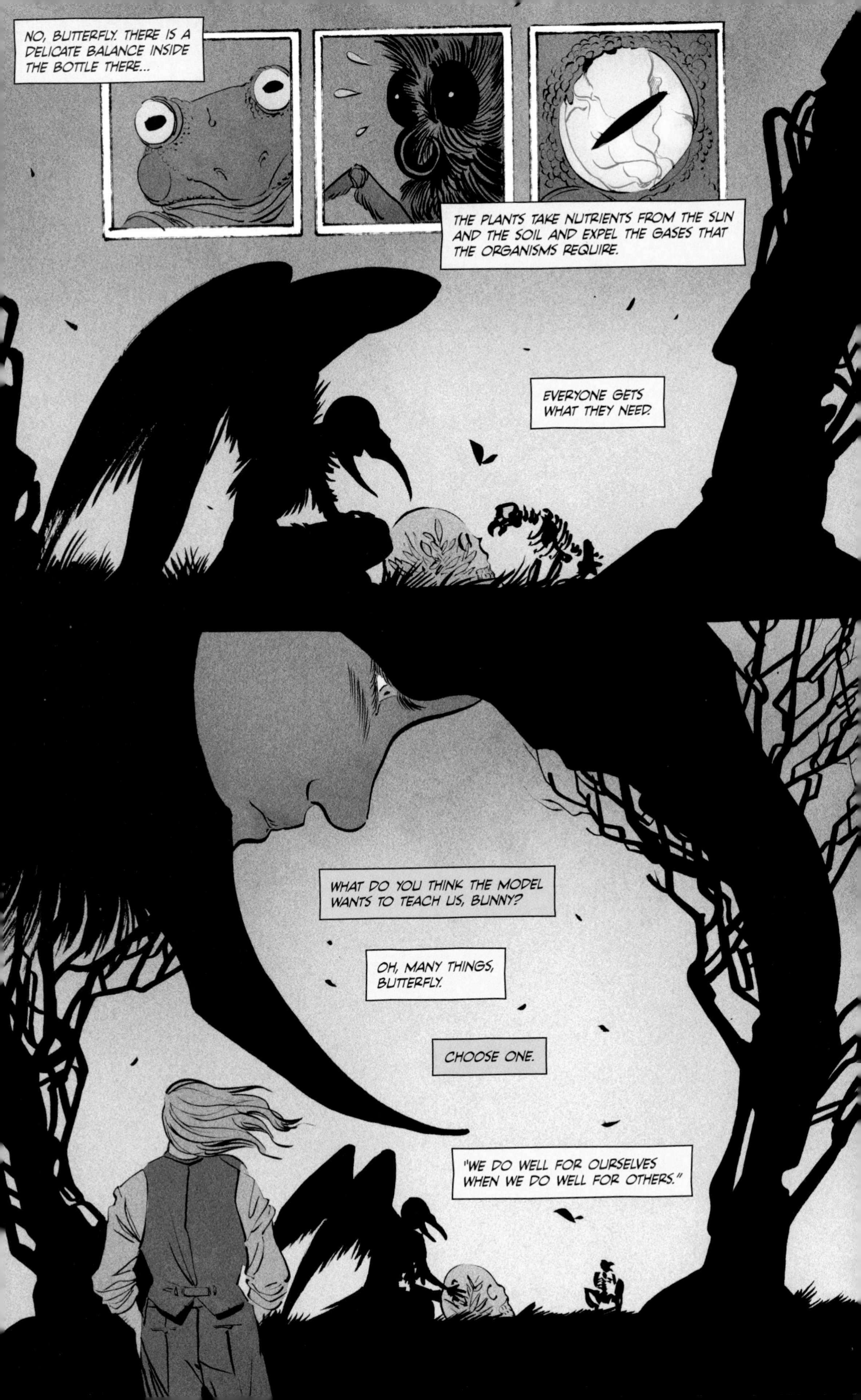
NO, BUTTERFLY. THERE IS A DELICATE BALANCE INSIDE THE BOTTLE THERE...
THE PLANTS TAKE NUTRIENTS FROM THE SUN AND THE SOIL AND EXPEL THE GASES THAT THE ORGANISMS REQUIRE.
EVERYONE GETS WHAT THEY NEED.
WHAT DO YOU THINK THE MODEL WANTS TO TEACH US, BUNNY?
OH, MANY THINGS, BUTTERFLY.
CHOOSE ONE.
"WE DO WELL FOR OURSELVES WHEN WE DO WELL FOR OTHERS."

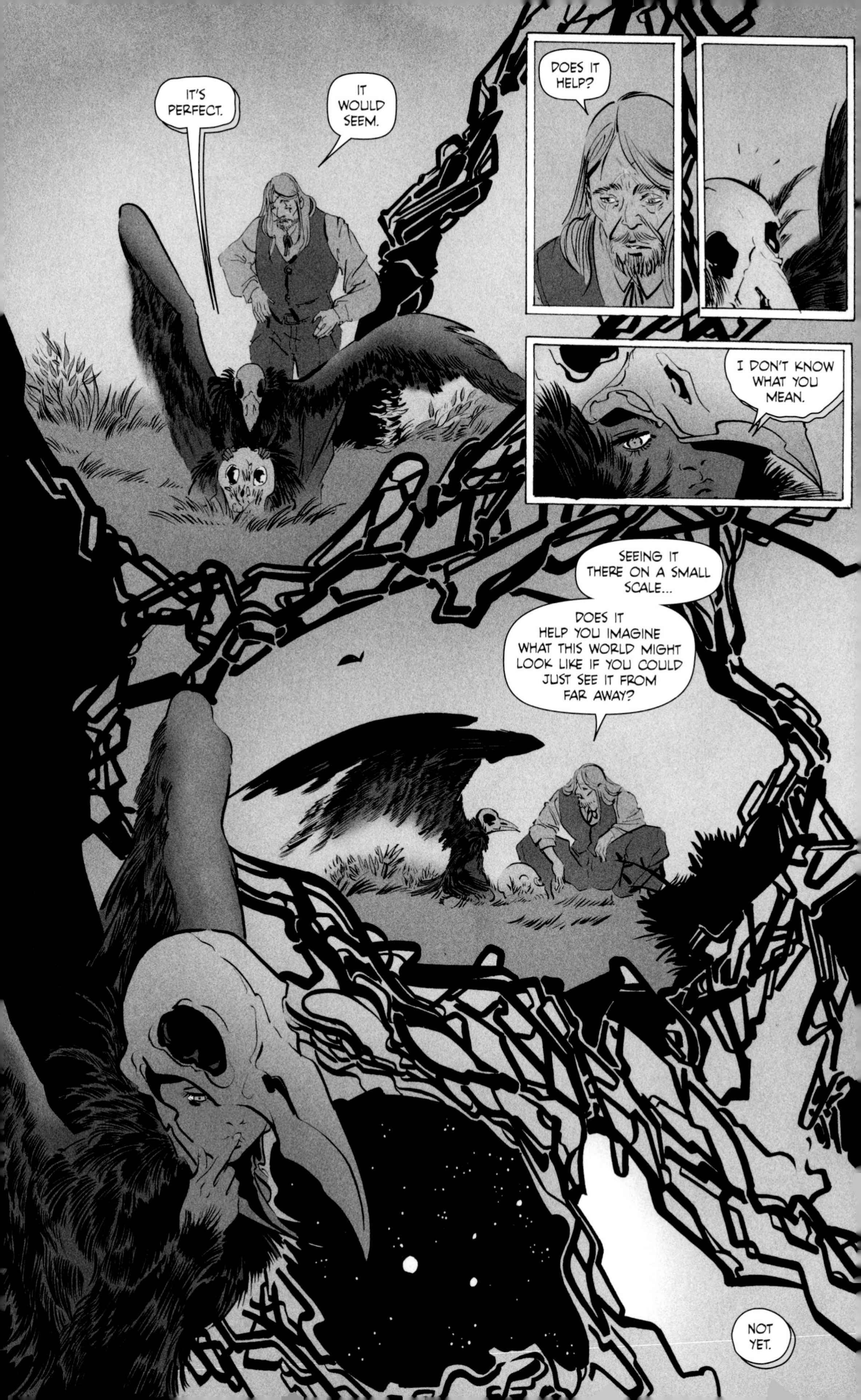
IT'S PERFECT.
IT WOULD SEEM.
DOES IT HELP?
I DON'T KNOW WHAT YOU MEAN.
SEEING IT THERE ON A SMALL SCALE...
DOES IT HELP YOU IMAGINE WHAT THIS WORLD MIGHT LOOK LIKE IF YOU COULD JUST SEE IT FROM FAR AWAY?
NOT YET.

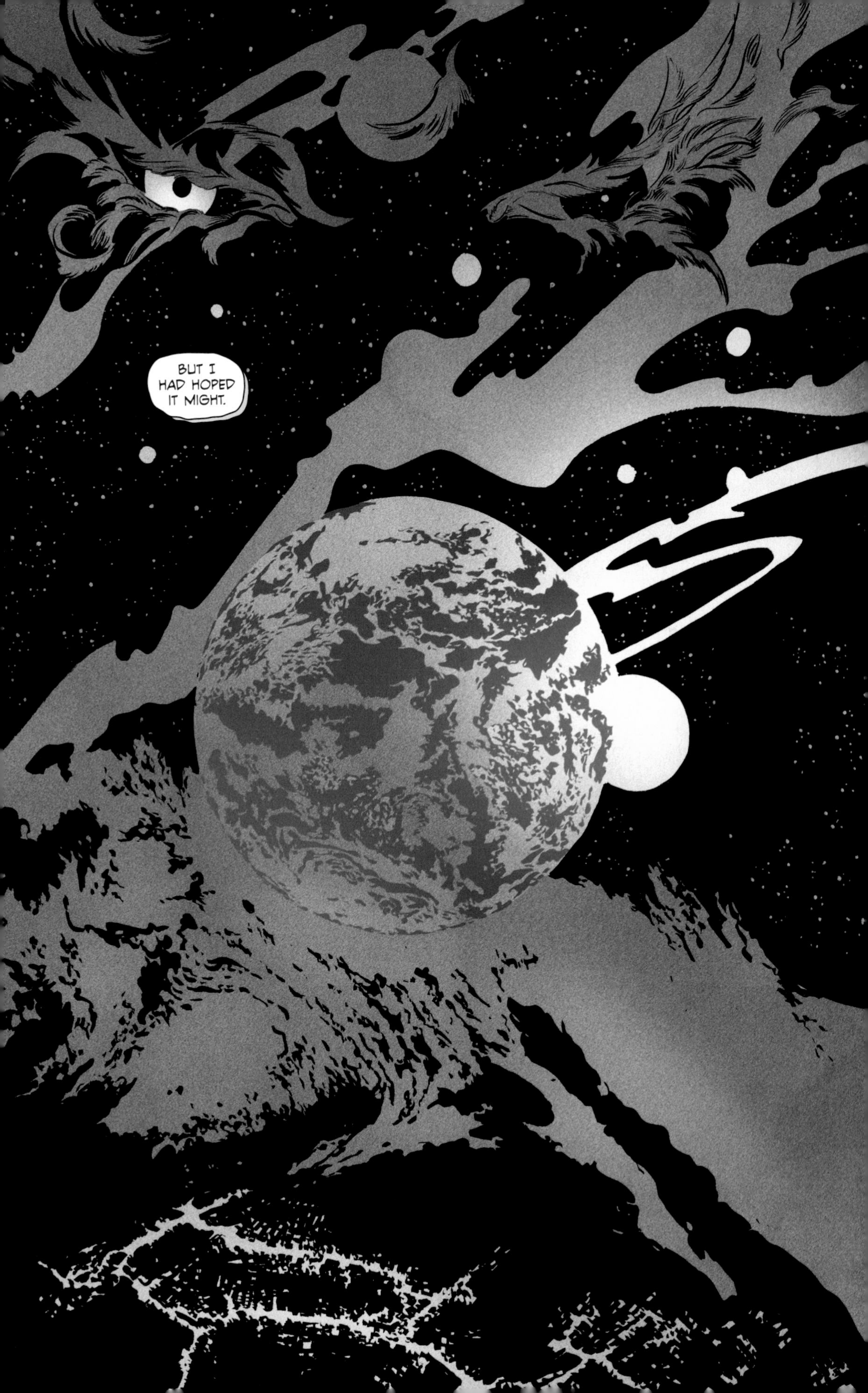
BUT I HAD HOPED IT MIGHT.

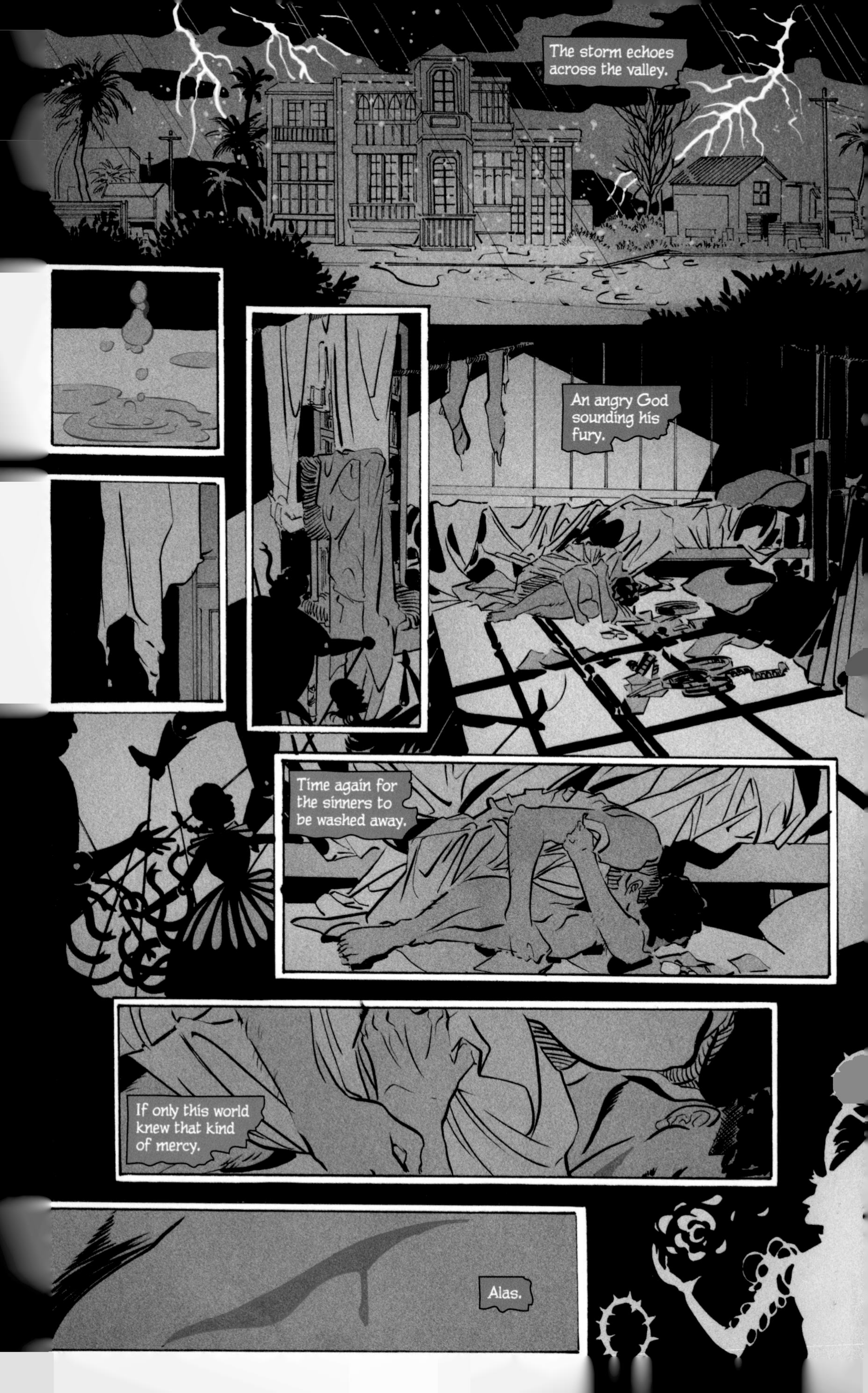

The storm echoes across the valley.
An angry God sounding his fury.
Time again for the sinners to be washed away.
If only this world knew that kind of mercy.
Alas.

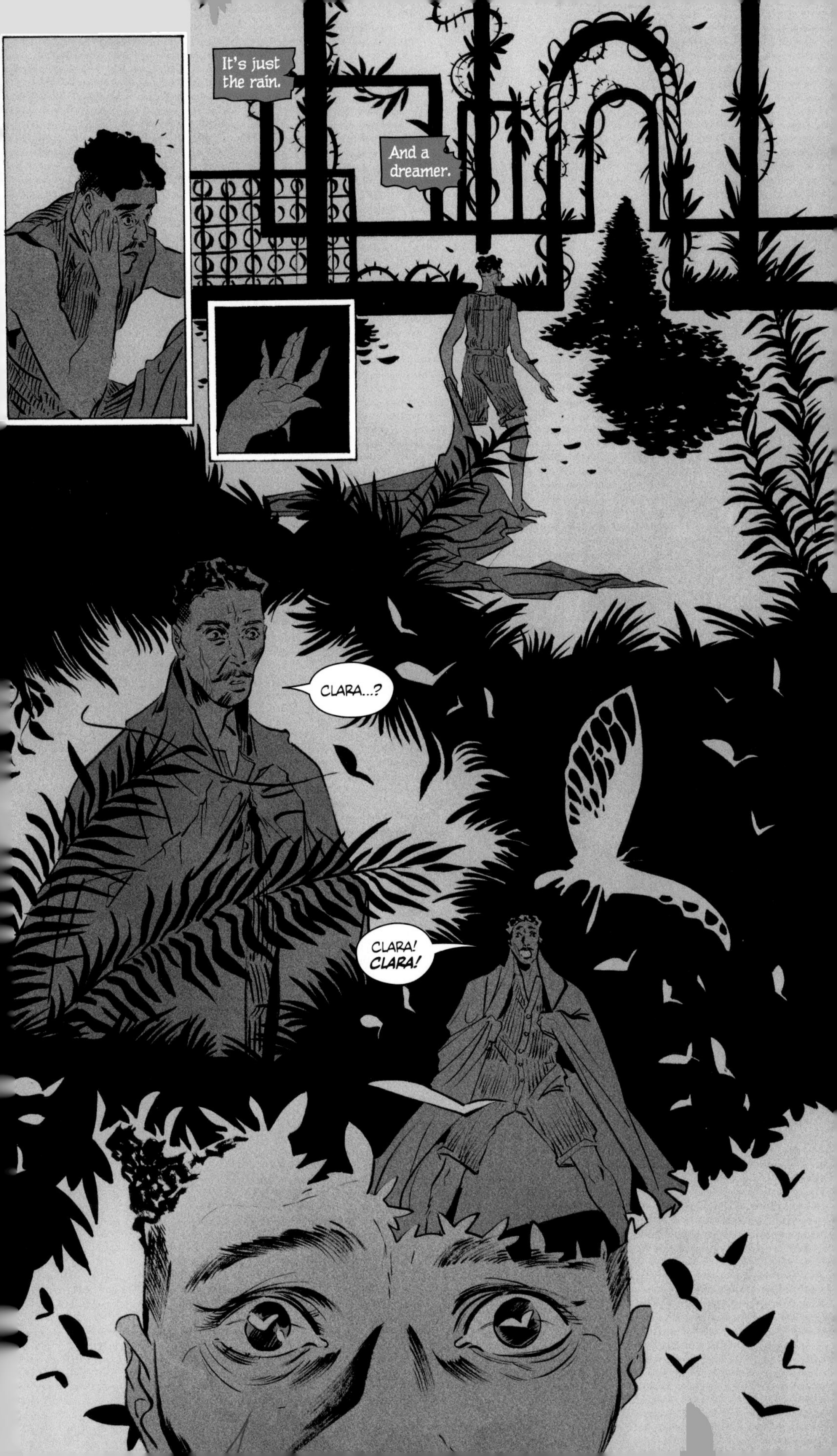
It's just the rain.
And a dreamer.
CLARA...?
CLARA! CLARA!

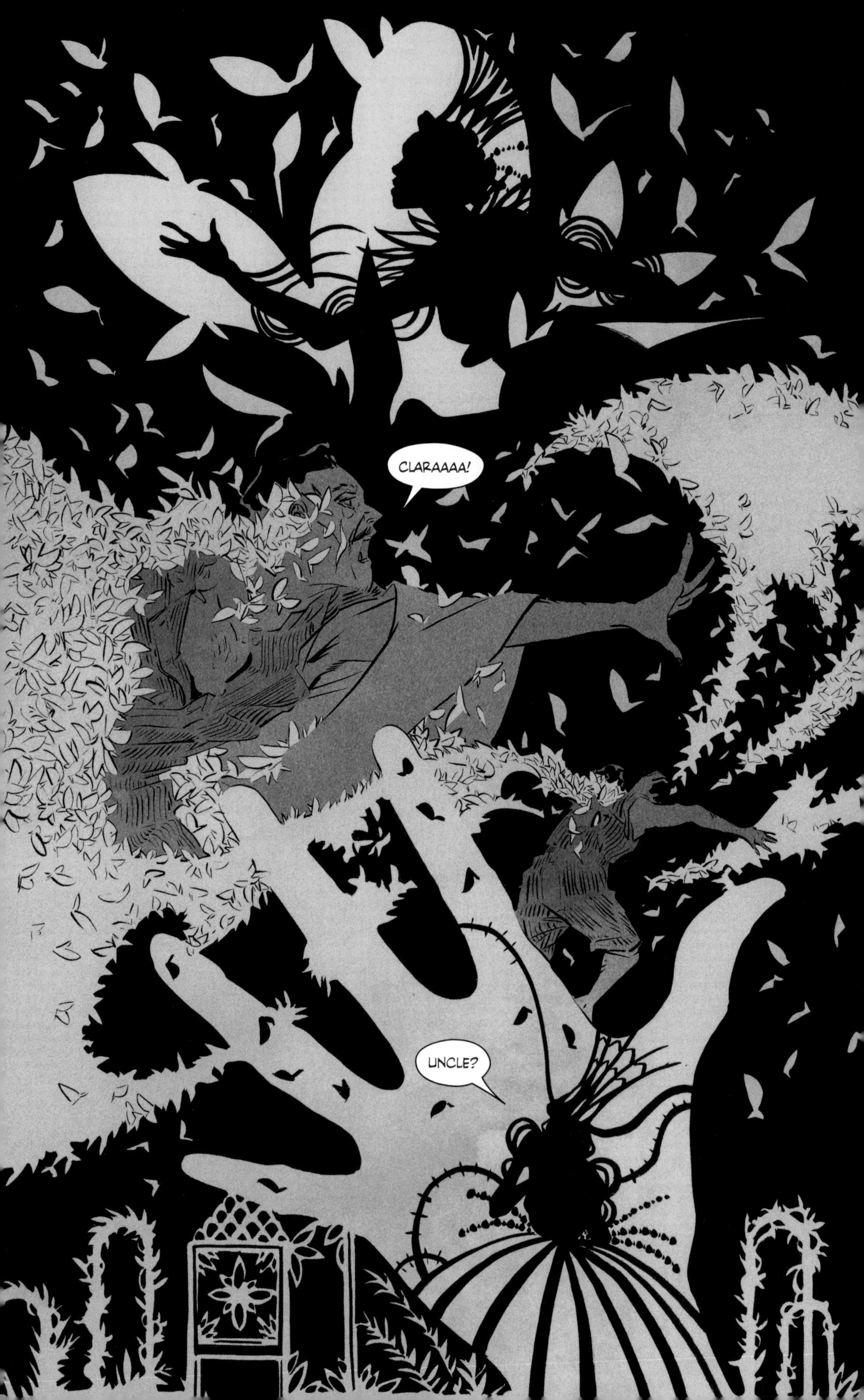
CLARAAAA!
UNCLE?

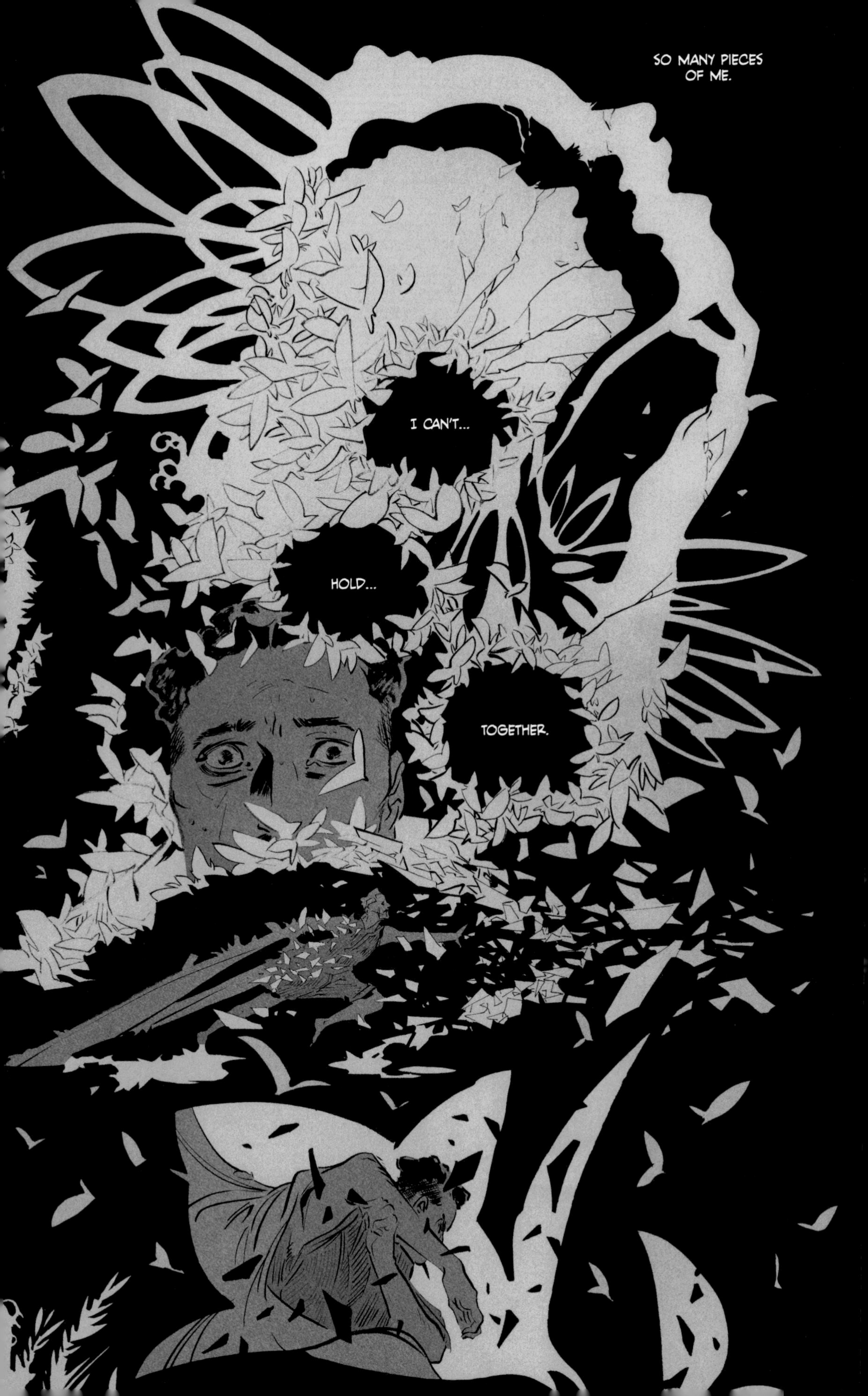
SO MANY PIECES OF ME.
I CAN'T...
HOLD...
TOGETHER.

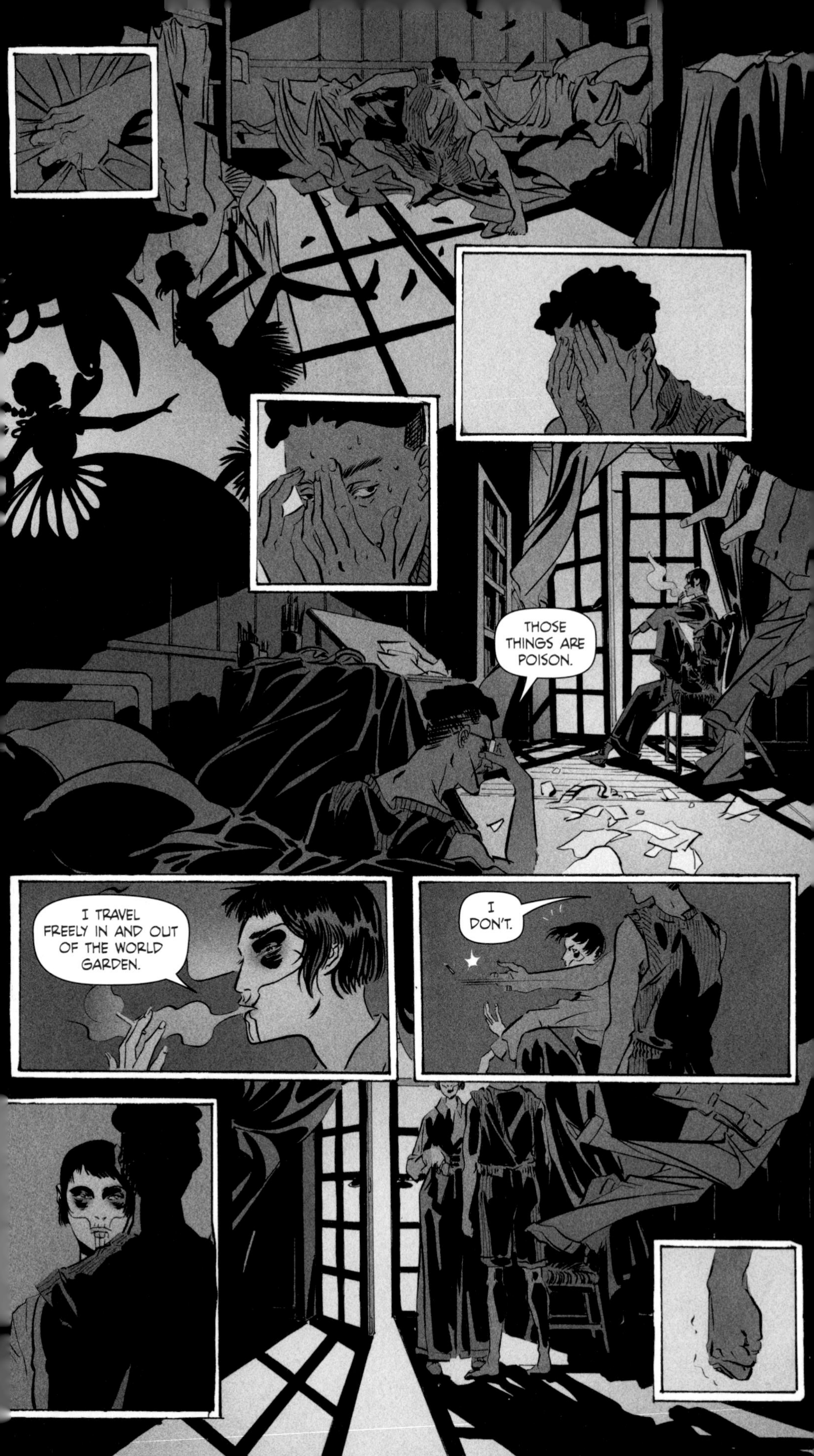
THOSE THINGS ARE POISON.
I TRAVEL FREELY IN AND OUT OF THE WORLD GARDEN.
I DON'T.

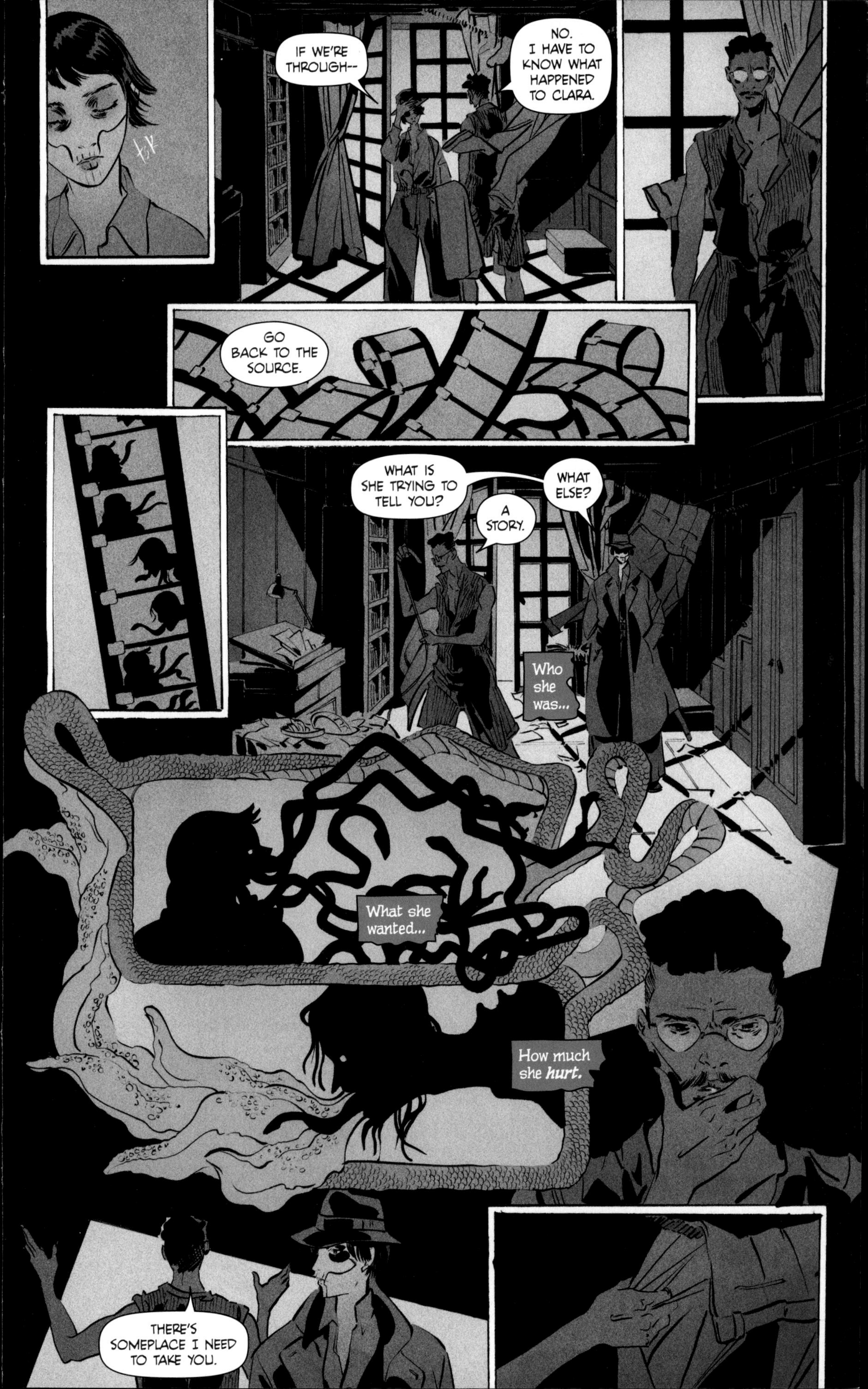

IF WE'RE THROUGH--
NO. I HAVE TO KNOW WHAT HAPPENED TO CLARA.
GO BACK TO THE SOURCE.
WHAT IS SHE TRYING TO TELL YOU?
A STORY.
WHAT ELSE?
Who she was...
What she wanted...
How much she *hurt.*
THERE'S SOMEPLACE I NEED TO TAKE YOU.

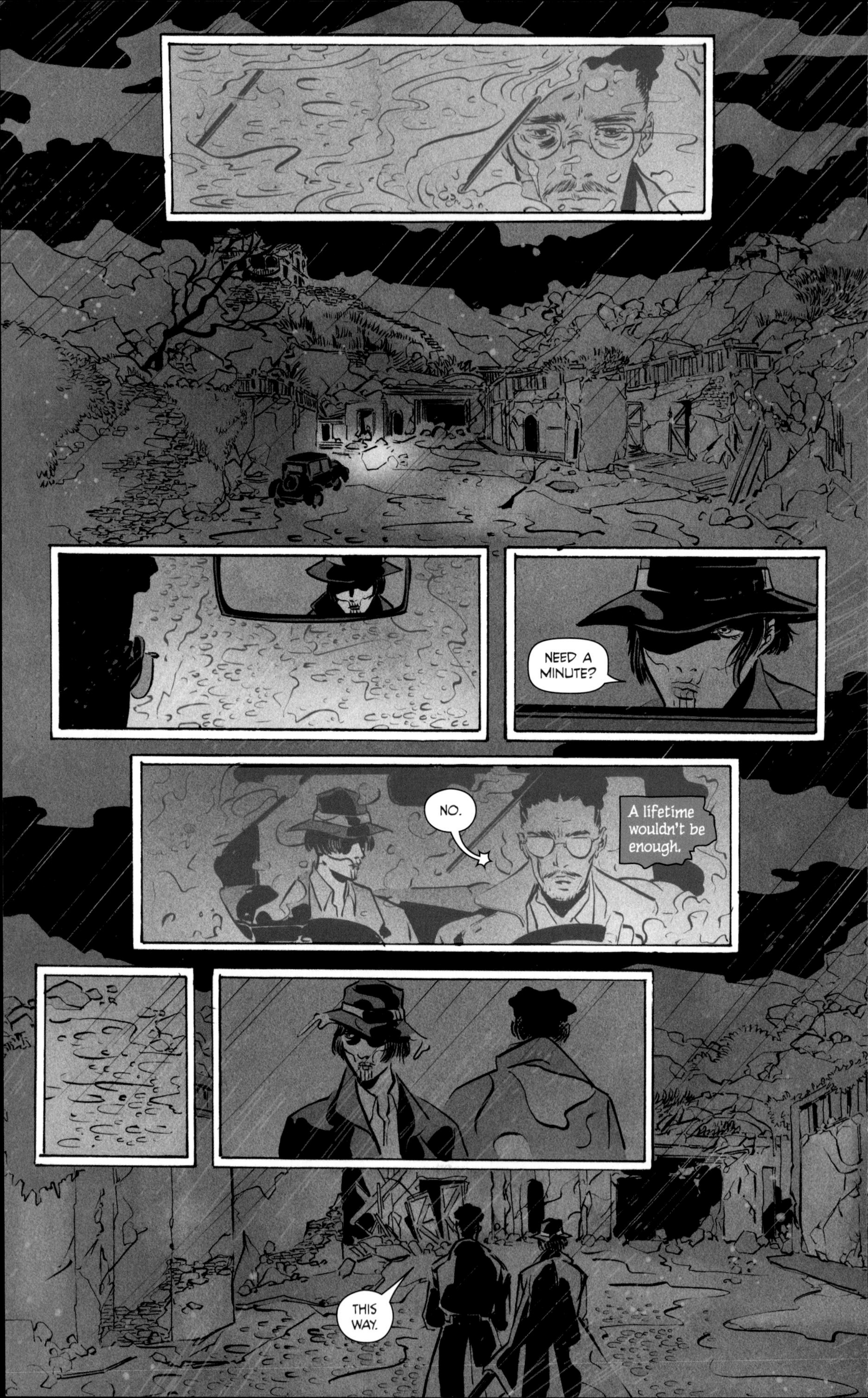
NEED A MINUTE?
NO.
A lifetime wouldn't be enough.
THIS WAY.

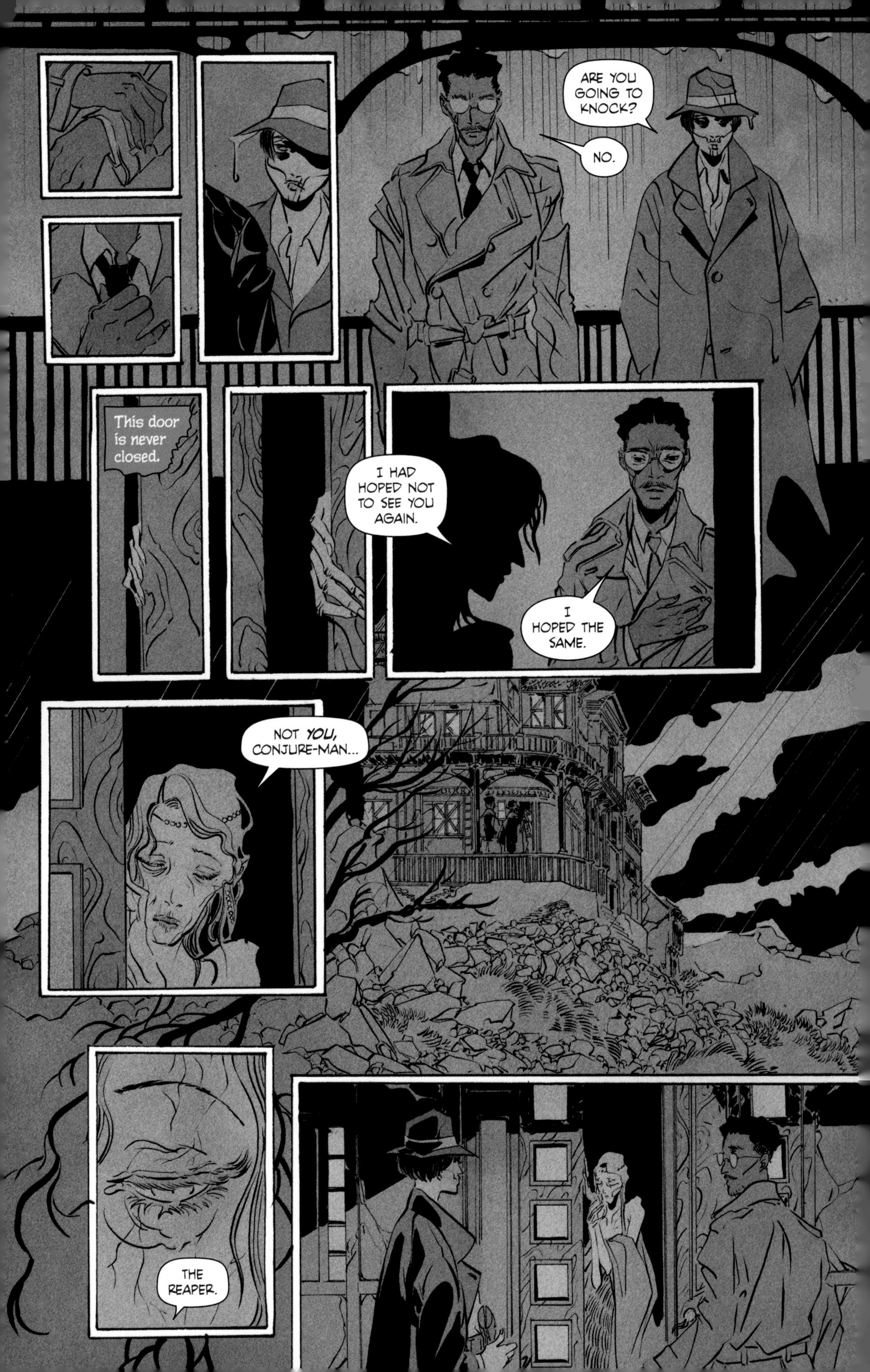

ARE YOU GOING TO KNOCK?
NO.
This door is never closed.
I HAD HOPED NOT TO SEE YOU AGAIN.
I HOPED THE SAME.
NOT *YOU*, CONJURE-MAN...
THE REAPER.

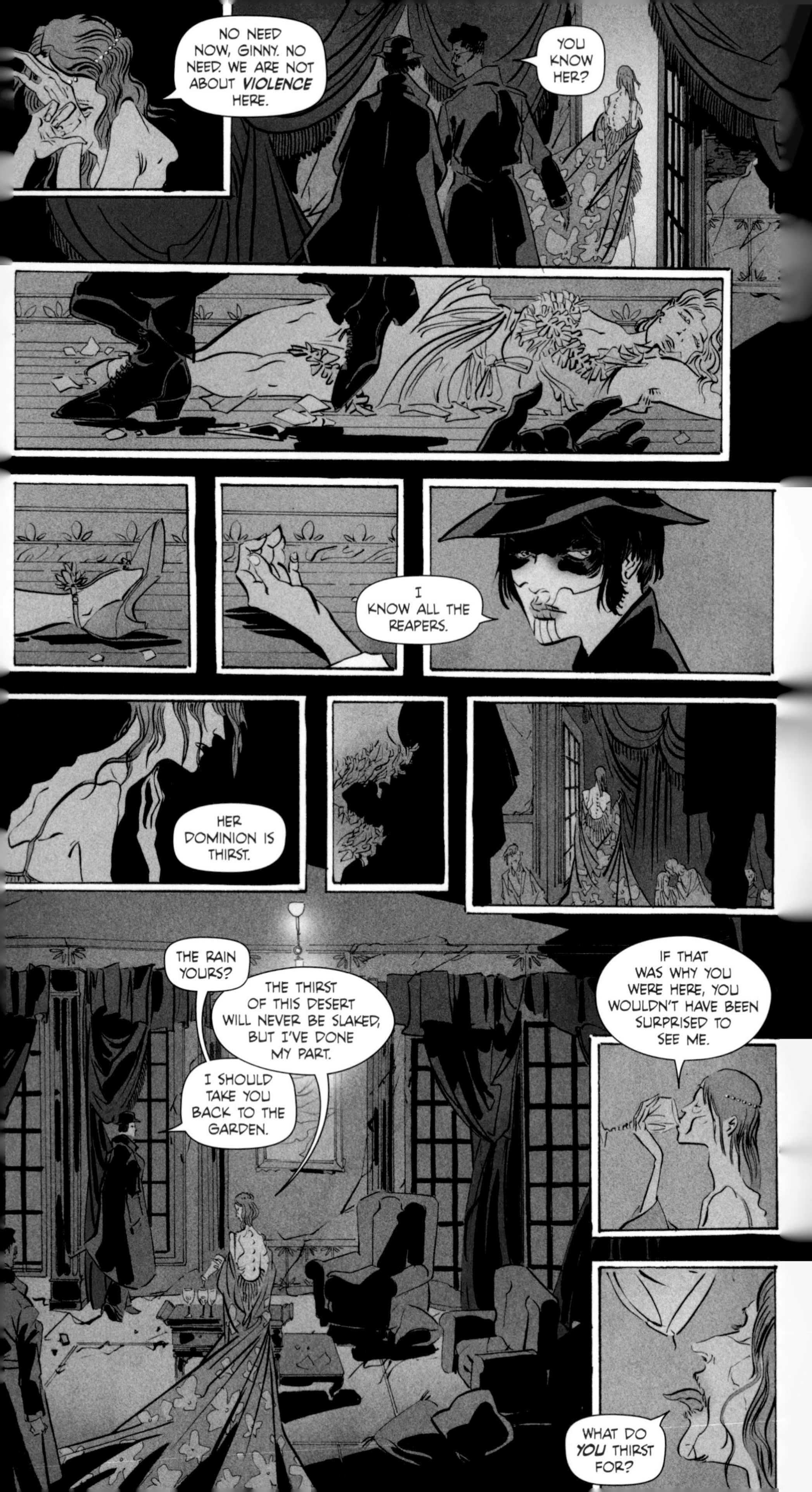
NO NEED NOW, GINNY. NO NEED. WE ARE NOT ABOUT *VIOLENCE* HERE.
YOU KNOW HER?
I KNOW ALL THE REAPERS.
HER DOMINION IS THIRST.
THE RAIN YOURS?
THE THIRST OF THIS DESERT WILL NEVER BE SLAKED, BUT I'VE DONE MY PART.
I SHOULD TAKE YOU BACK TO THE GARDEN.
IF THAT WAS WHY YOU WERE HERE, YOU WOULDN'T HAVE BEEN SURPRISED TO SEE ME.
WHAT DO *YOU* THIRST FOR?

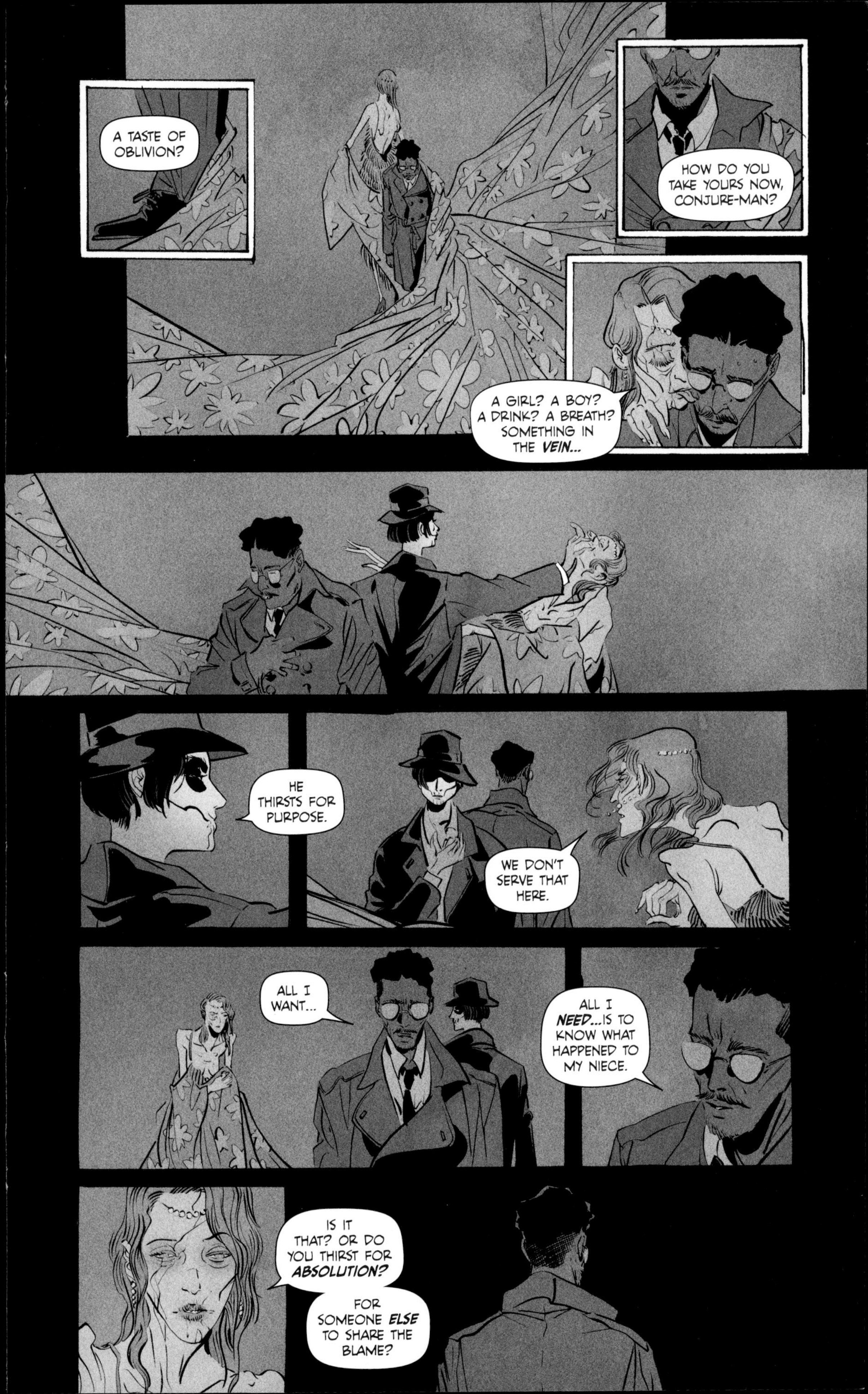
A TASTE OF OBLIVION?
HOW DO YOU TAKE YOURS NOW, CONJURE-MAN?
A GIRL? A BOY? A DRINK? A BREATH? SOMETHING IN THE VEIN...
HE THIRSTS FOR PURPOSE.
WE DON'T SERVE THAT HERE.
ALL I WANT...
ALL I NEED...IS TO KNOW WHAT HAPPENED TO MY NIECE.
IS IT THAT? OR DO YOU THIRST FOR ABSOLUTION?
FOR SOMEONE ELSE TO SHARE THE BLAME?

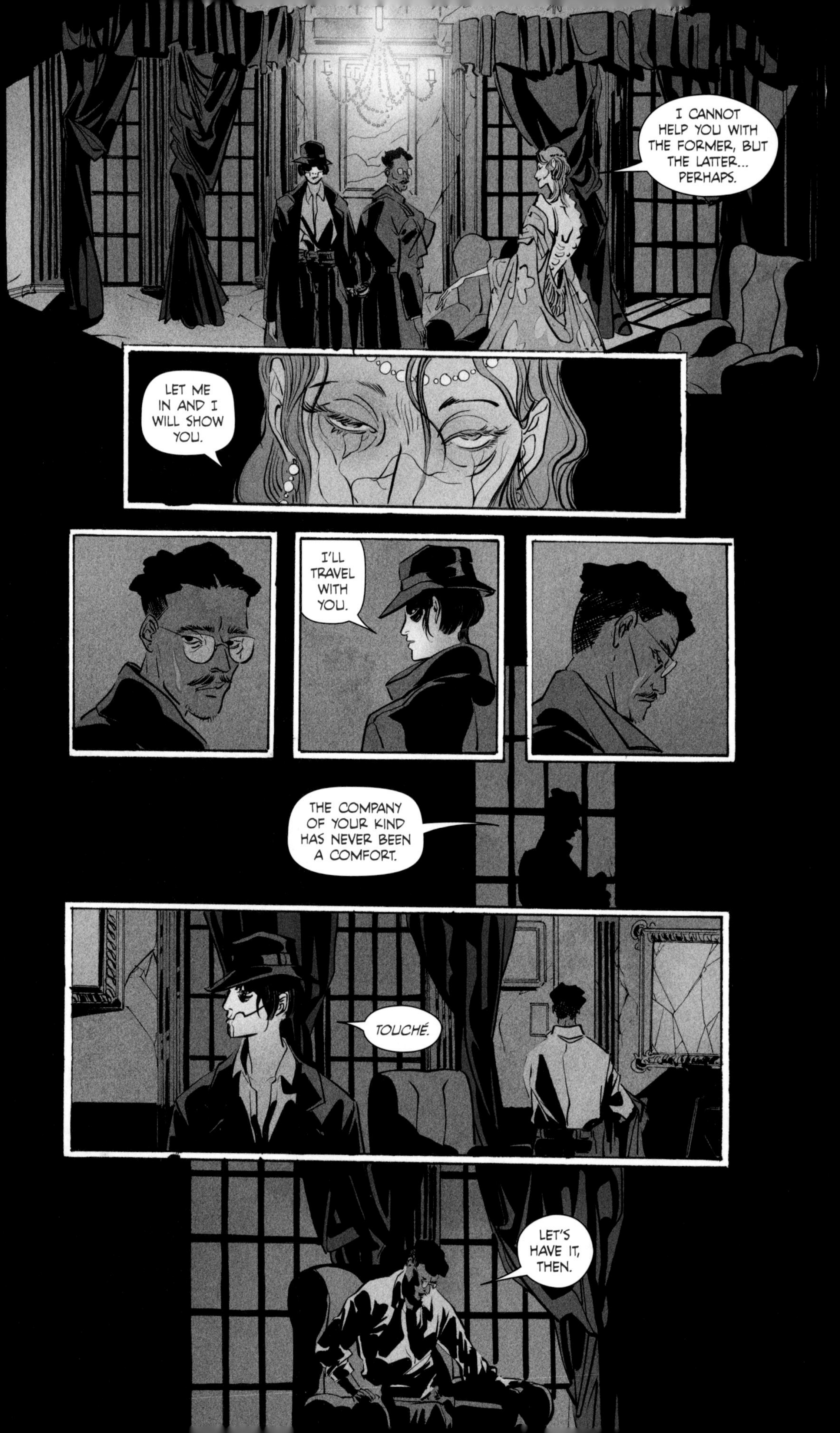
I CANNOT HELP YOU WITH THE FORMER, BUT THE LATTER... PERHAPS.
LET ME IN AND I WILL SHOW YOU.
I'LL TRAVEL WITH YOU.
THE COMPANY OF YOUR KIND HAS NEVER BEEN A COMFORT.
TOUCHÉ.
LET'S HAVE IT, THEN.

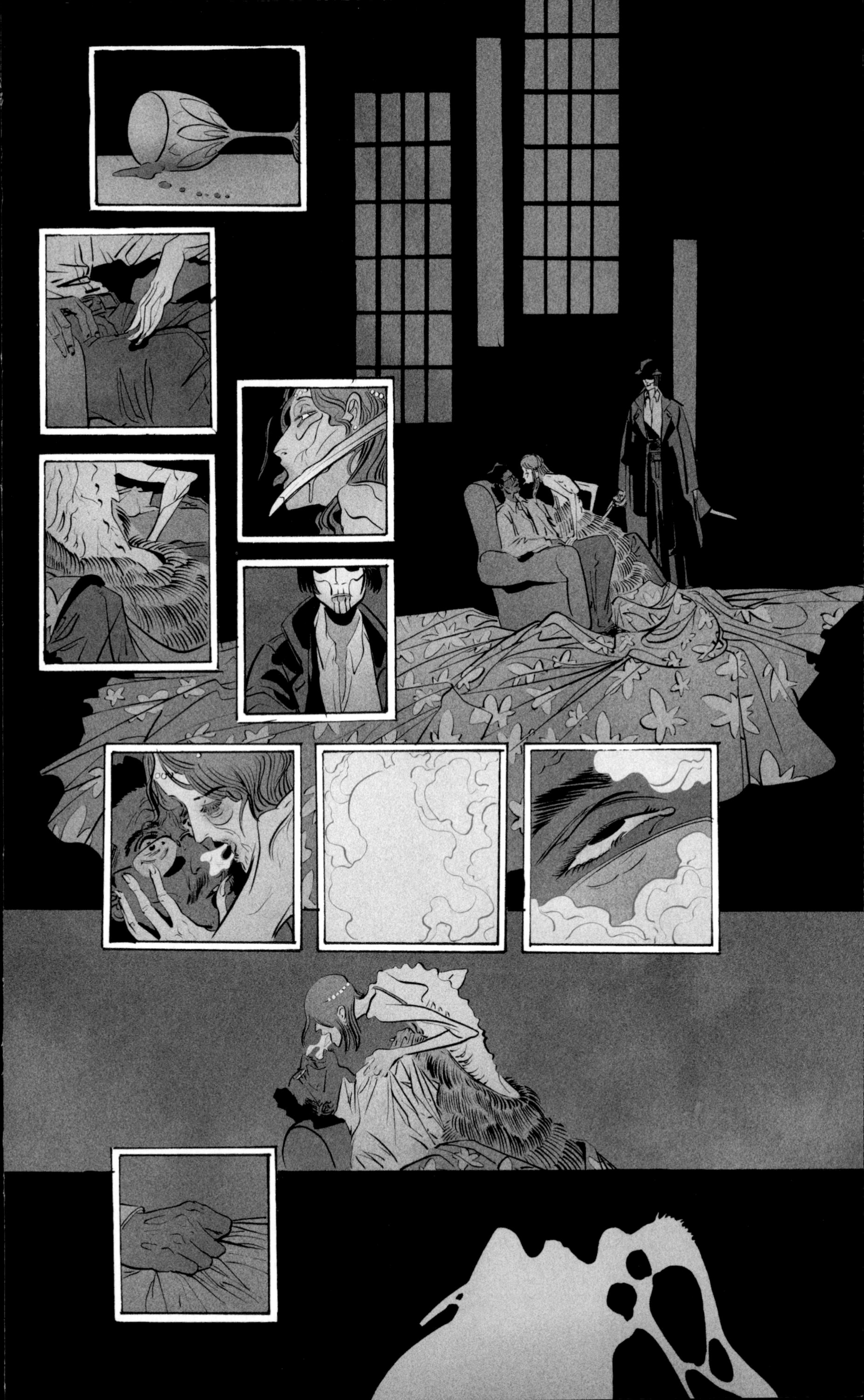

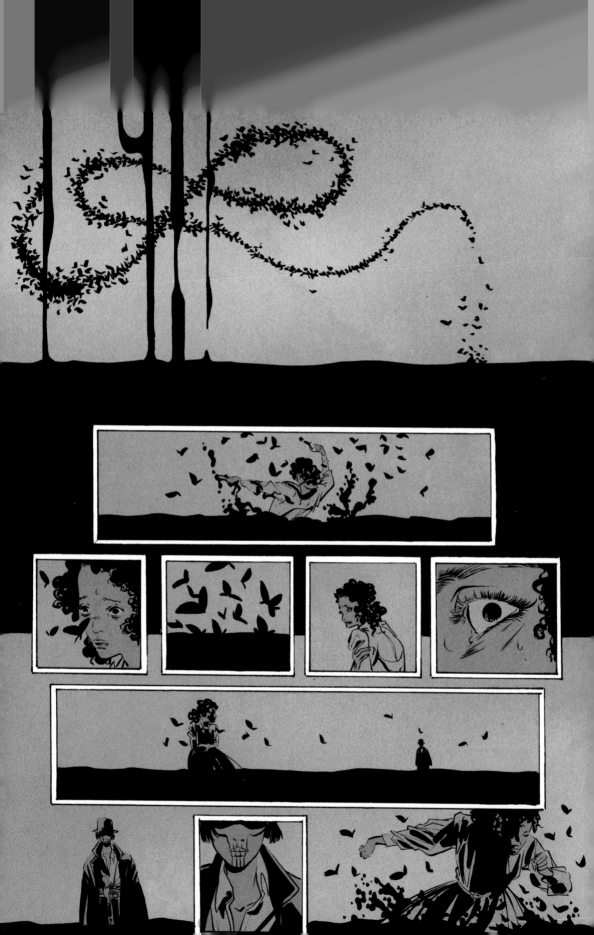

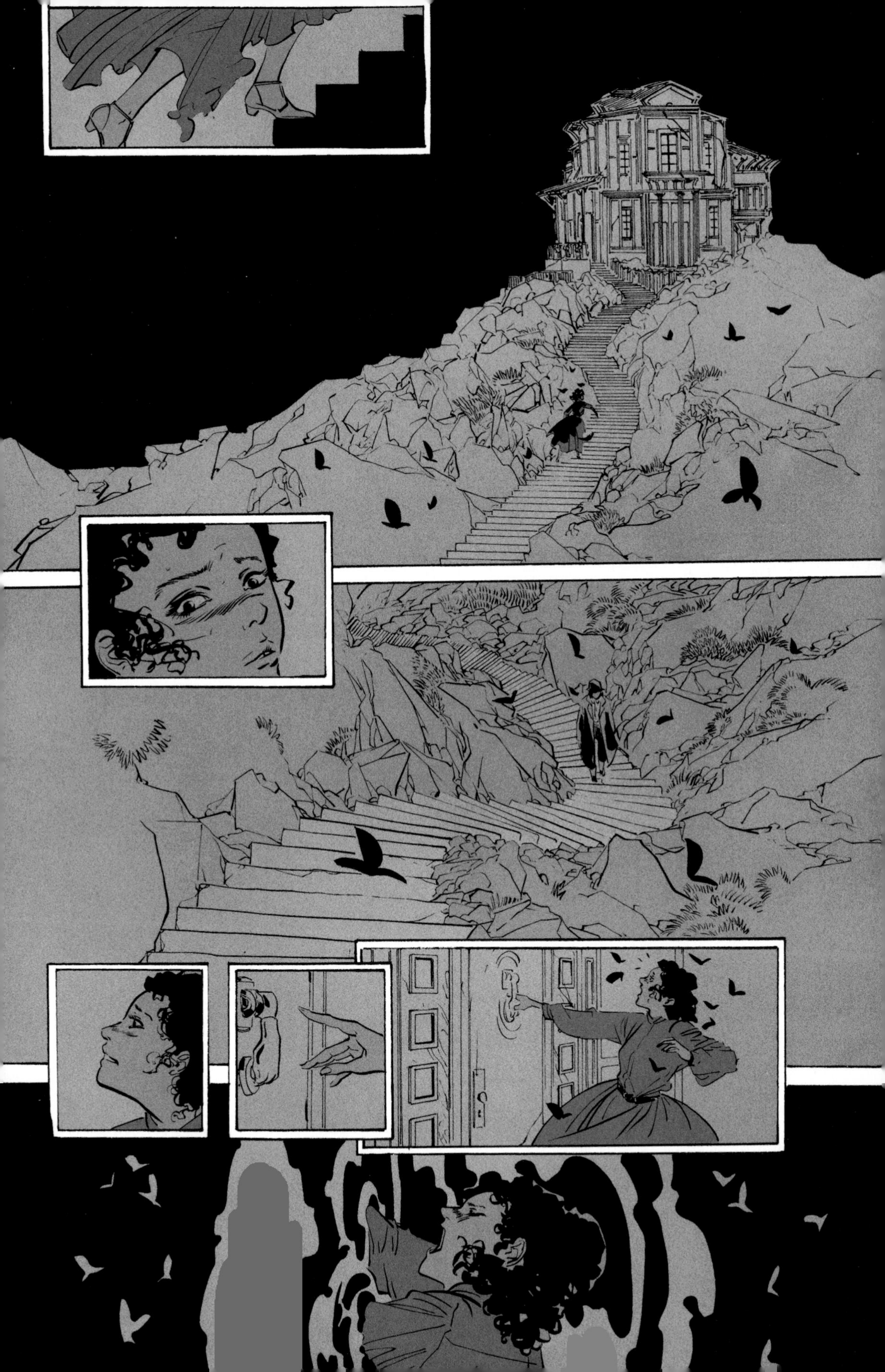

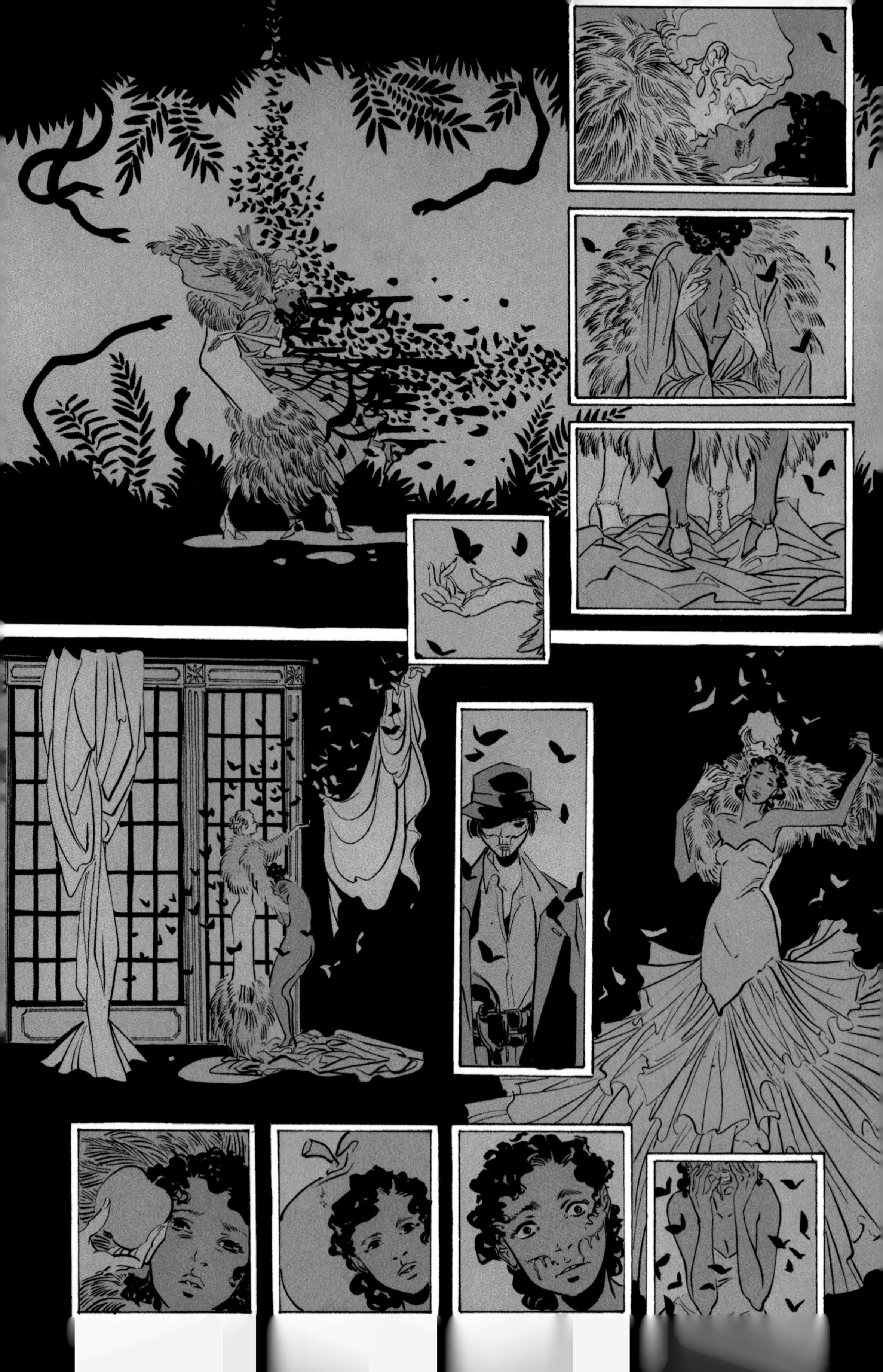

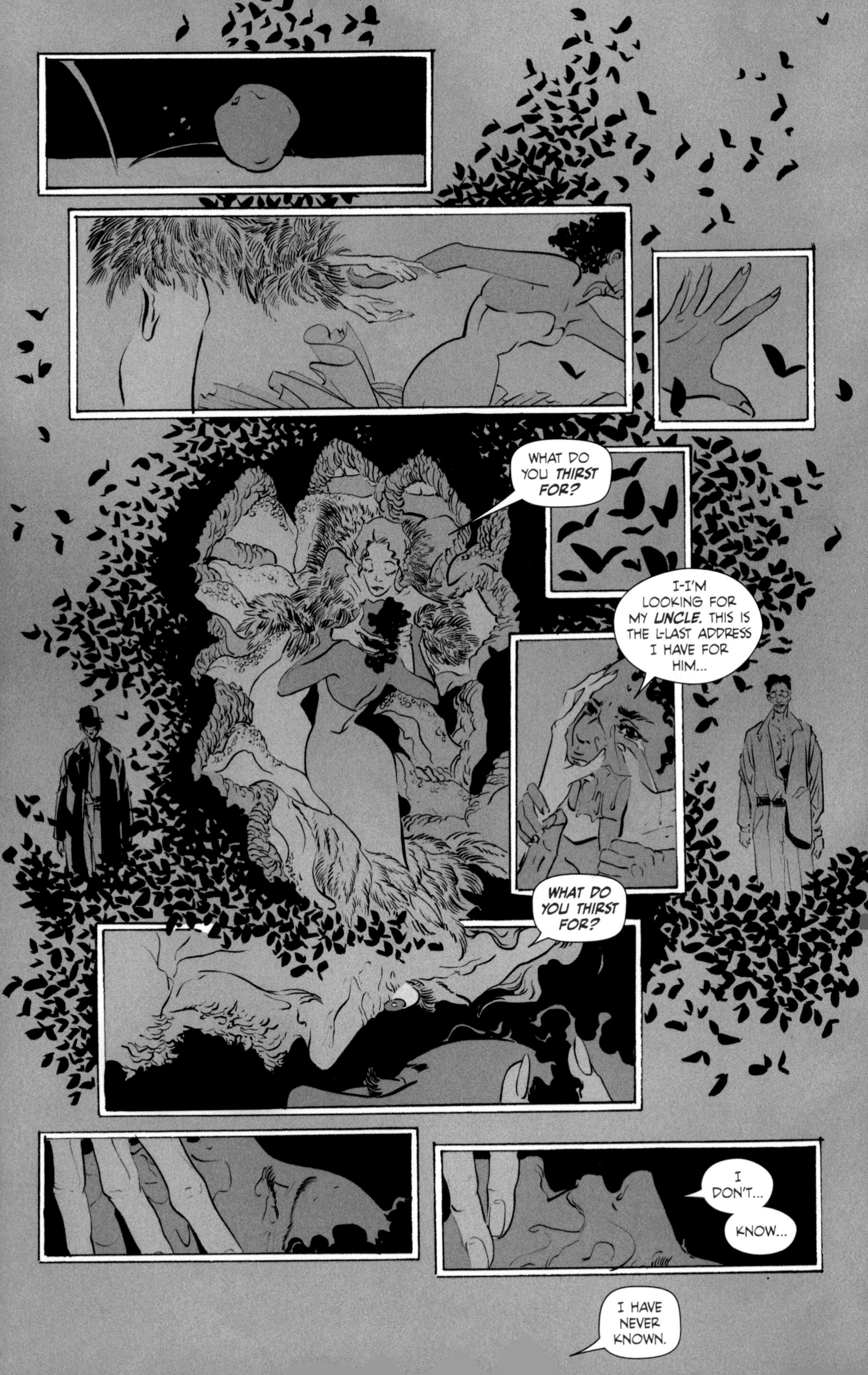
WHAT DO YOU *THIRST* FOR?
I-I'M LOOKING FOR MY ***UNCLE.*** THIS IS THE L-LAST ADDRESS I HAVE FOR HIM...
WHAT DO YOU THIRST FOR?
I DON'T...
KNOW...
I HAVE NEVER KNOWN.

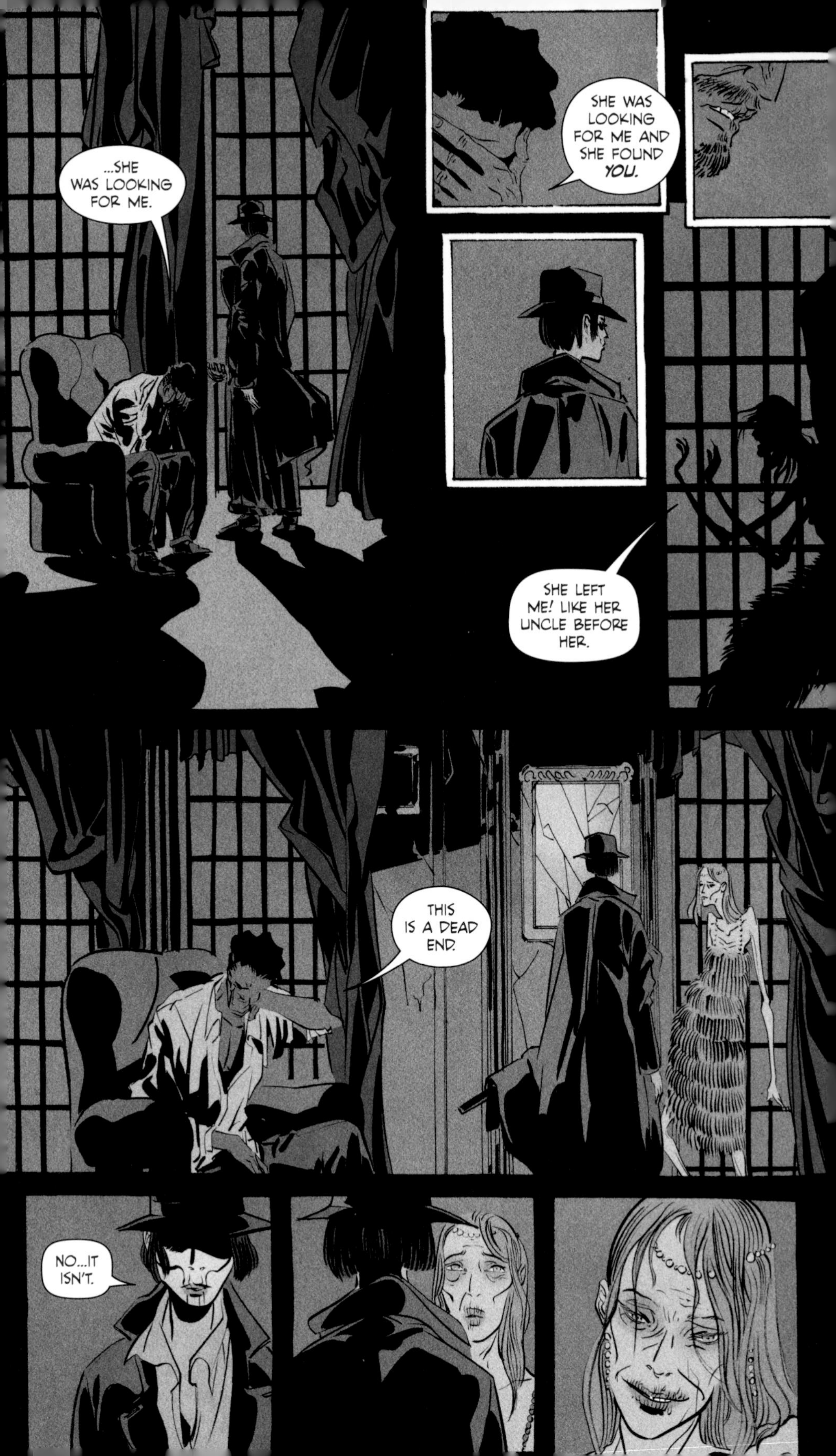
...SHE WAS LOOKING FOR ME.
SHE WAS LOOKING FOR ME AND SHE FOUND *YOU.*
SHE LEFT ME! LIKE HER UNCLE BEFORE HER.
THIS IS A DEAD END.
NO...IT ISN'T.

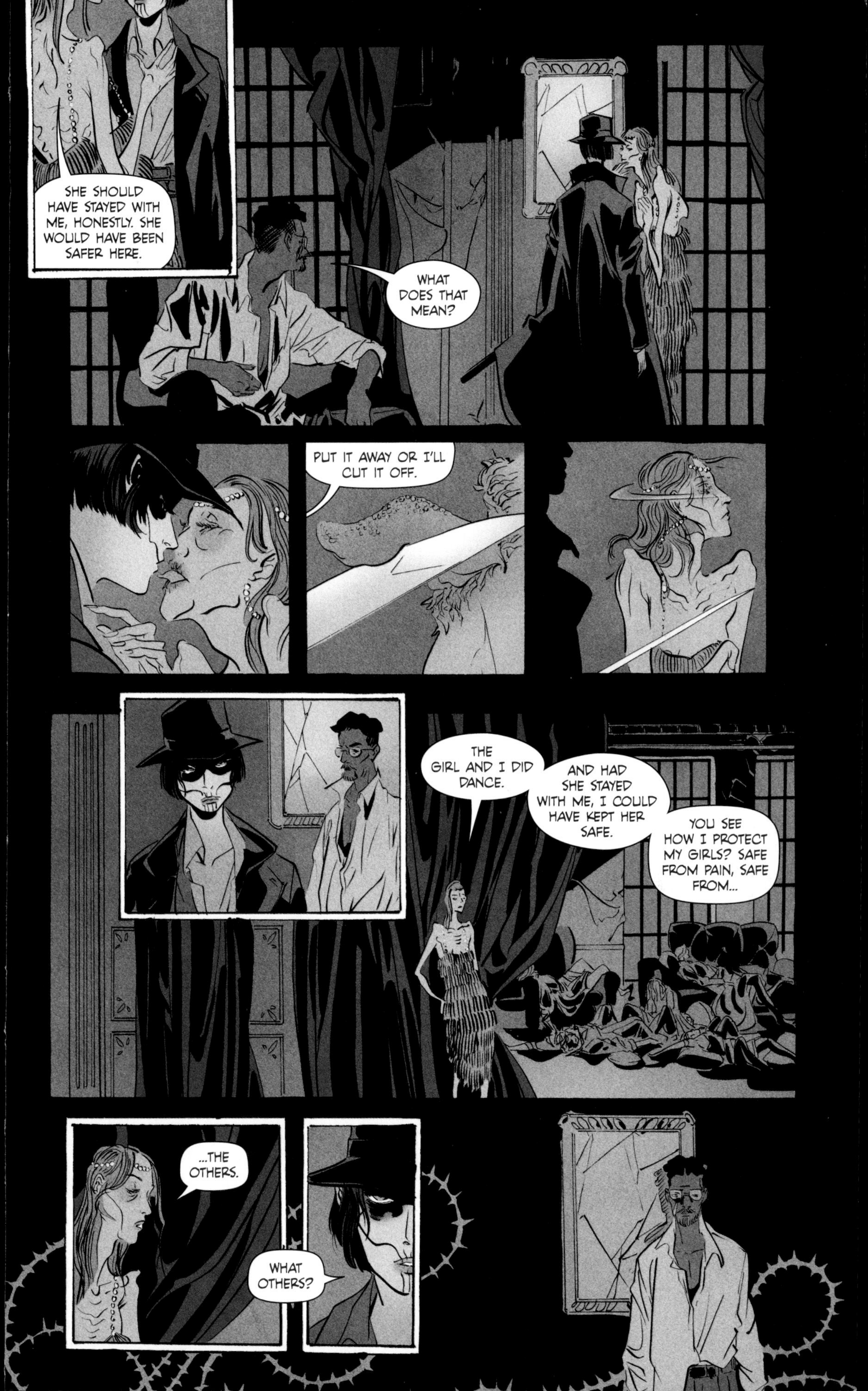
SHE SHOULD HAVE STAYED WITH ME, HONESTLY. SHE WOULD HAVE BEEN SAFER HERE.
WHAT DOES THAT MEAN?
PUT IT AWAY OR I'LL CUT IT OFF.
THE GIRL AND I DID DANCE.
AND HAD SHE STAYED WITH ME, I COULD HAVE KEPT HER SAFE.
YOU SEE HOW I PROTECT MY GIRLS? SAFE FROM PAIN, SAFE FROM...
...THE OTHERS.
WHAT OTHERS?

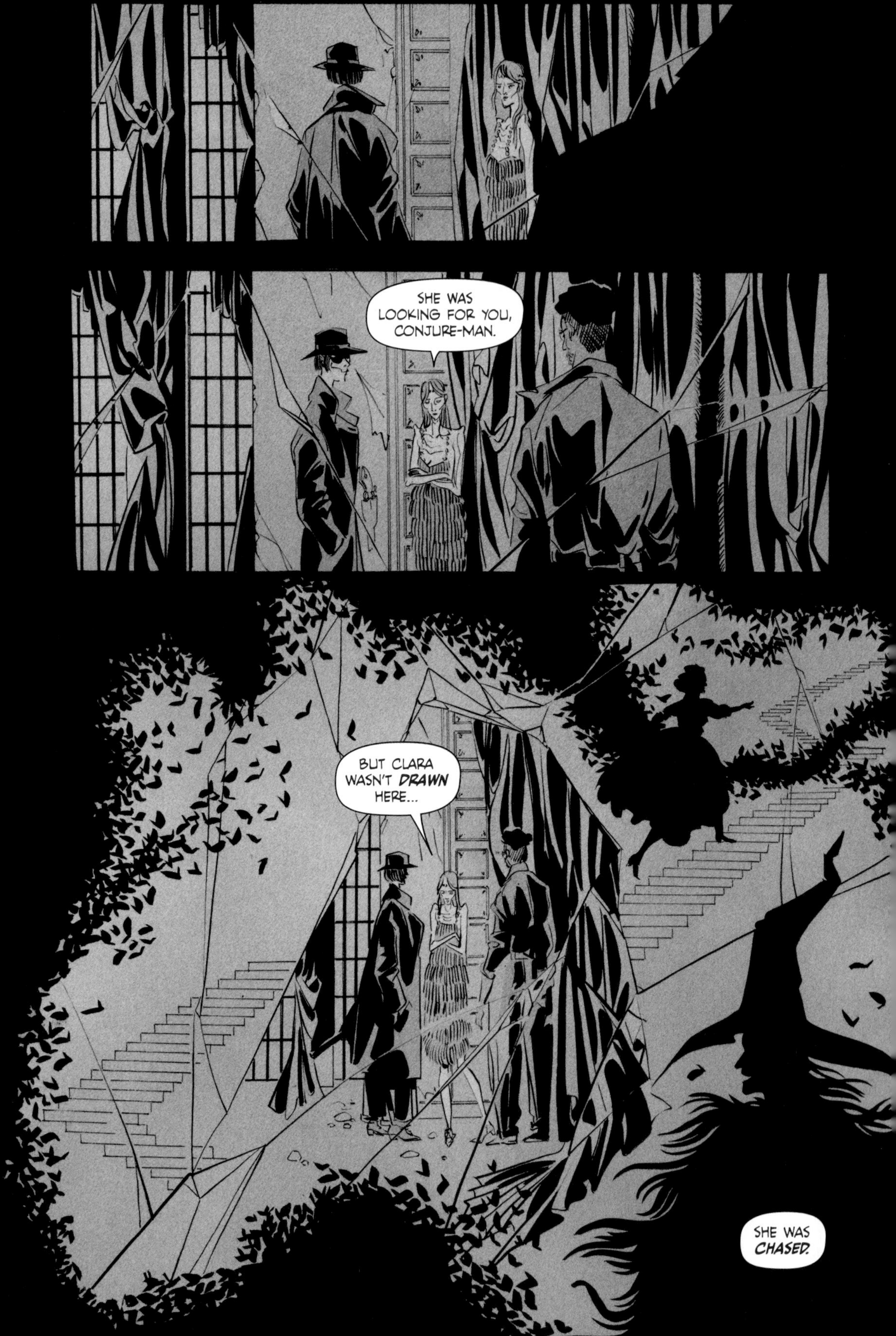
SHE WAS LOOKING FOR YOU, CONJURE-MAN.
BUT CLARA WASN'T DRAWN HERE...
SHE WAS CHASED.

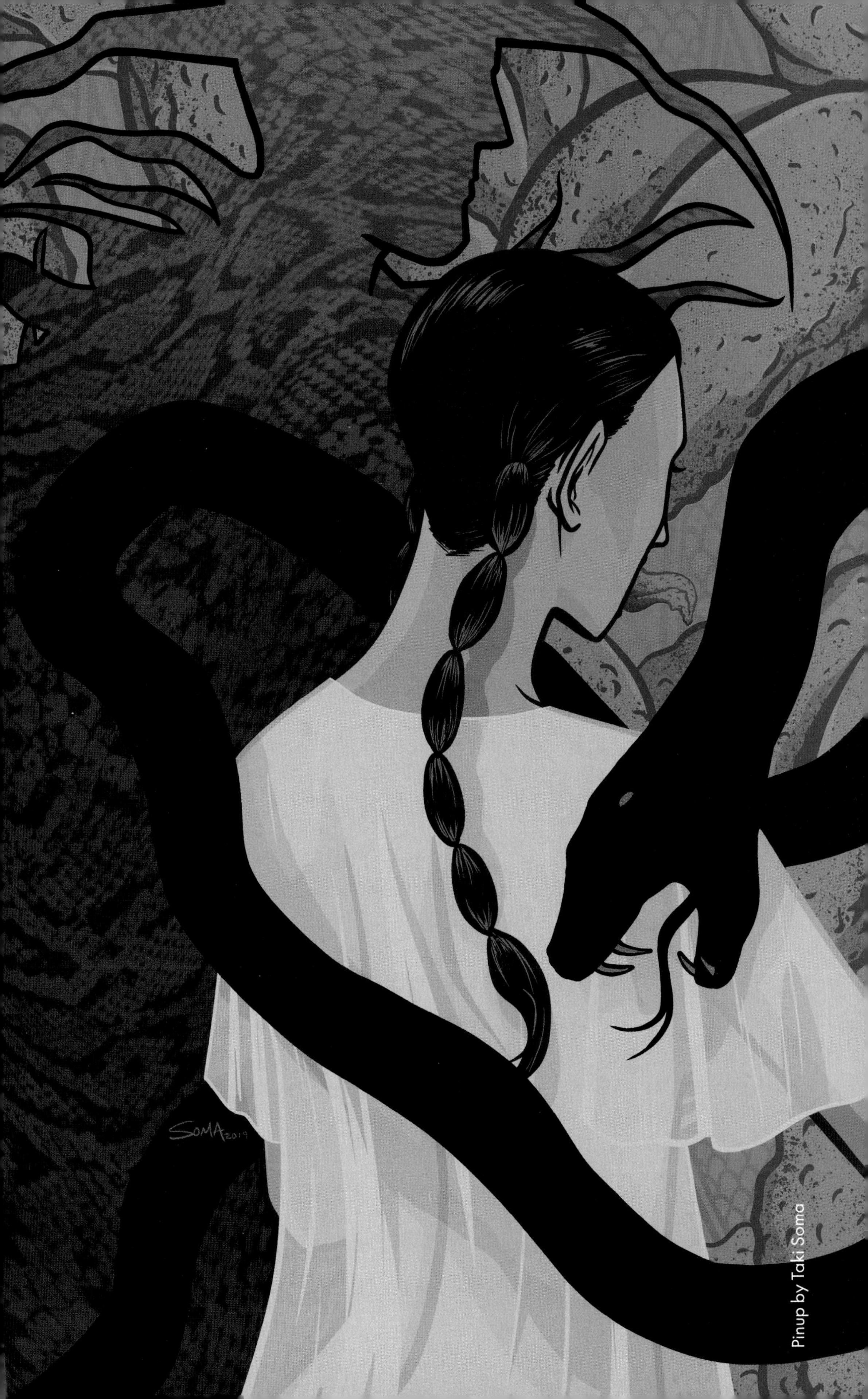
SOMA 2019
Pinup by Taki Soma

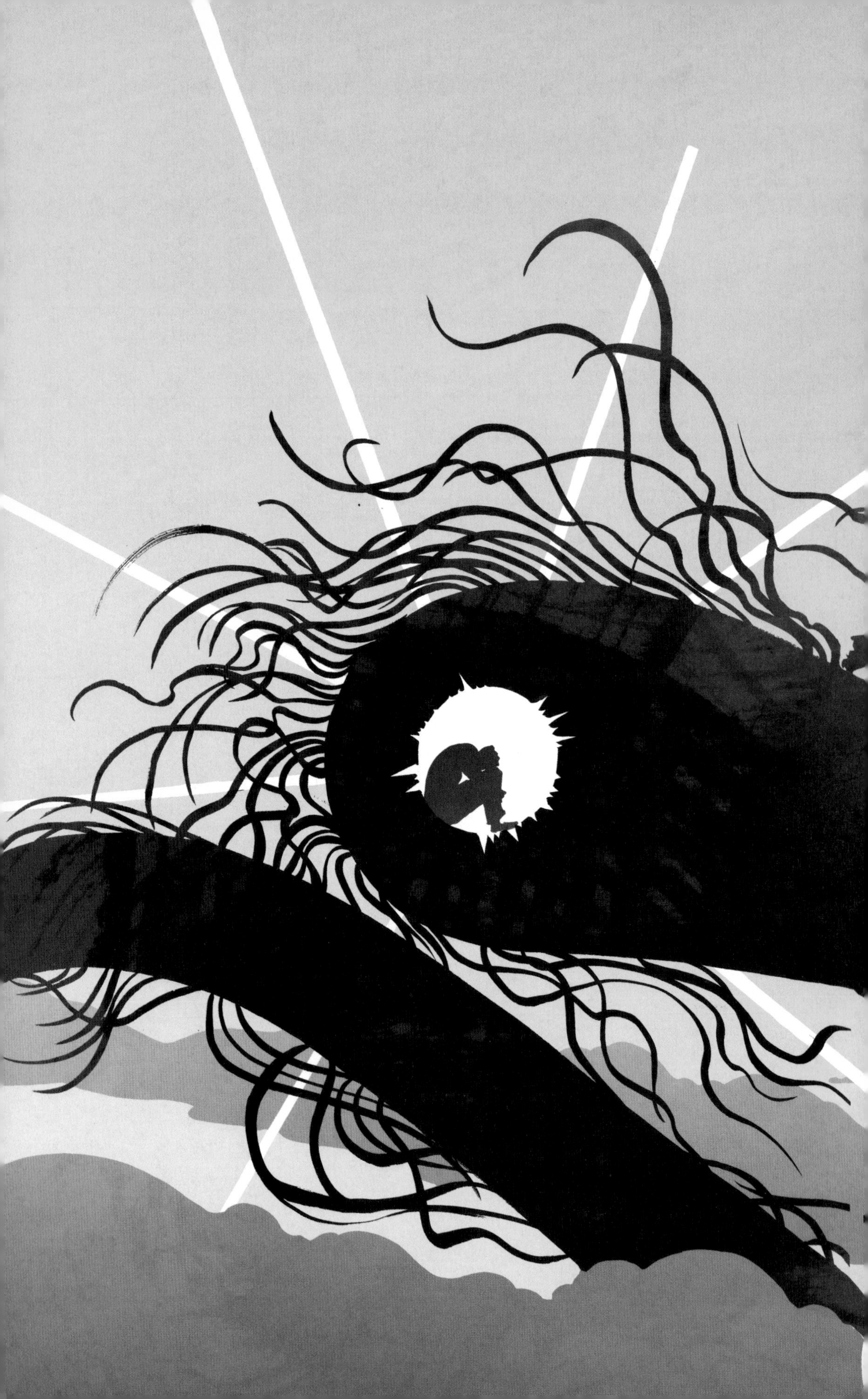

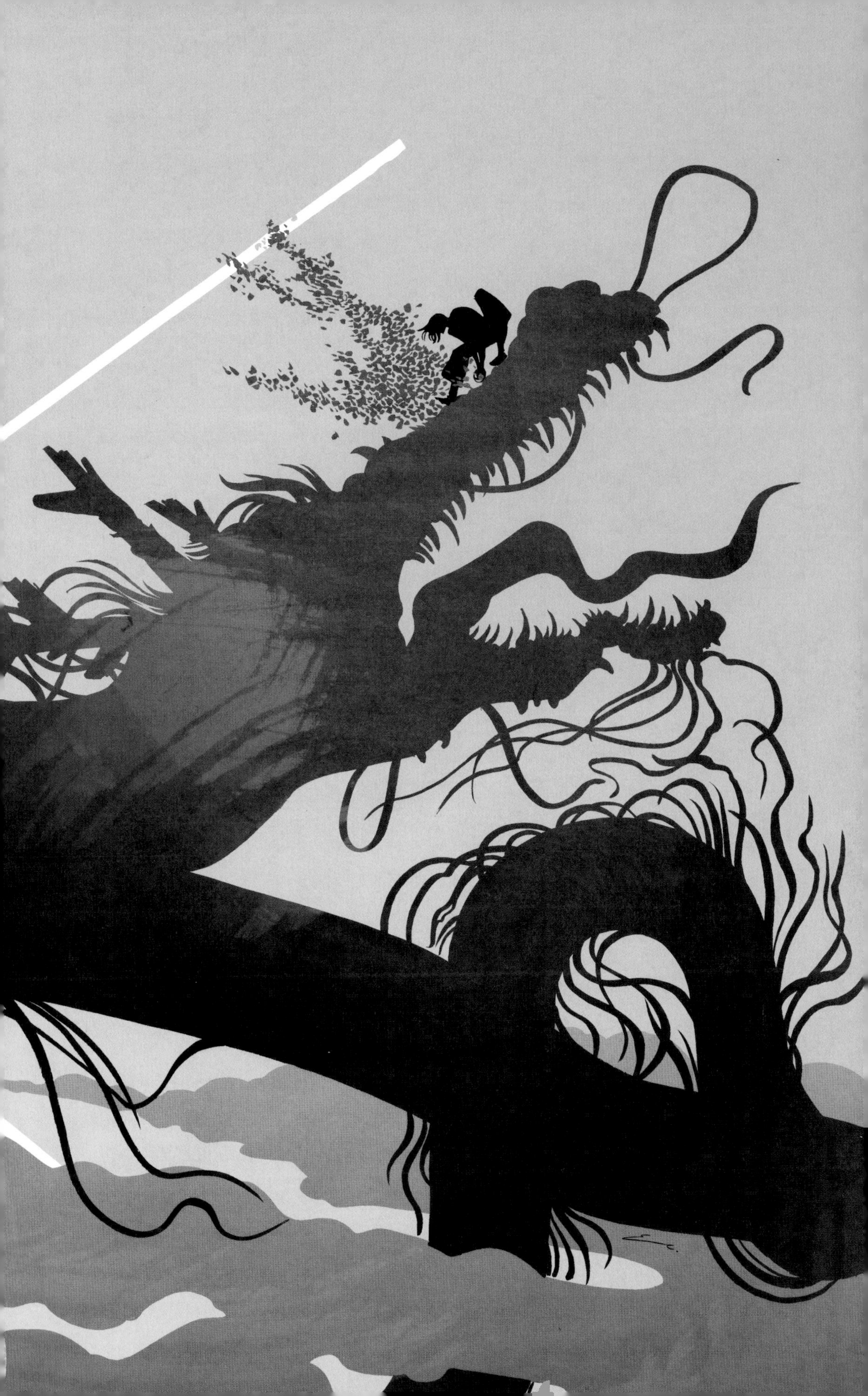

Bones Bunny tells Butterfly the tale.

The Ballad was a history. With Death's daughter Ginny at her side, Sissy, the child of blood and violence raised on love, defeated Old Death in his own domain and took his place in the long-fallow World Garden. Having assumed the mantle of Death, Sissy must bring the Garden back to life and seek out the errant Reapers, and return them to the fold. In the mortal realm, Sarah Fields, the woman who pulled Sissy from the river of blood that bore her, died. Her children, and their connection to the Reapers, live on. Striking out from their birthplace, Sarah's progeny have found themselves as far-flung as the bloody trenches of France to the arid streets of Hollywoodland.

In between the glitz, the glamour, and the bright lights, Clara Fields is found dead. Her uncle Frank, the Conjure-Man, sets out to solve the mystery of her death. As he desperately searches for answers, Ginny, Death's daughter and the reaper of Vengeance, sets aside her duties to assist the Conjure-Man on his quest.

They started their investigation with Director Jack Kaufman, who took advantage of Clara's talent before she disappeared. The trail led them to the Reaper of Thirst, who gave Clara distractions, for a time. But Clara left her domain as well. Now they search for the Reaper who stalked her…

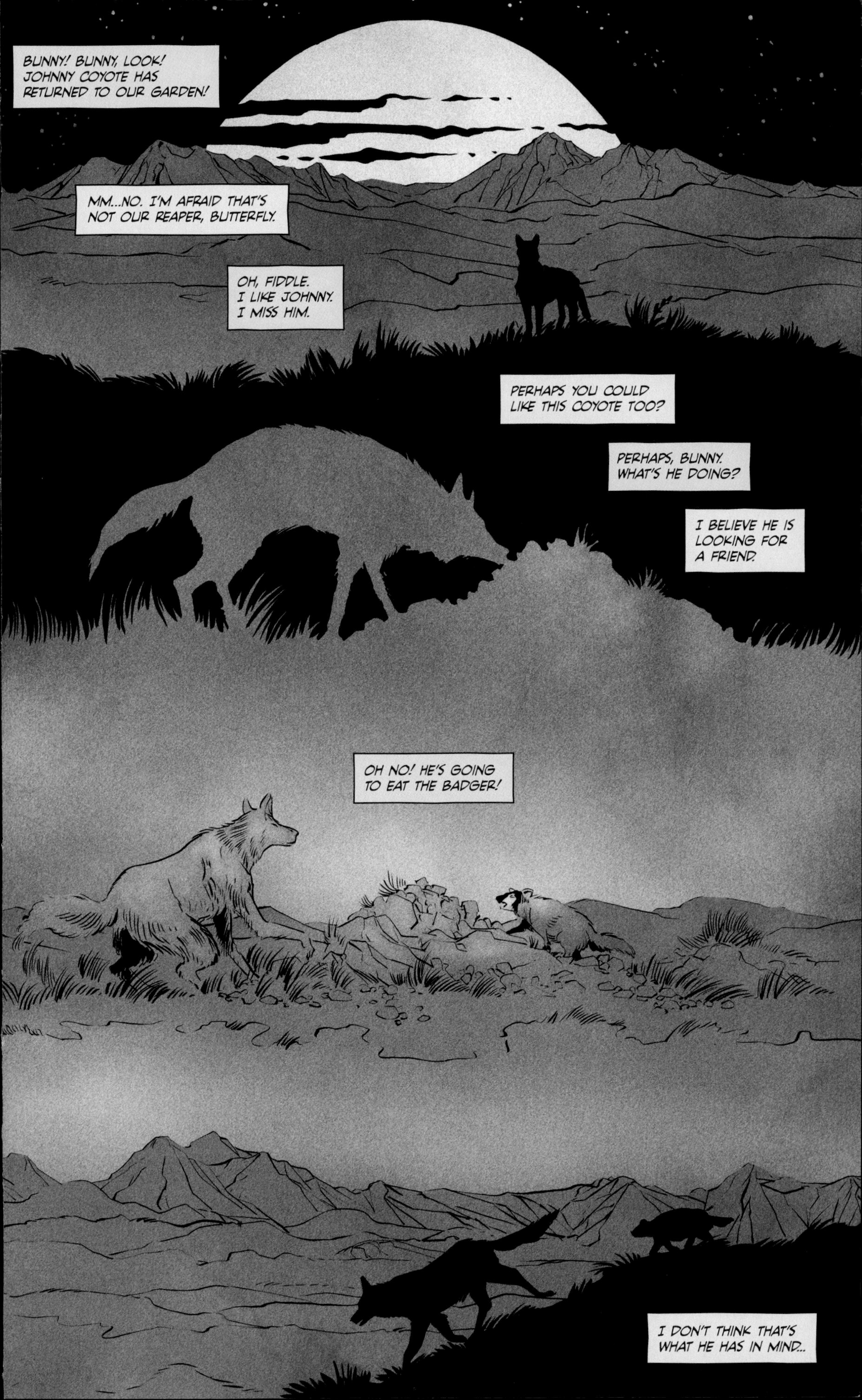
BUNNY! BUNNY, LOOK! JOHNNY COYOTE HAS RETURNED TO OUR GARDEN!
MM...NO. I'M AFRAID THAT'S NOT OUR REAPER, BUTTERFLY.
OH, FIDDLE. I LIKE JOHNNY. I MISS HIM.
PERHAPS YOU COULD LIKE THIS COYOTE TOO?
PERHAPS, BUNNY. WHAT'S HE DOING?
I BELIEVE HE IS LOOKING FOR A FRIEND.
OH NO! HE'S GOING TO EAT THE BADGER!
I DON'T THINK THAT'S WHAT HE HAS IN MIND...

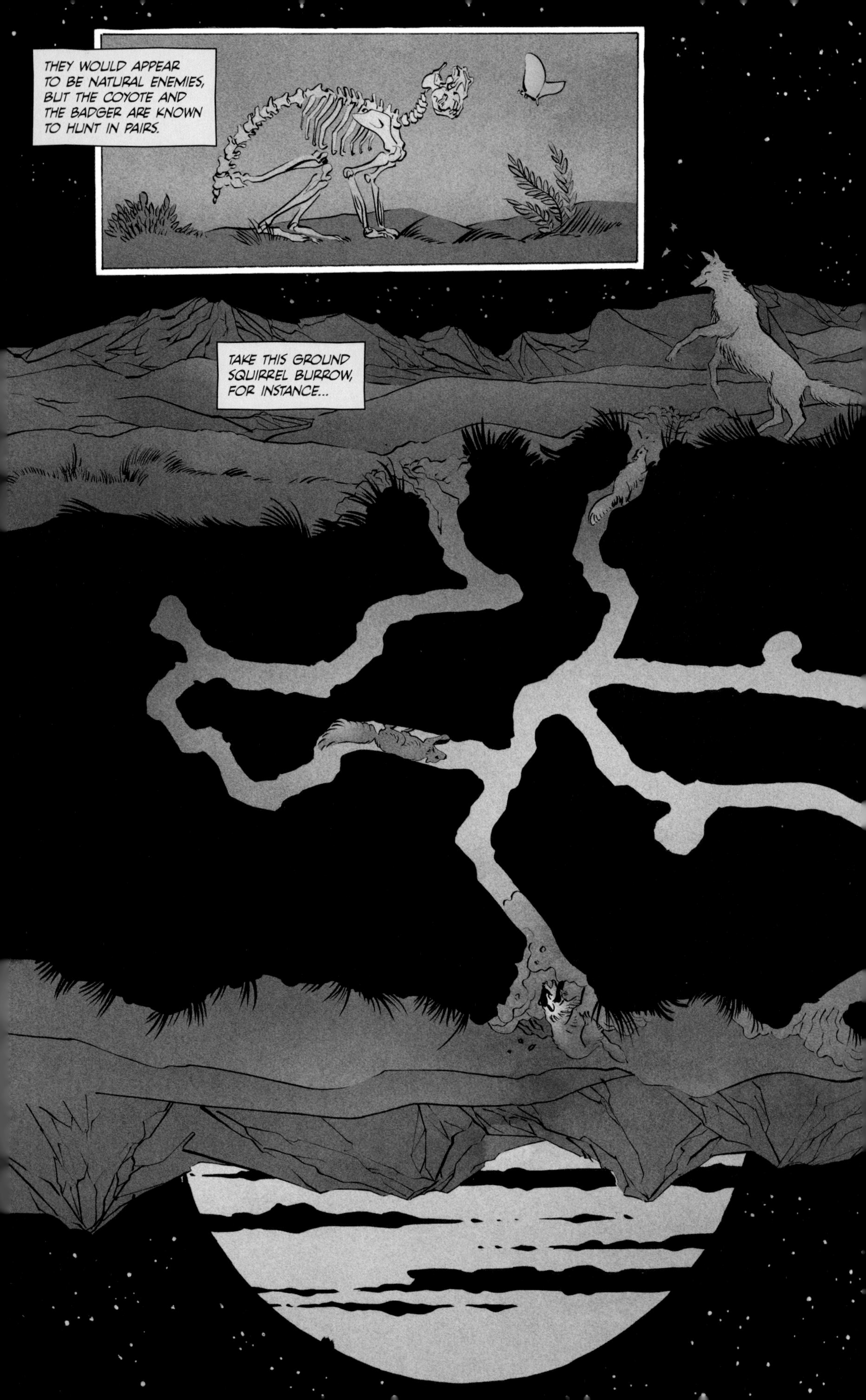
THEY WOULD APPEAR TO BE NATURAL ENEMIES, BUT THE COYOTE AND THE BADGER ARE KNOWN TO HUNT IN PAIRS.
TAKE THIS GROUND SQUIRREL BURROW, FOR INSTANCE...

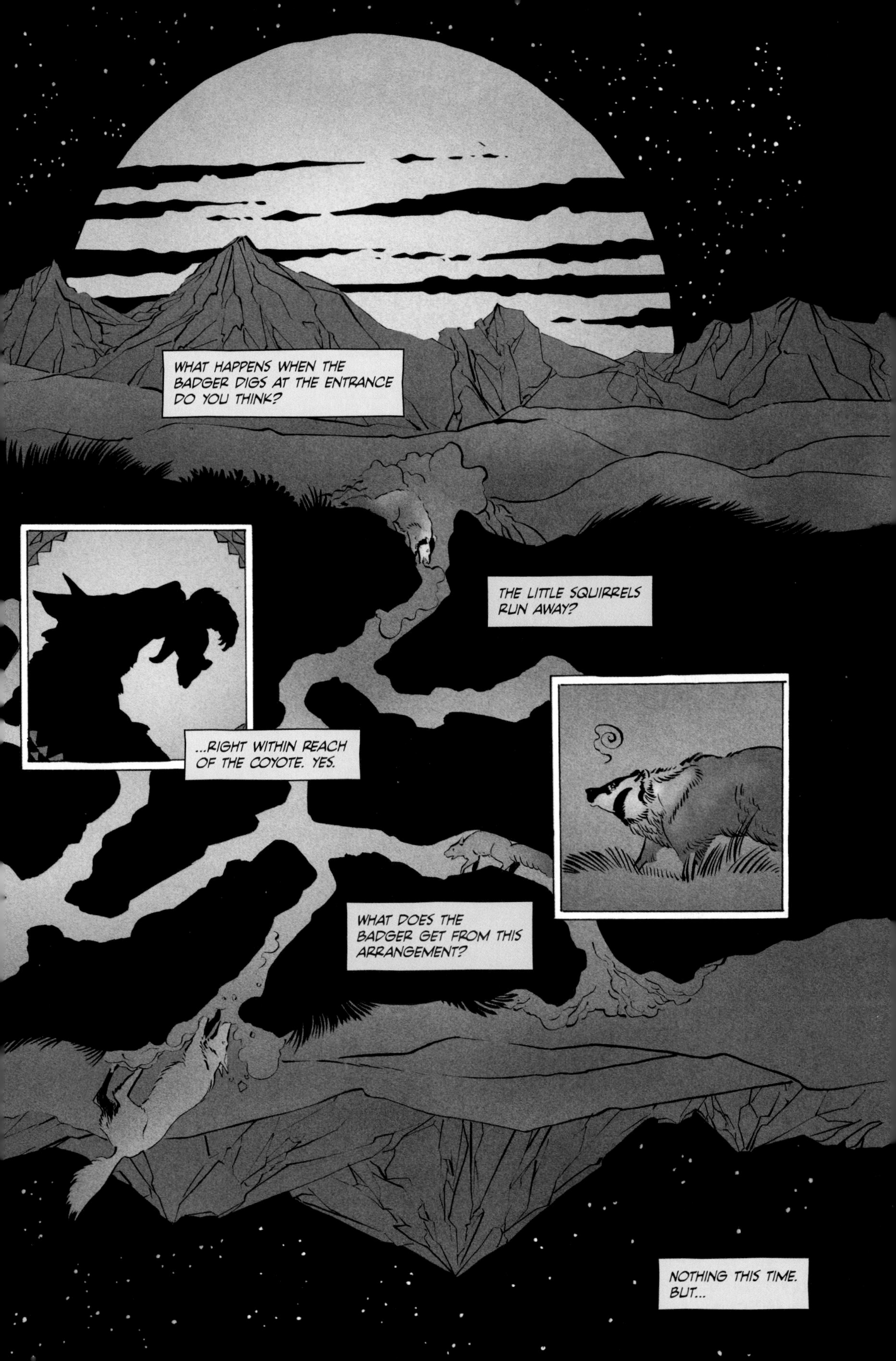
WHAT HAPPENS WHEN THE BADGER DIGS AT THE ENTRANCE DO YOU THINK?
THE LITTLE SQUIRRELS RUN AWAY?
...RIGHT WITHIN REACH OF THE COYOTE. YES.
WHAT DOES THE BADGER GET FROM THIS ARRANGEMENT?
NOTHING THIS TIME. BUT...

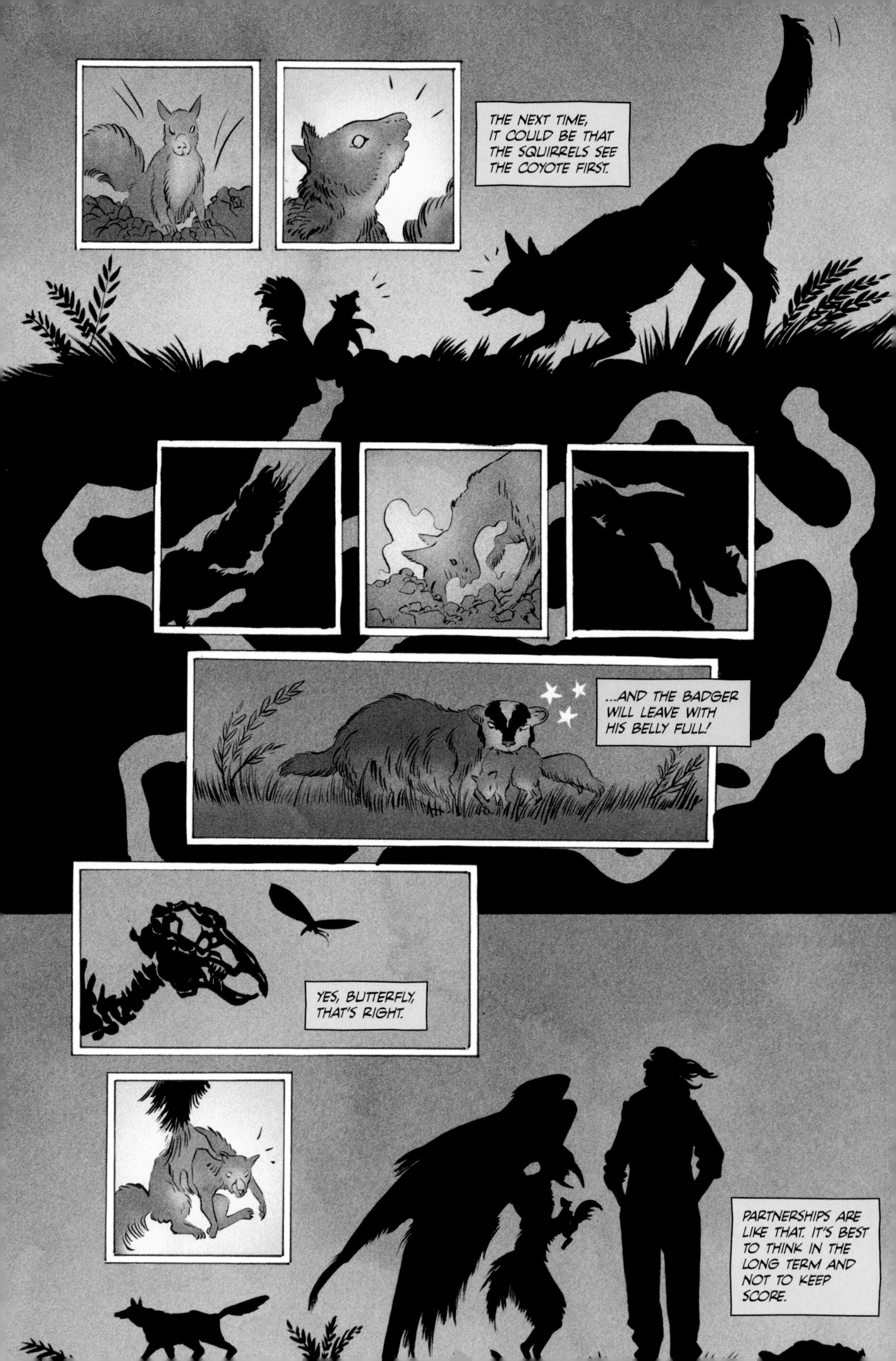
THE NEXT TIME, IT COULD BE THAT THE SQUIRRELS SEE THE COYOTE FIRST.
...AND THE BADGER WILL LEAVE WITH HIS BELLY FULL!
YES, BUTTERFLY, THAT'S RIGHT.
PARTNERSHIPS ARE LIKE THAT. IT'S BEST TO THINK IN THE LONG TERM AND NOT TO KEEP SCORE.

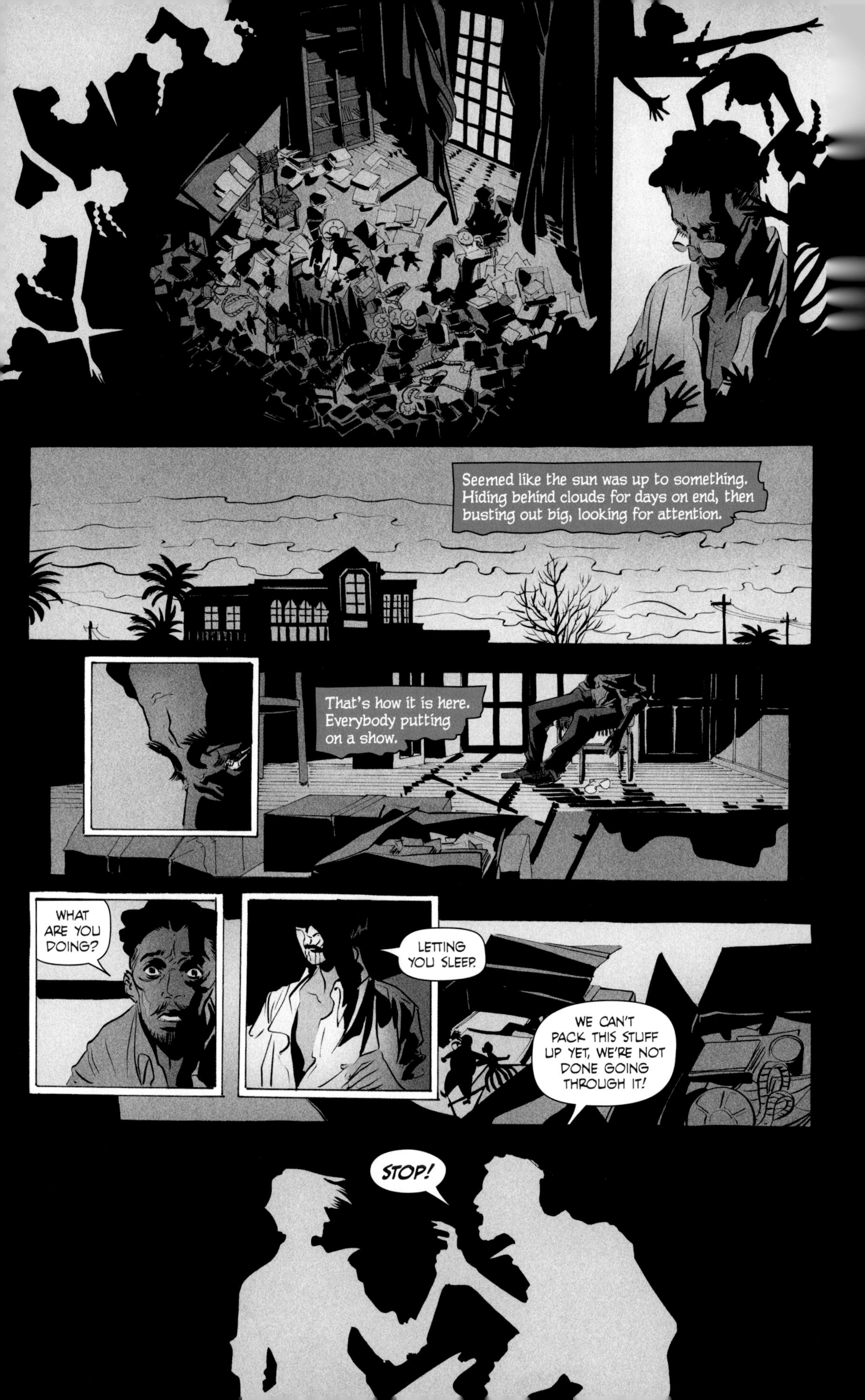
Seemed like the sun was up to something. Hiding behind clouds for days on end, then busting out big, looking for attention.
That's how it is here. Everybody putting on a show.
WHAT ARE YOU DOING?
LETTING YOU SLEEP.
WE CAN'T PACK THIS STUFF UP YET, WE'RE NOT DONE GOING THROUGH IT!
STOP!

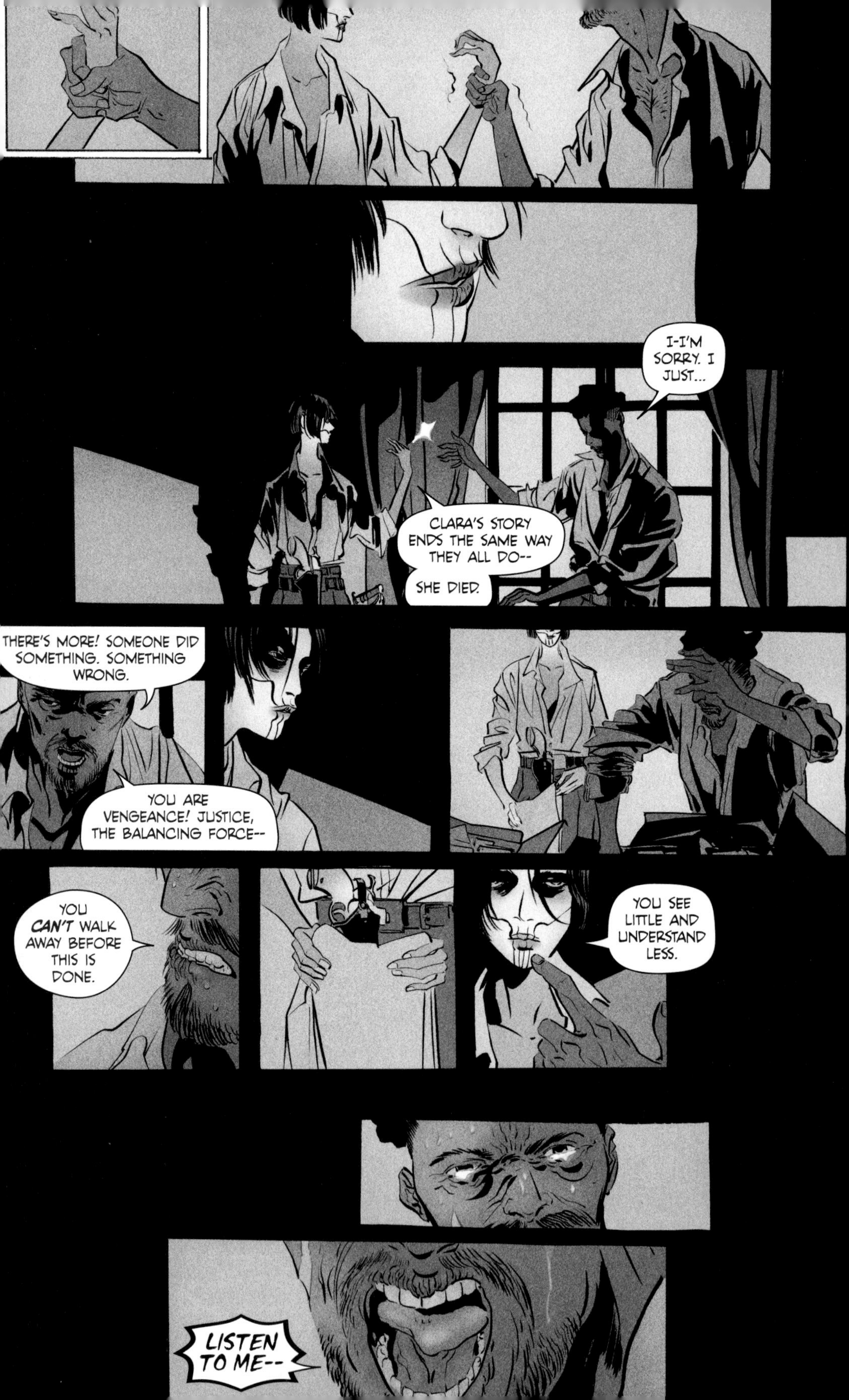
I-I'M SORRY. I JUST...
CLARA'S STORY ENDS THE SAME WAY THEY ALL DO--
SHE DIED.
THERE'S MORE! SOMEONE DID SOMETHING. SOMETHING WRONG.
YOU ARE VENGEANCE! JUSTICE, THE BALANCING FORCE--
YOU CAN'T WALK AWAY BEFORE THIS IS DONE.
YOU SEE LITTLE AND UNDERSTAND LESS.
LISTEN TO ME--

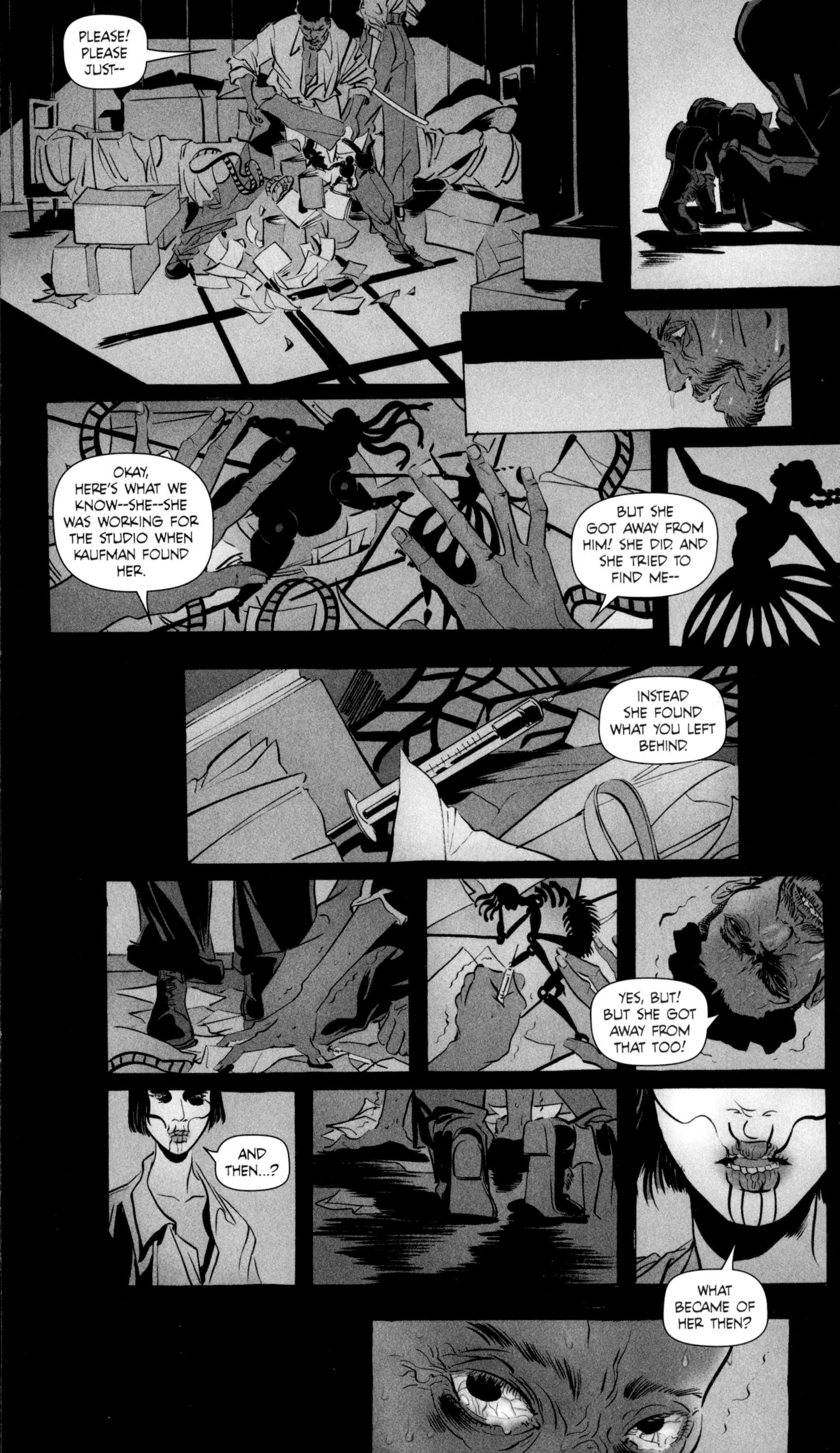
PLEASE! PLEASE JUST--
OKAY, HERE'S WHAT WE KNOW--SHE--SHE WAS WORKING FOR THE STUDIO WHEN KAUFMAN FOUND HER.
BUT SHE GOT AWAY FROM HIM! SHE DID. AND SHE TRIED TO FIND ME--
INSTEAD SHE FOUND WHAT YOU LEFT BEHIND.
YES, BUT! BUT SHE GOT AWAY FROM THAT TOO!
AND THEN...?
WHAT BECAME OF HER THEN?

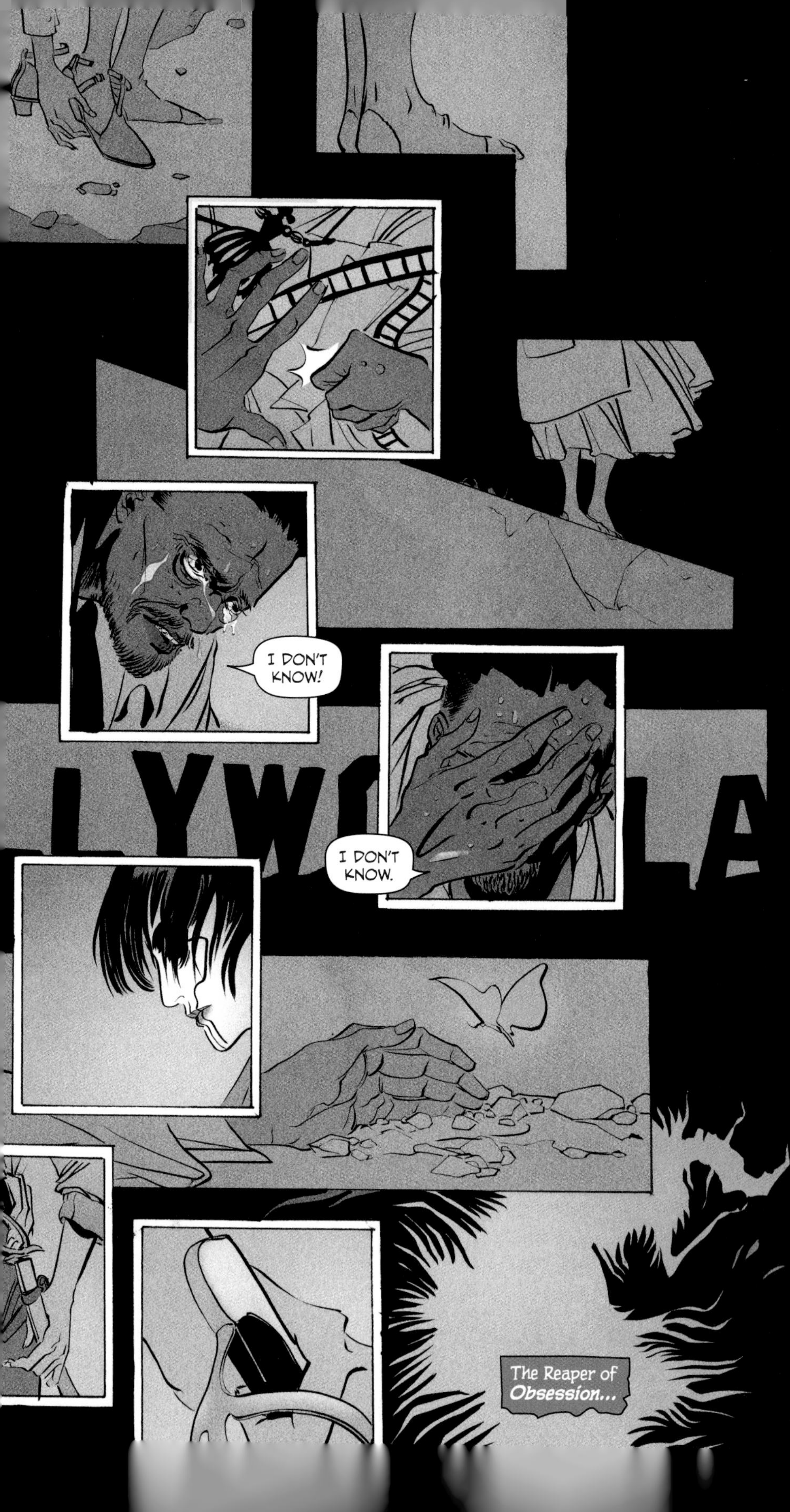
I DON'T KNOW!
I DON'T KNOW.
The Reaper of Obsession...

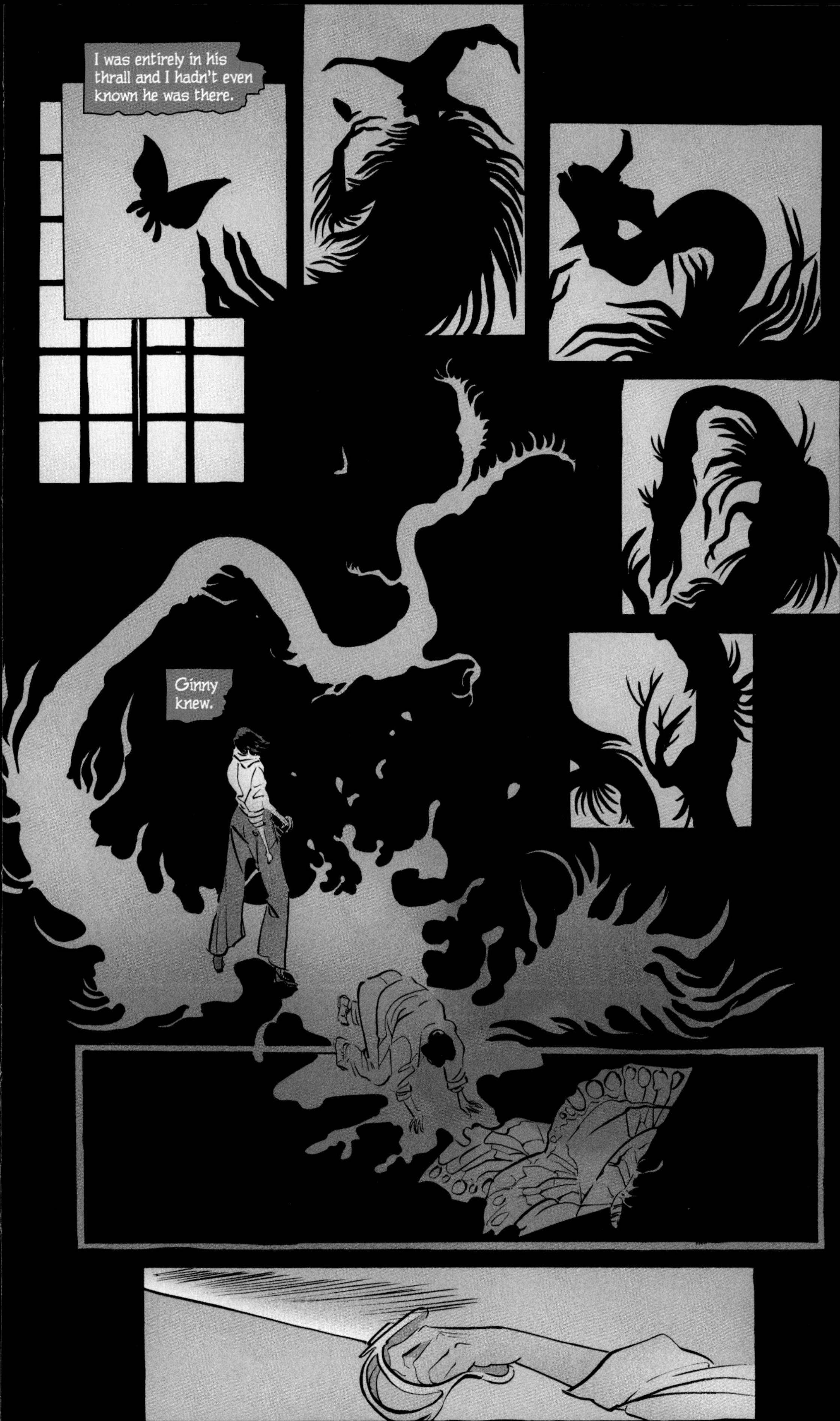
I was entirely in his thrall and I hadn't even known he was there.
Ginny knew.

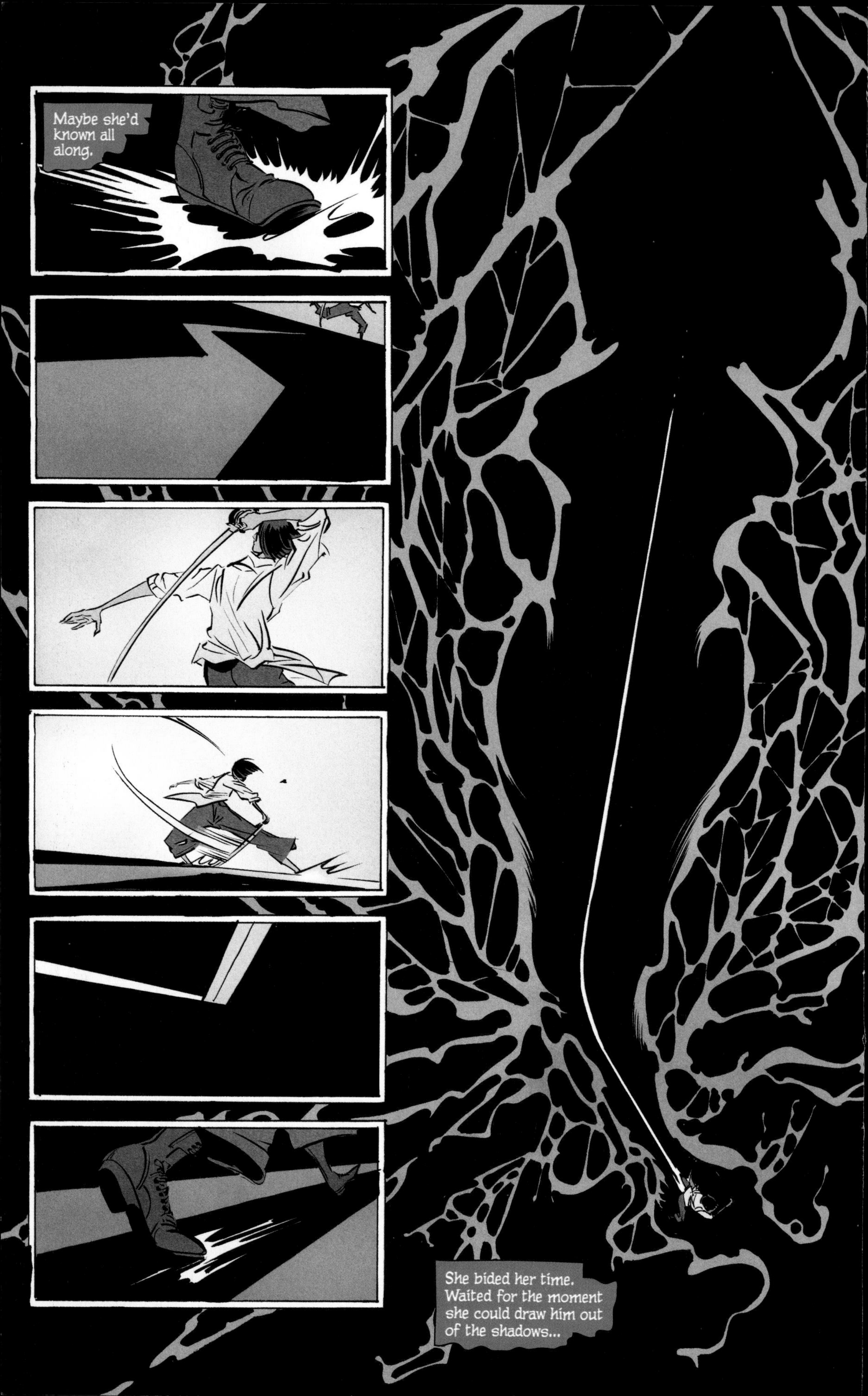
Maybe she'd known all along.
She bided her time. Waited for the moment she could draw him out of the shadows...

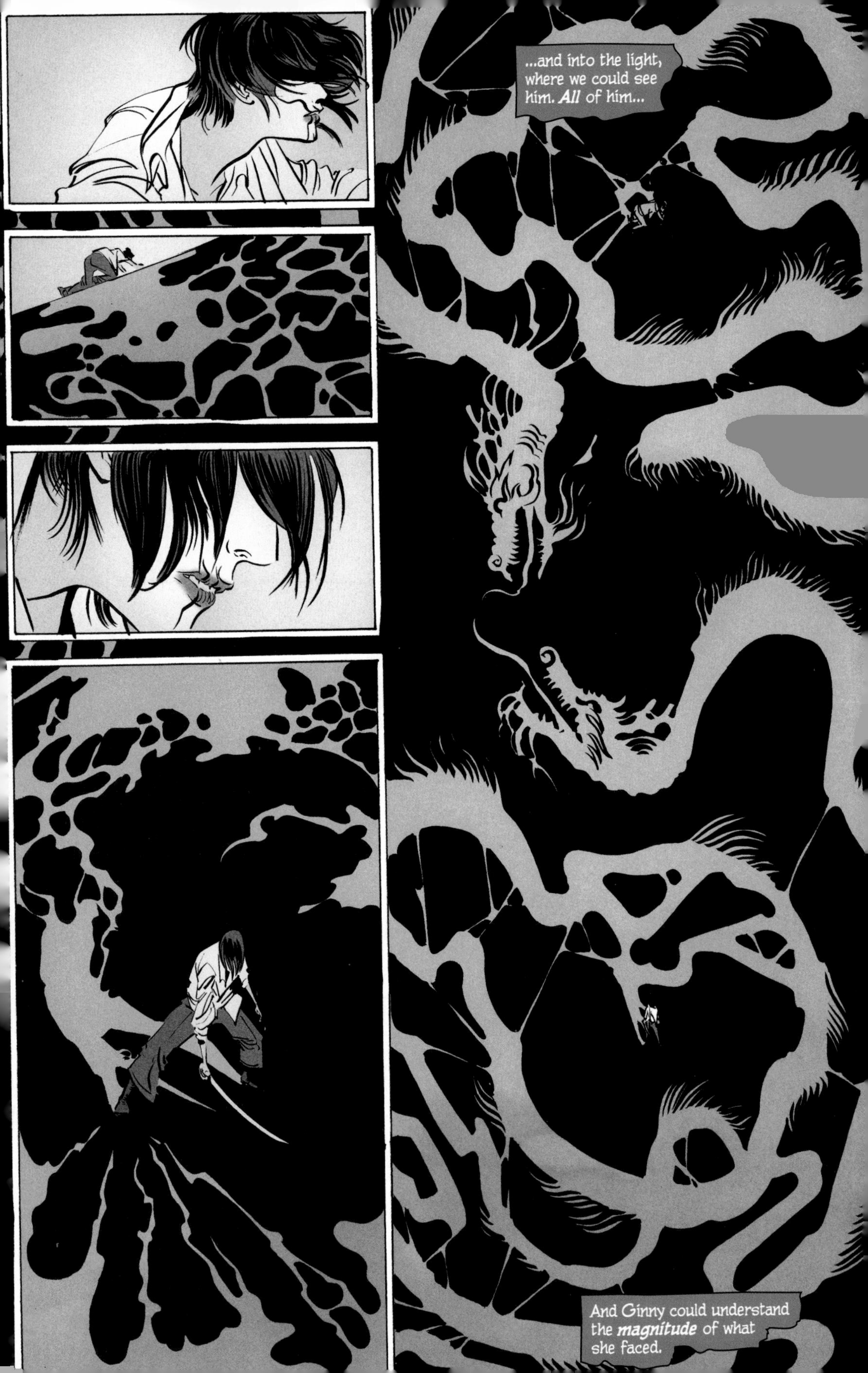
...and into the light, where we could see him. *All* of him...
And Ginny could understand the *magnitude* of what she faced.

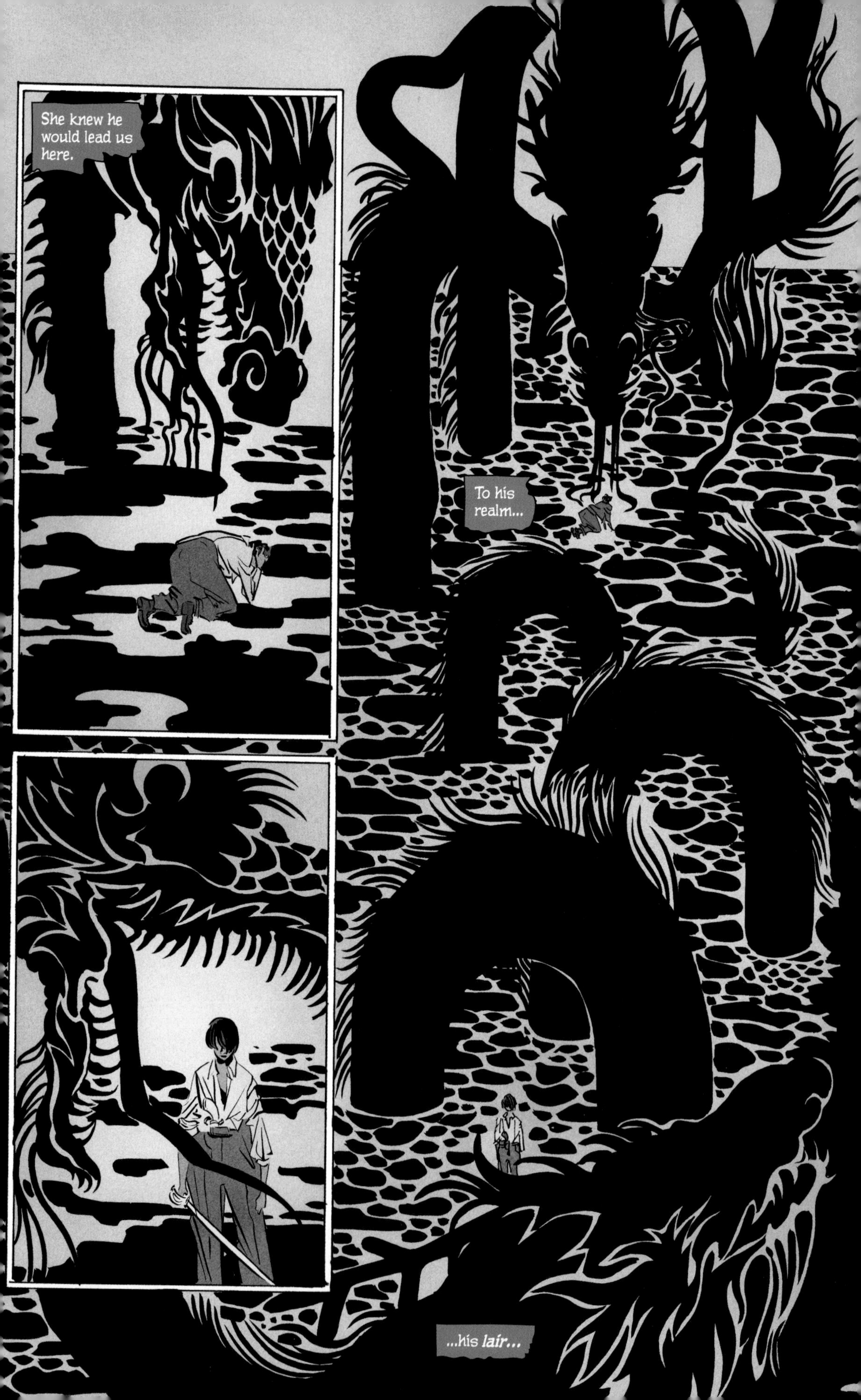
She knew he would lead us here.
To his realm...
...his lair...

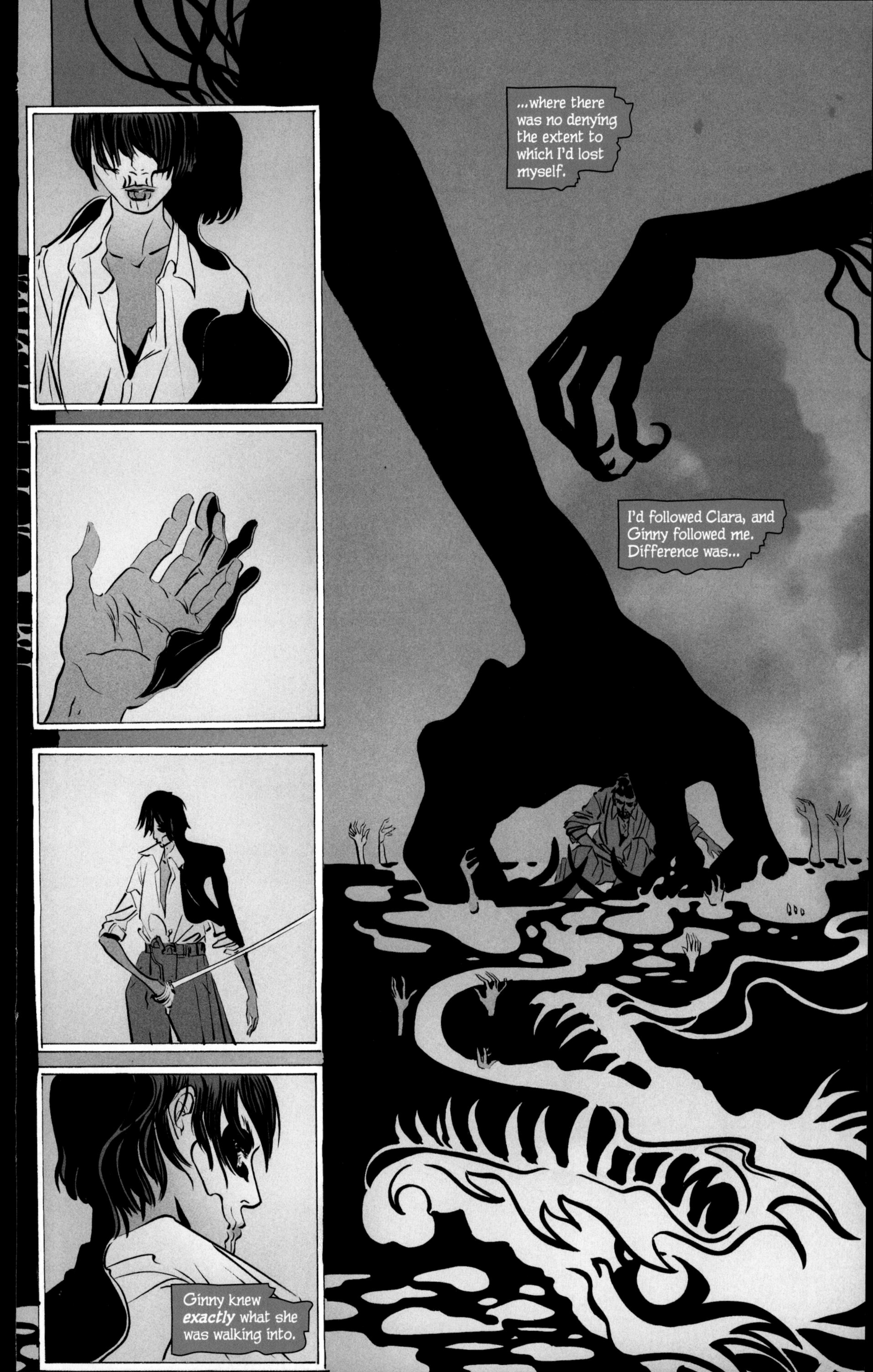
...where there was no denying the extent to which I'd lost myself.
I'd followed Clara, and Ginny followed me. Difference was...
Ginny knew *exactly* what she was walking into.

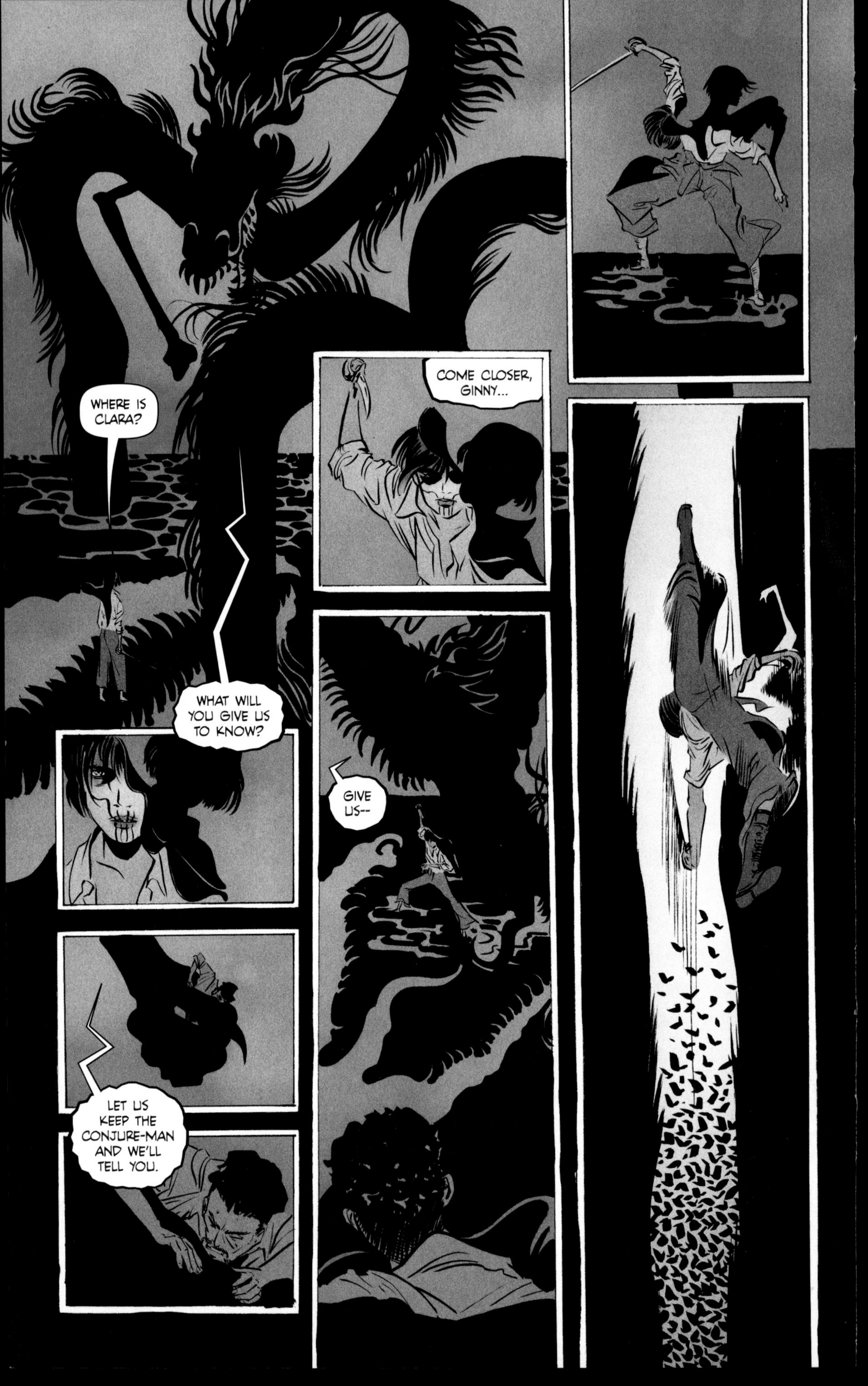
WHERE IS CLARA?
WHAT WILL YOU GIVE US TO KNOW?
LET US KEEP THE CONJURE-MAN AND WE'LL TELL YOU.
COME CLOSER, GINNY...
GIVE US--

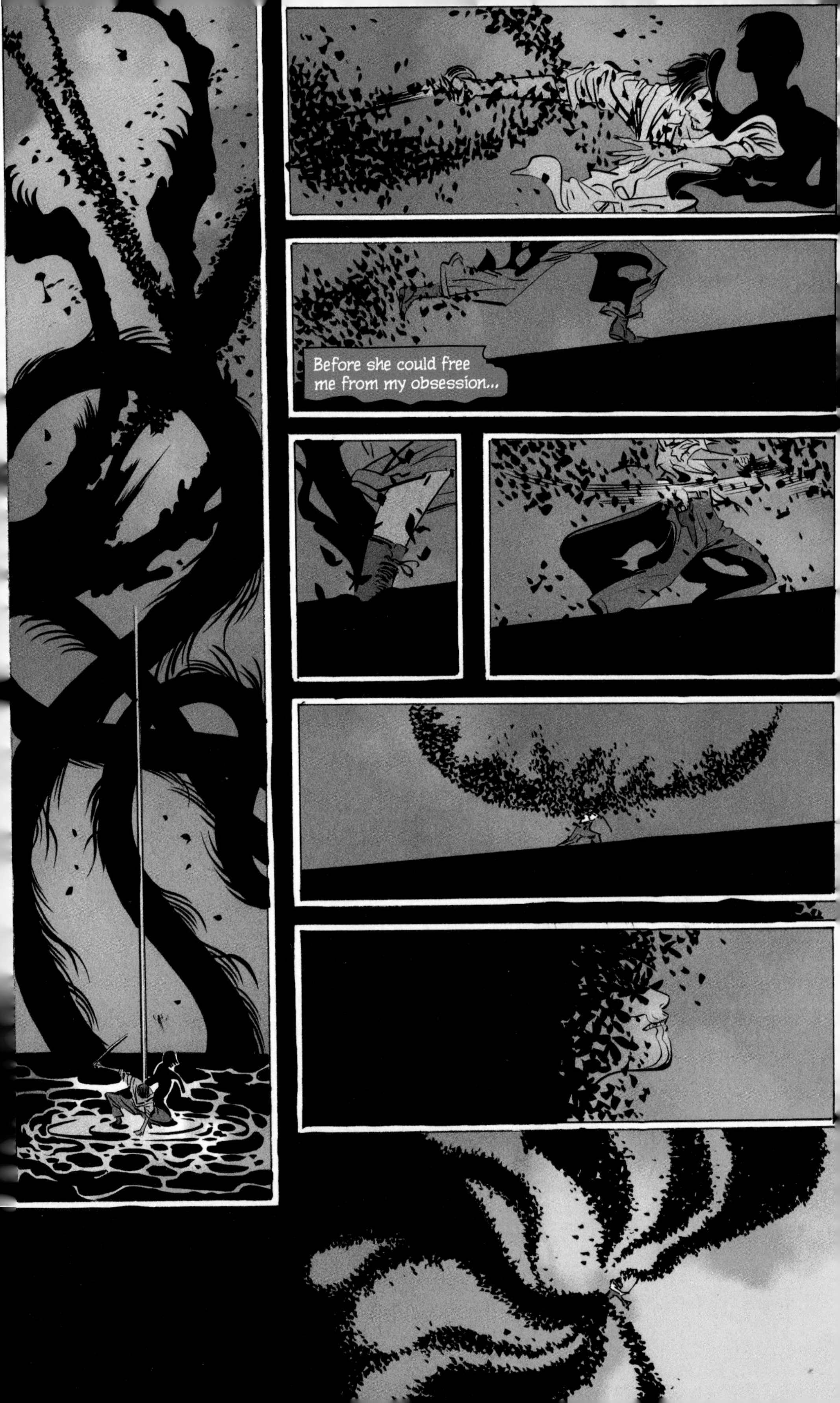
Before she could free
me from my obsession...

...she had to face her own.

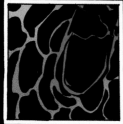

Big Alice, The Reaper of Cruelty.

They were meant to be a pair, Ginny and Alice. Cruelty and Vengeance.

But Ginny preferred to ride alone. And Alice...

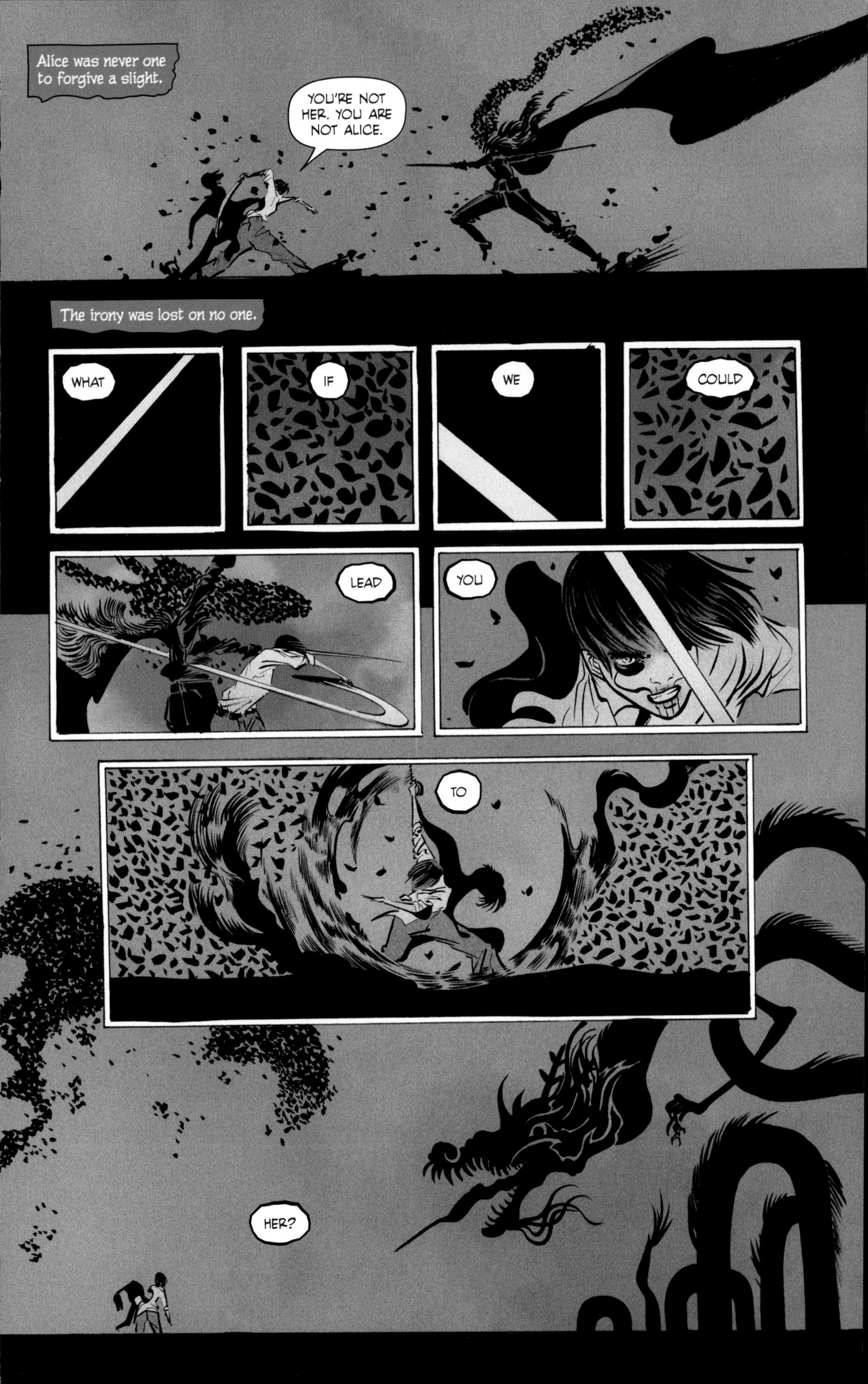
Alice was never one to forgive a slight.
YOU'RE NOT HER. YOU ARE NOT ALICE.
The irony was lost on no one.
WHAT
IF
WE
COULD
LEAD
YOU
TO
HER?

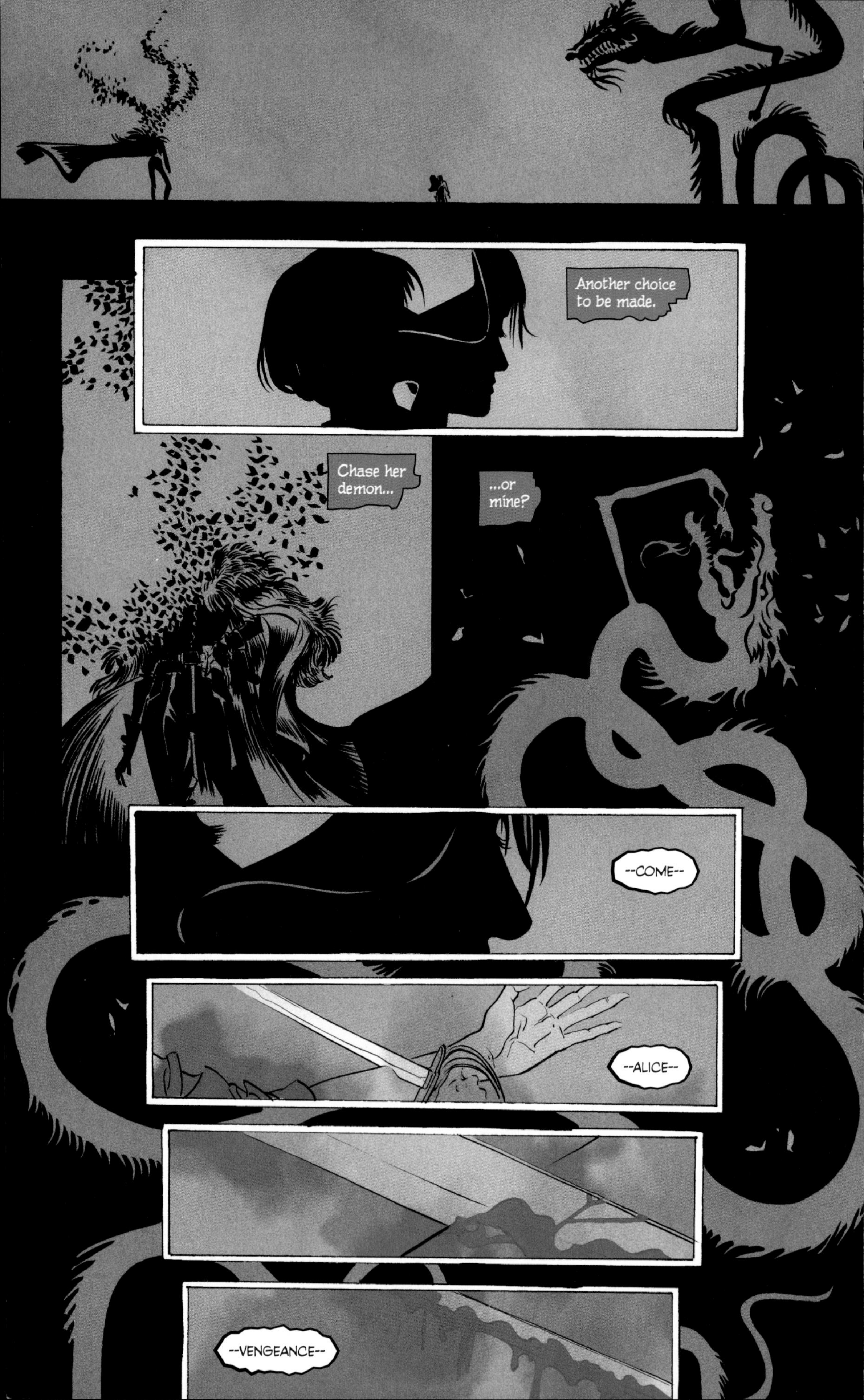
Another choice to be made.
Chase her demon...
...or mine?
--COME--
--ALICE--
--VENGEANCE--

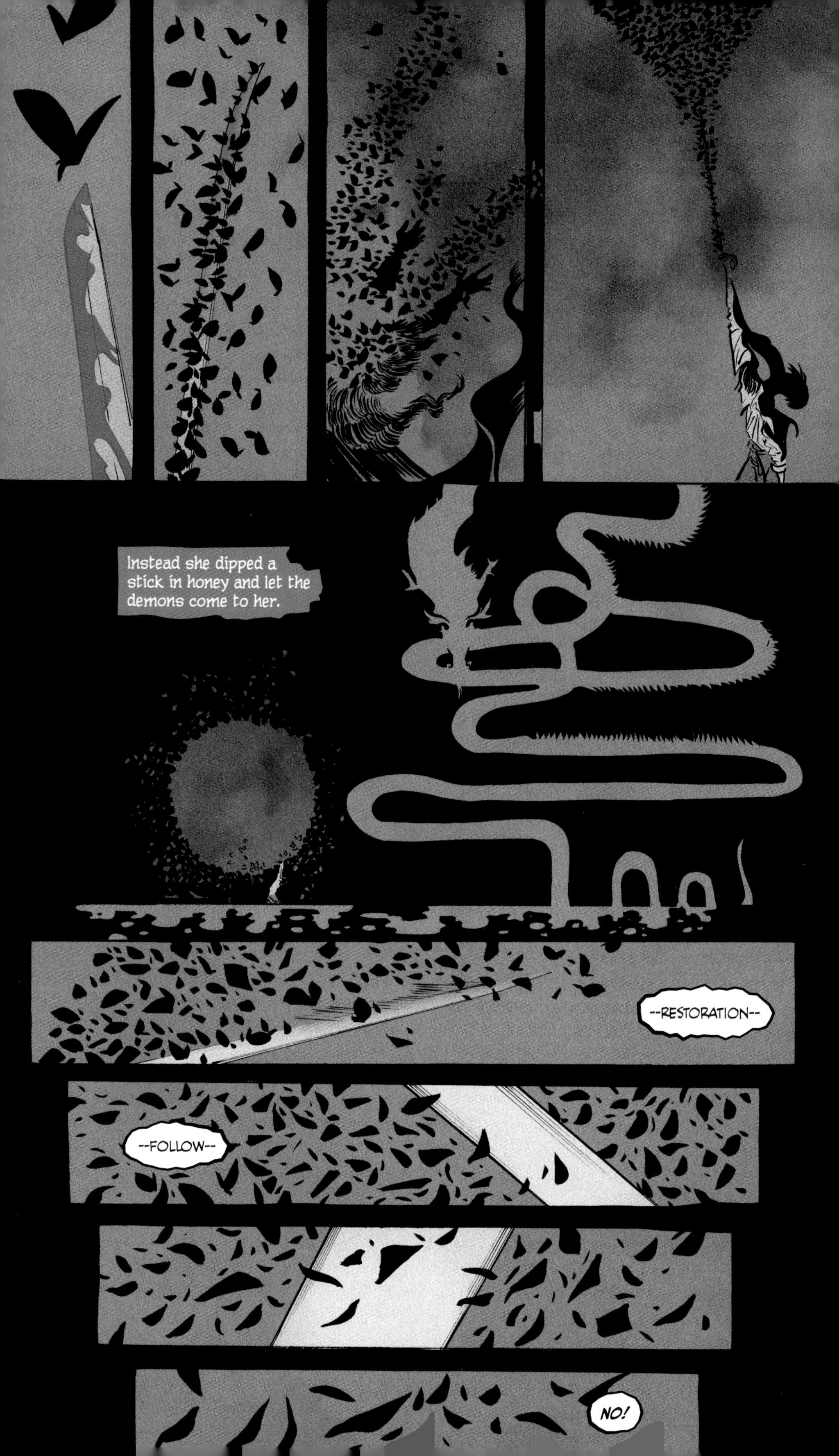
Instead she dipped a stick in honey and let the demons come to her.
--RESTORATION--
--FOLLOW--
NO!

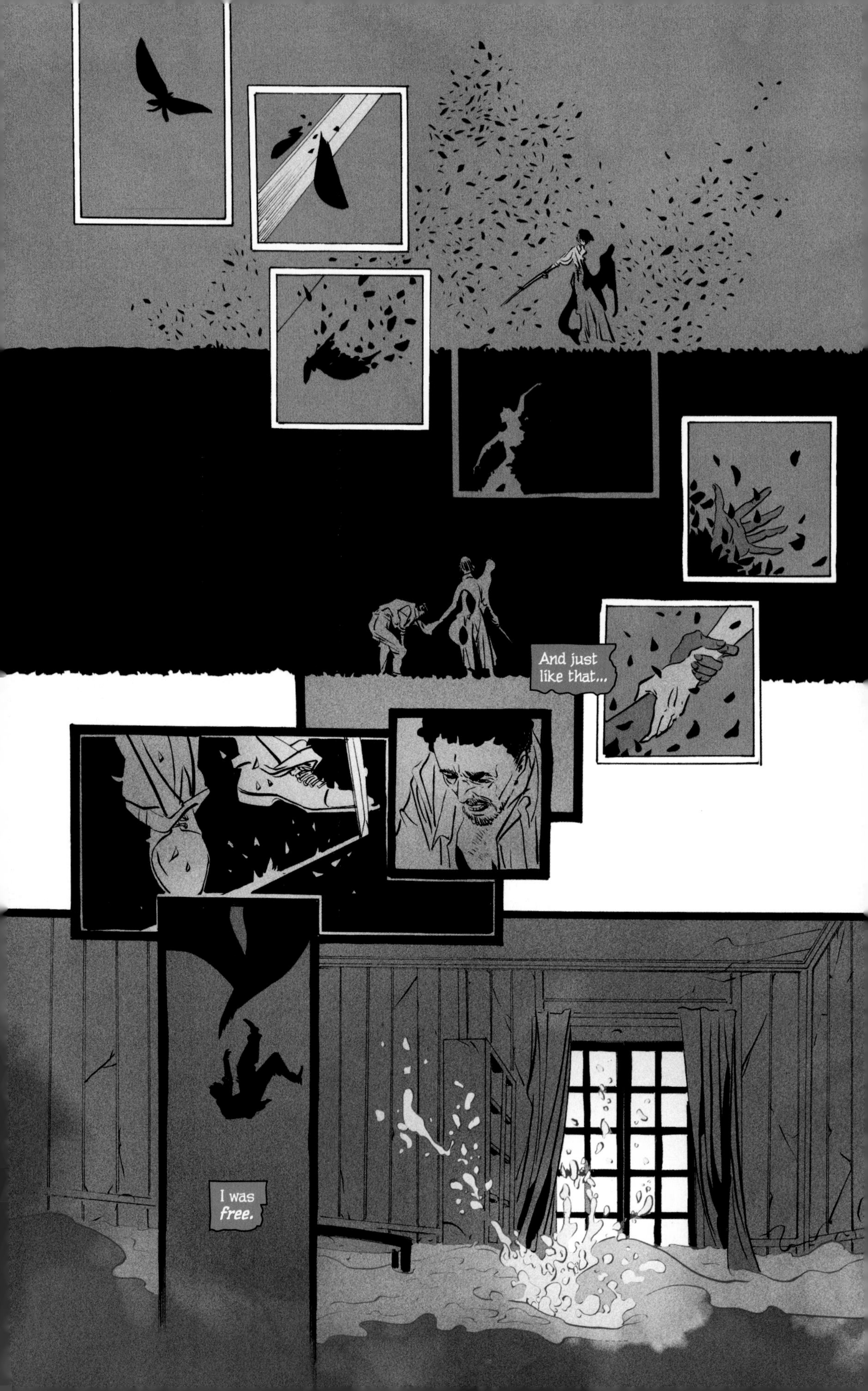
And just like that...
I was free.

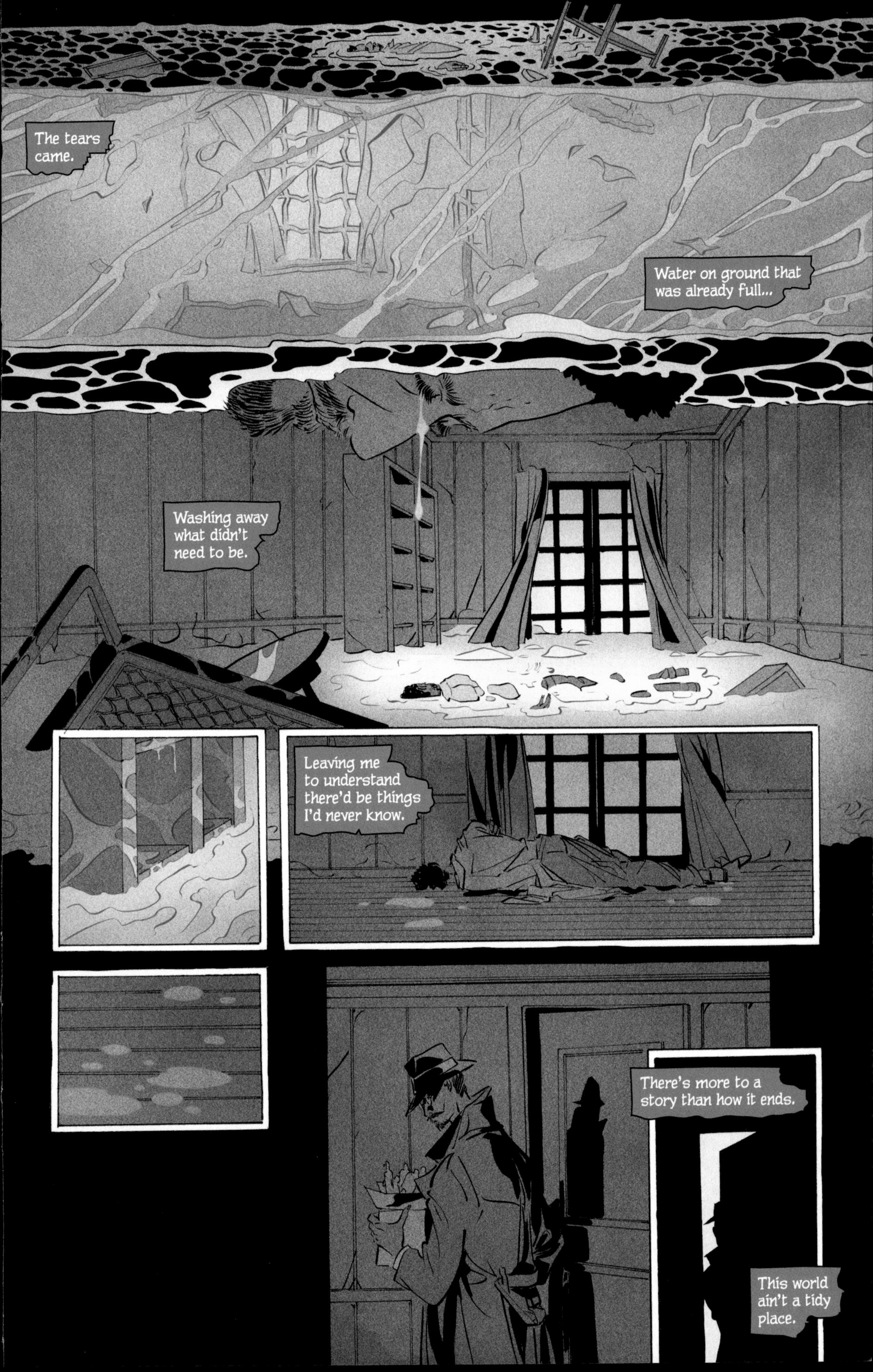
The tears came.
Water on ground that was already full...
Washing away what didn't need to be.
Leaving me to understand there'd be things I'd never know.
There's more to a story than how it ends.
This world ain't a tidy place.

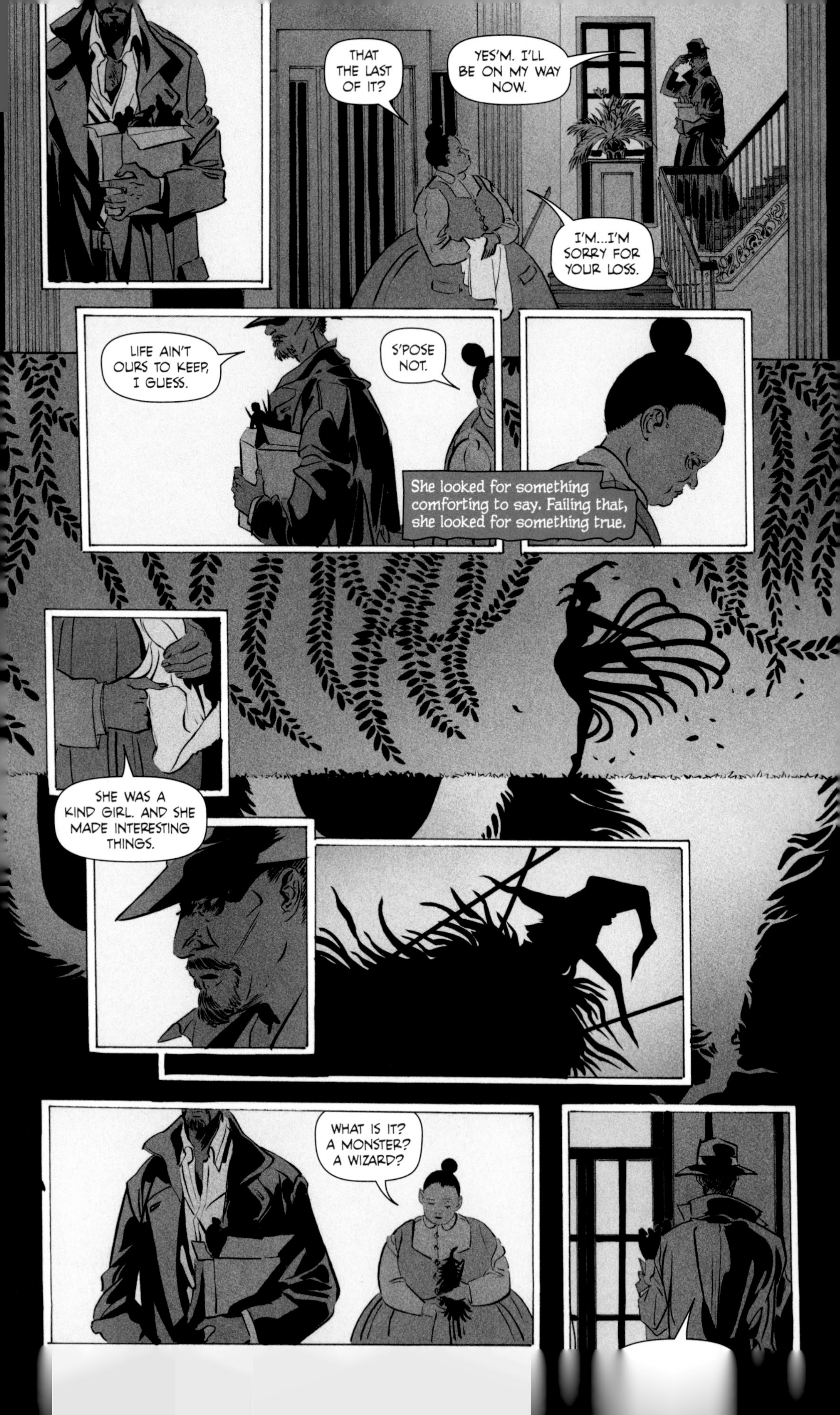

THAT THE LAST OF IT?
YES'M. I'LL BE ON MY WAY NOW.
I'M...I'M SORRY FOR YOUR LOSS.
LIFE AIN'T OURS TO KEEP, I GUESS.
S'POSE NOT.
She looked for something comforting to say. Failing that, she looked for something true.
SHE WAS A KIND GIRL. AND SHE MADE INTERESTING THINGS.
WHAT IS IT? A MONSTER? A WIZARD?

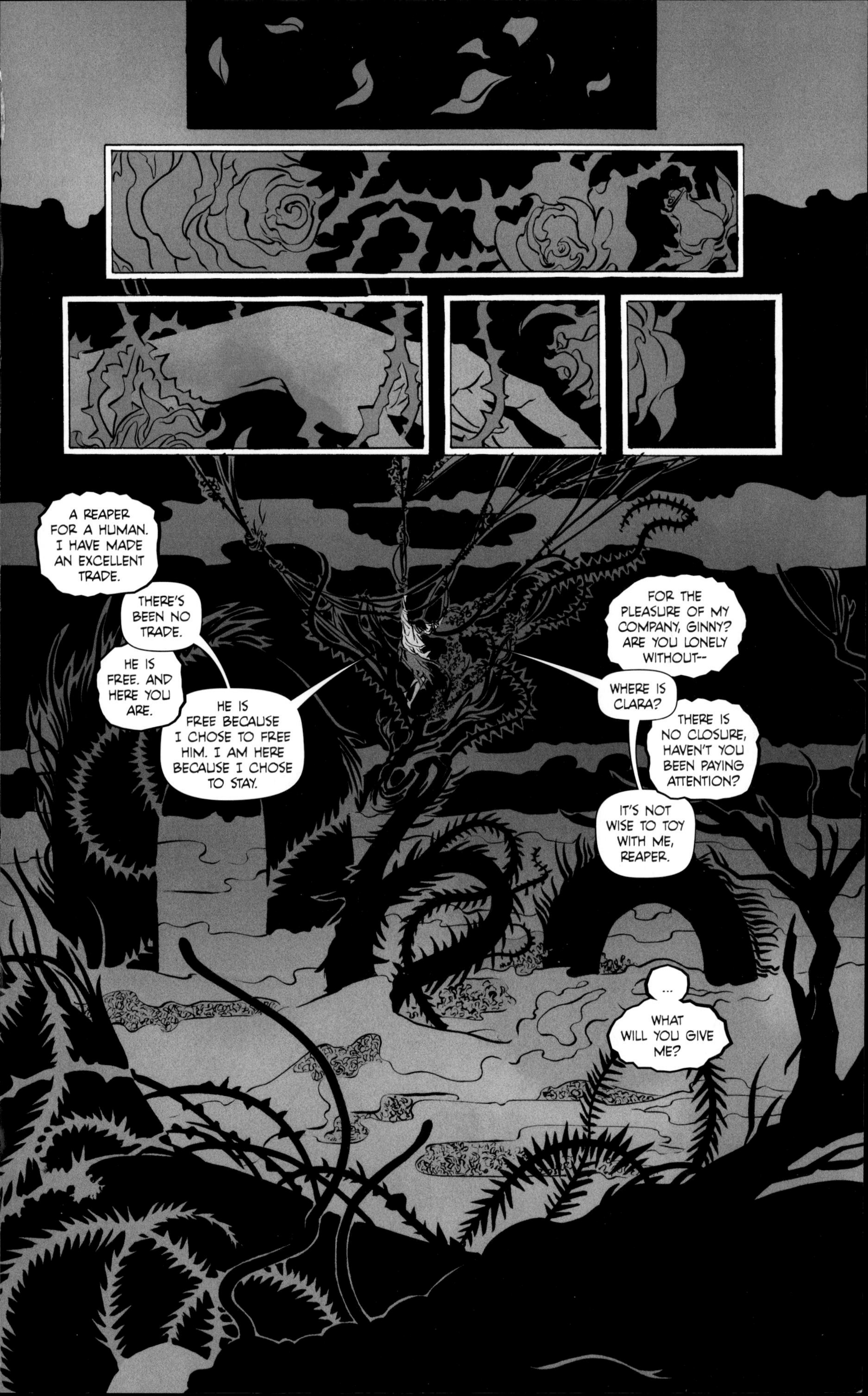
A REAPER FOR A HUMAN. I HAVE MADE AN EXCELLENT TRADE.
THERE'S BEEN NO TRADE.
HE IS FREE. AND HERE YOU ARE.
HE IS FREE BECAUSE I CHOSE TO FREE HIM. I AM HERE BECAUSE I CHOSE TO STAY.
FOR THE PLEASURE OF MY COMPANY, GINNY? ARE YOU LONELY WITHOUT--
WHERE IS CLARA?
THERE IS NO CLOSURE, HAVEN'T YOU BEEN PAYING ATTENTION?
IT'S NOT WISE TO TOY WITH ME, REAPER.
...
WHAT WILL YOU GIVE ME?

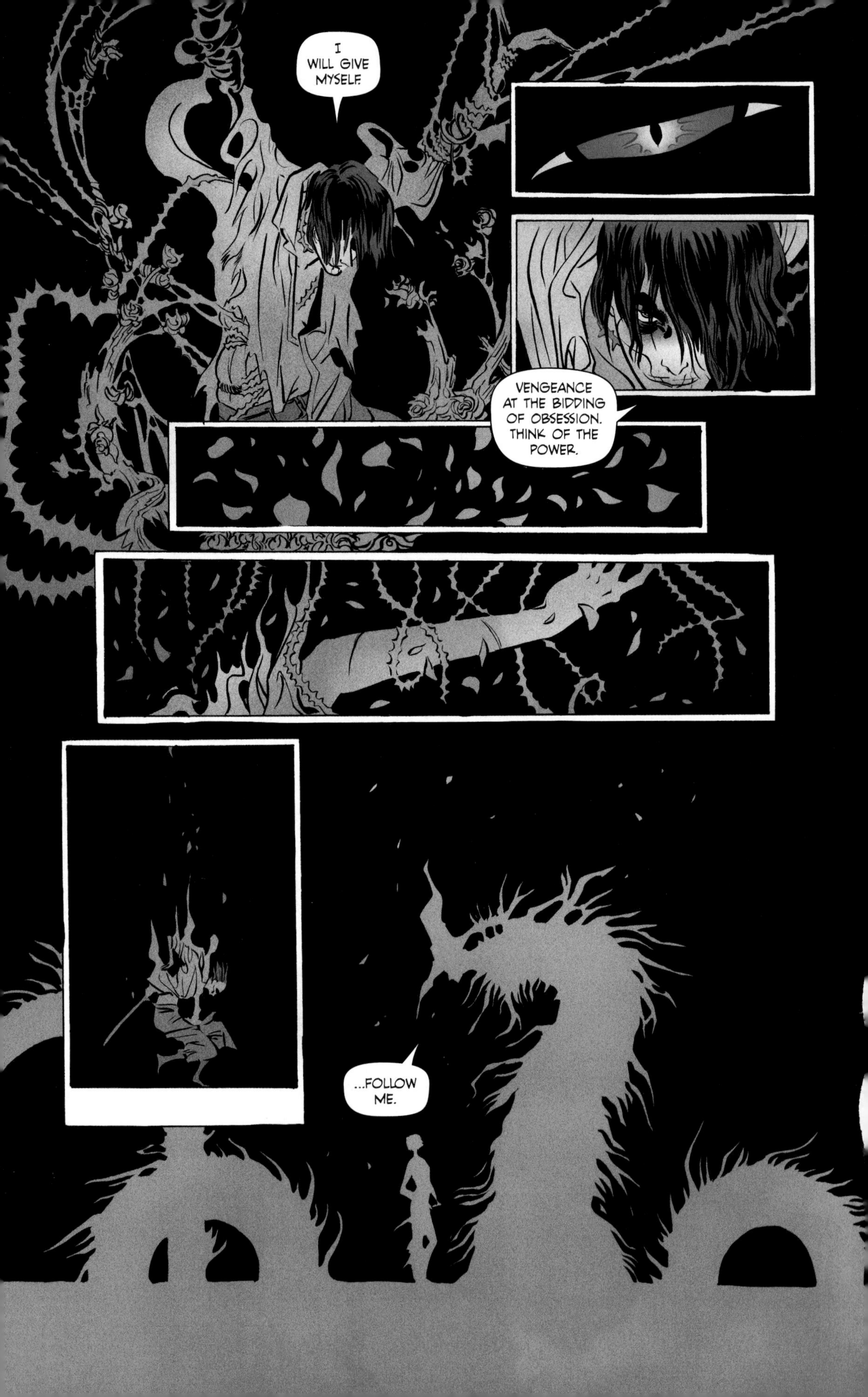
I WILL GIVE MYSELF.
VENGEANCE AT THE BIDDING OF OBSESSION. THINK OF THE POWER.
...FOLLOW ME.

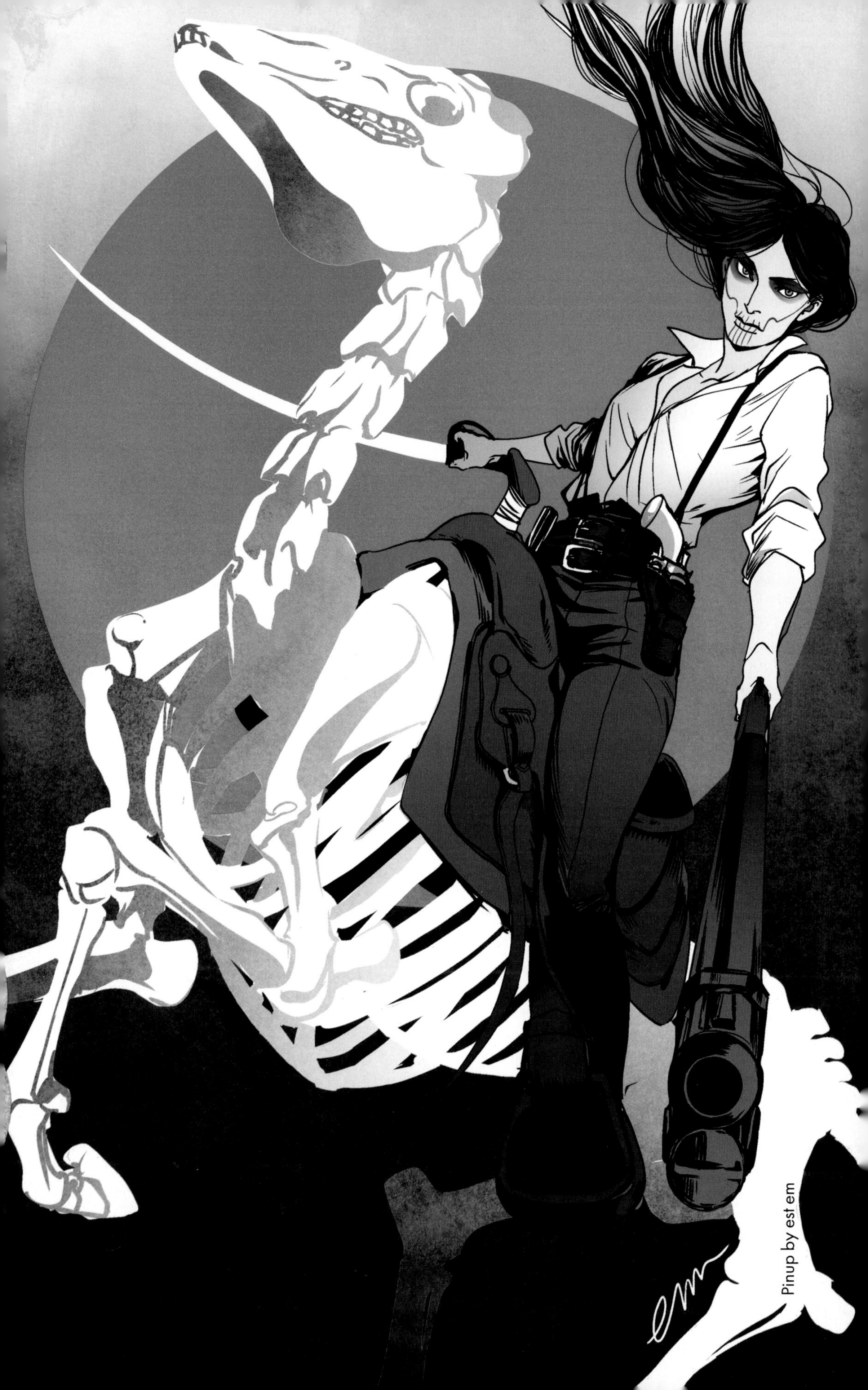

Pinup by est em

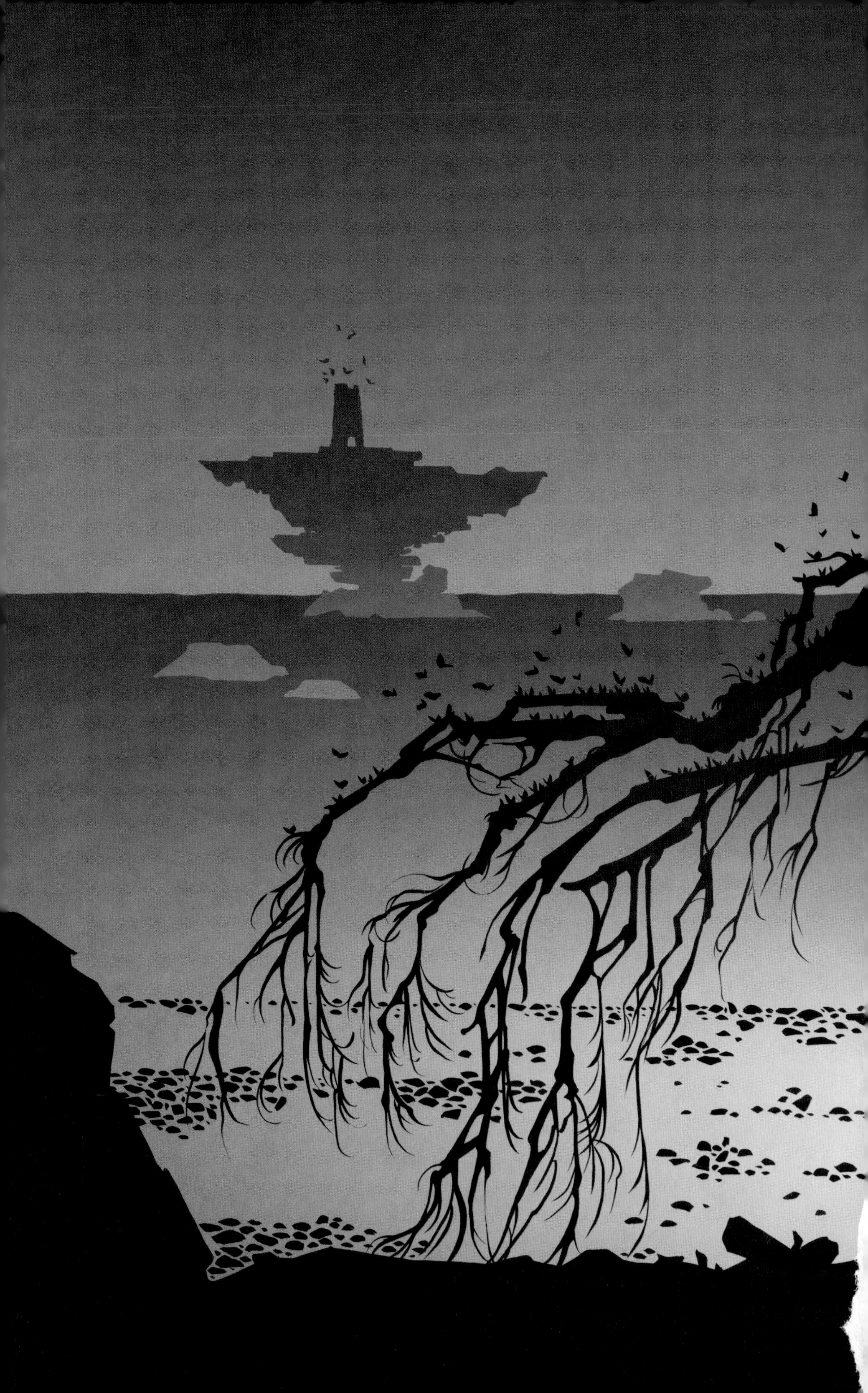

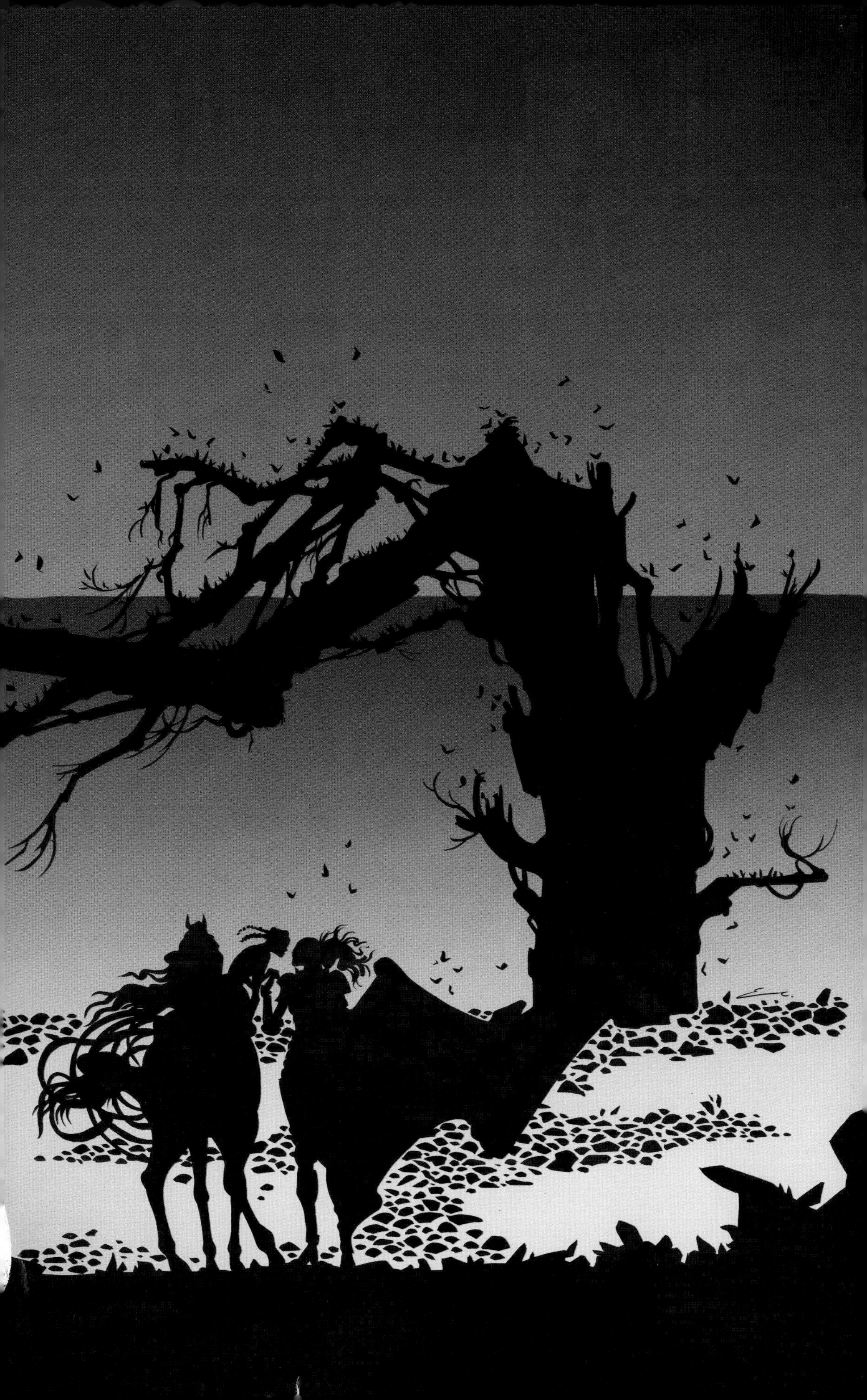

Bones Bunny tells Butterfly the tale.

The Ballad was a history.

In between the glitz, the glamour, and the bright lights, Clara Fields was found dead. Her grief-stricken uncle Frank, the Conjure-Man, set out to solve the mystery of her death. As he desperately searched for answers, Ginny, Death's daughter and the Reaper of Vengeance, set aside her duties to assist the Conjure-Man on his quest.

They started their investigation with Director, Jack Kaufman, who took advantage of Clara's talent before she disappeared. The trail led them to the Reaper of Thirst, who gave Clara distractions, for a time. But Clara fled and fell into the clutches of the Reaper of obsession.

Now, Clara speaks.

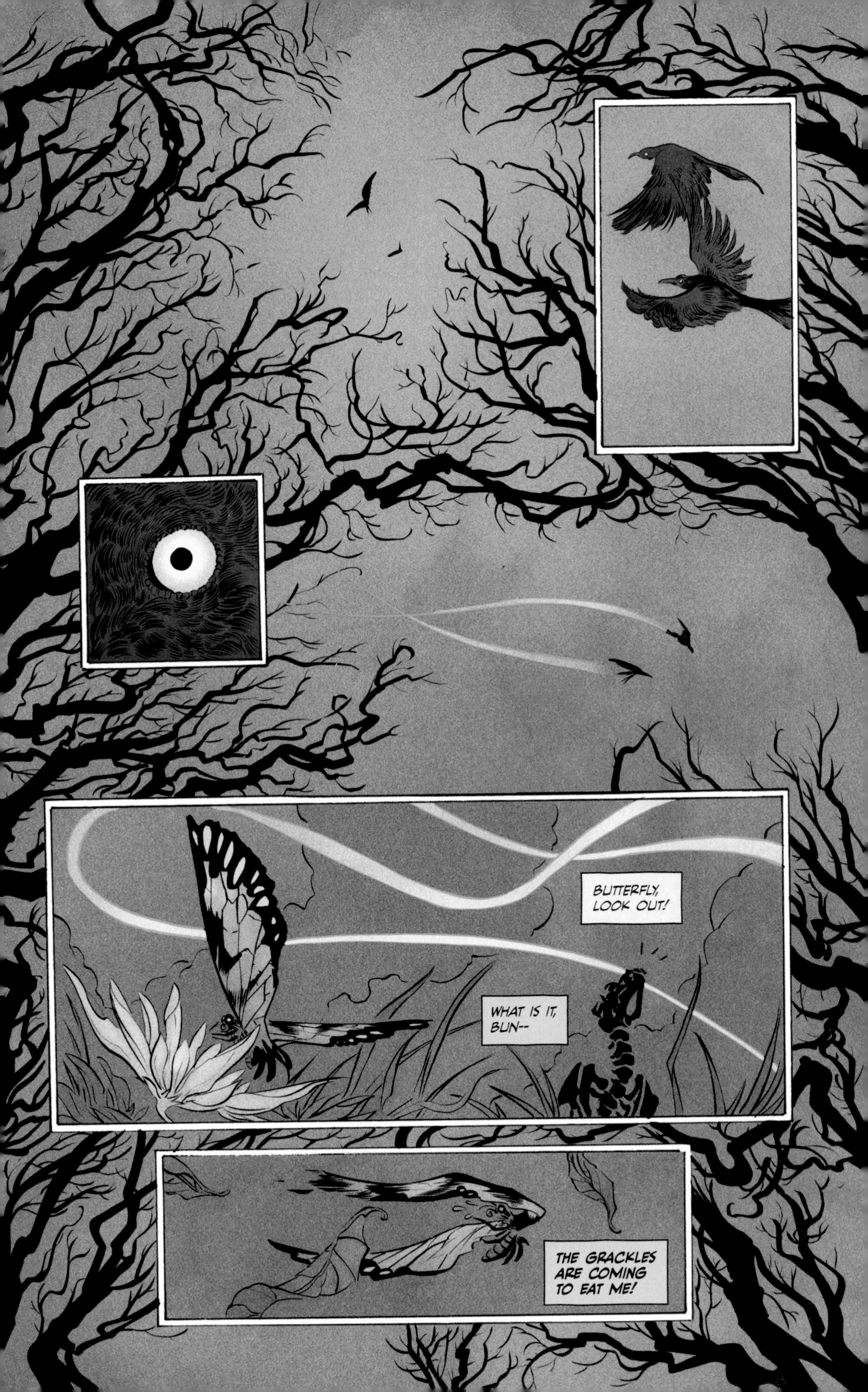
BUTTERFLY, LOOK OUT!
WHAT IS IT, BUN--
THE GRACKLES ARE COMING TO EAT ME!

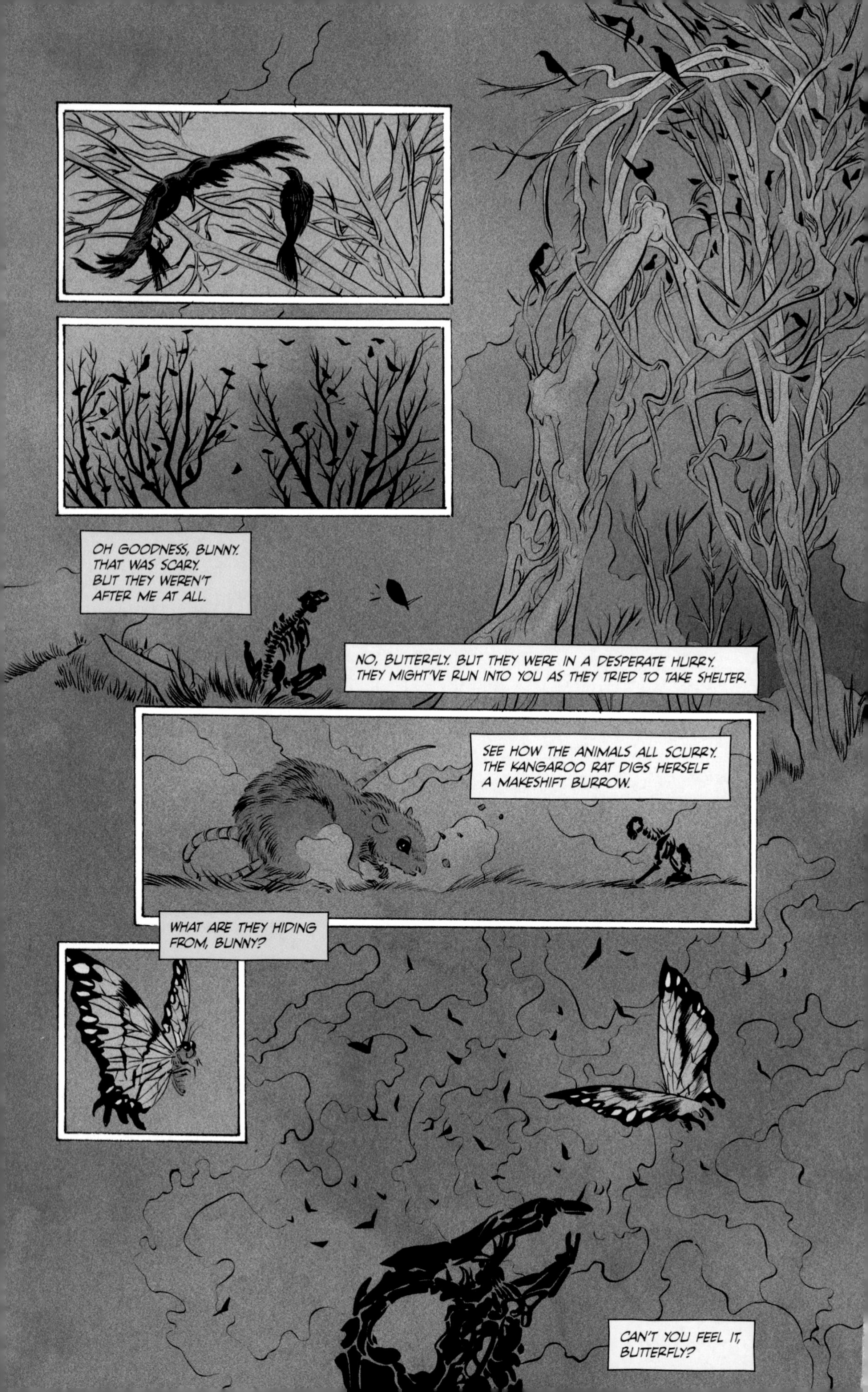
OH GOODNESS, BUNNY. THAT WAS SCARY. BUT THEY WEREN'T AFTER ME AT ALL.
NO, BUTTERFLY. BUT THEY WERE IN A DESPERATE HURRY. THEY MIGHT'VE RUN INTO YOU AS THEY TRIED TO TAKE SHELTER.
SEE HOW THE ANIMALS ALL SCURRY. THE KANGAROO RAT DIGS HERSELF A MAKESHIFT BURROW.
WHAT ARE THEY HIDING FROM, BUNNY?
CAN'T YOU FEEL IT, BUTTERFLY?

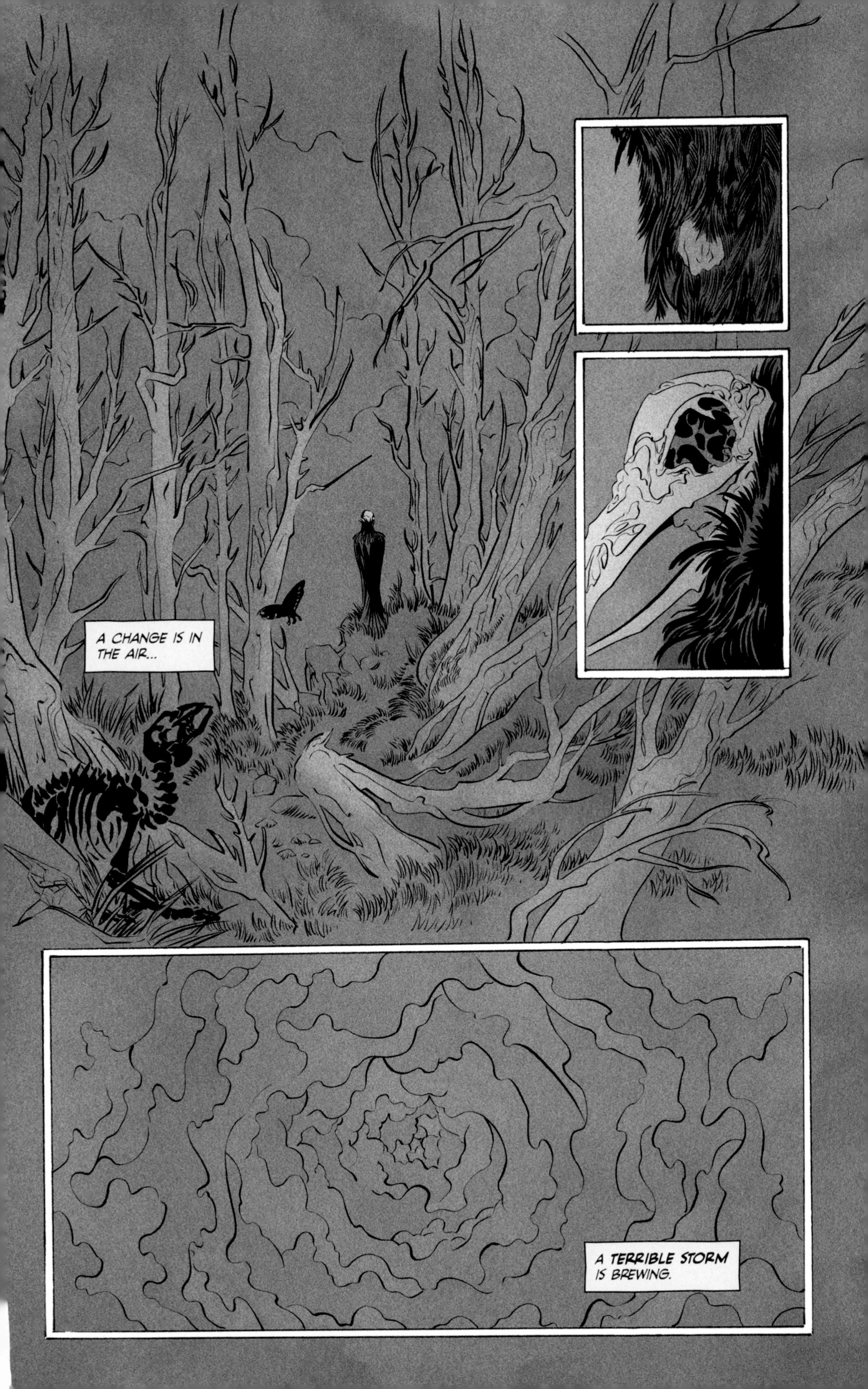
A CHANGE IS IN THE AIR...
A TERRIBLE STORM IS BREWING.

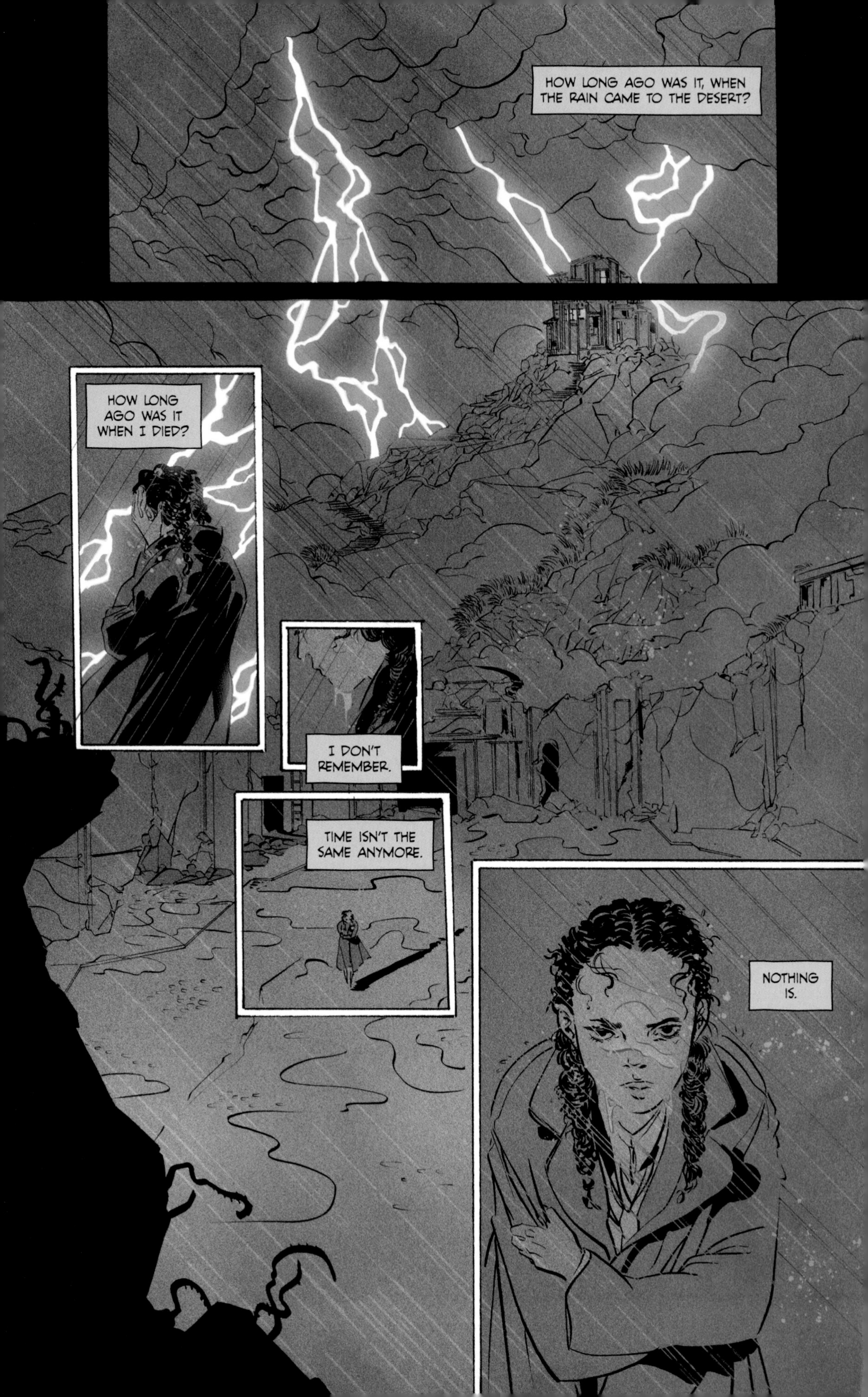
HOW LONG AGO WAS IT, WHEN THE RAIN CAME TO THE DESERT?
HOW LONG AGO WAS IT WHEN I DIED?
I DON'T REMEMBER.
TIME ISN'T THE SAME ANYMORE.
NOTHING IS.

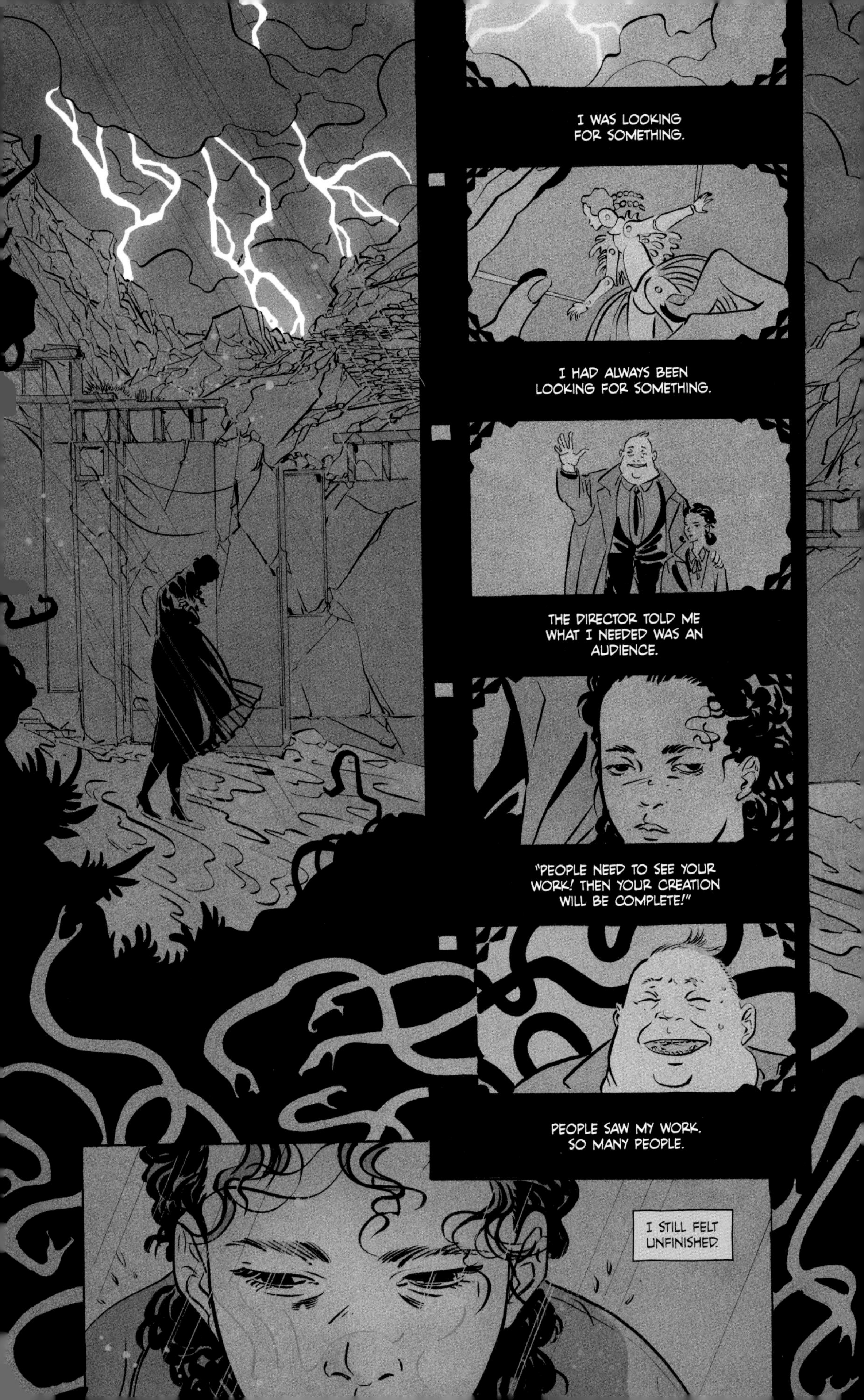
I WAS LOOKING FOR SOMETHING.
I HAD ALWAYS BEEN LOOKING FOR SOMETHING.
THE DIRECTOR TOLD ME WHAT I NEEDED WAS AN AUDIENCE.
"PEOPLE NEED TO SEE YOUR WORK! THEN YOUR CREATION WILL BE COMPLETE!"
PEOPLE SAW MY WORK. SO MANY PEOPLE.
I STILL FELT UNFINISHED.

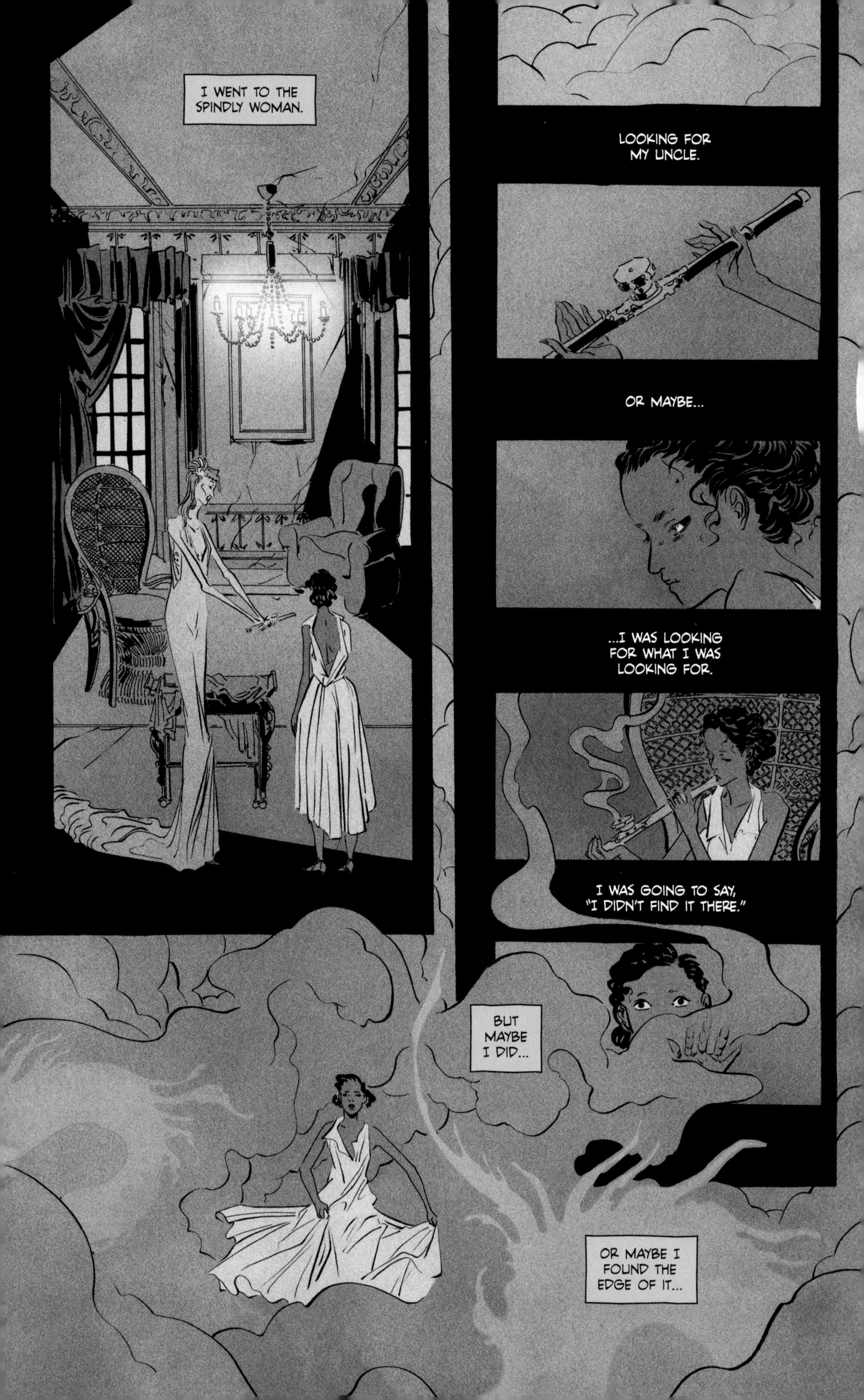
I WENT TO THE SPINDLY WOMAN.
LOOKING FOR MY UNCLE.
OR MAYBE...
...I WAS LOOKING FOR WHAT I WAS LOOKING FOR.
I WAS GOING TO SAY, "I DIDN'T FIND IT THERE."
BUT MAYBE I DID...
OR MAYBE I FOUND THE EDGE OF IT...

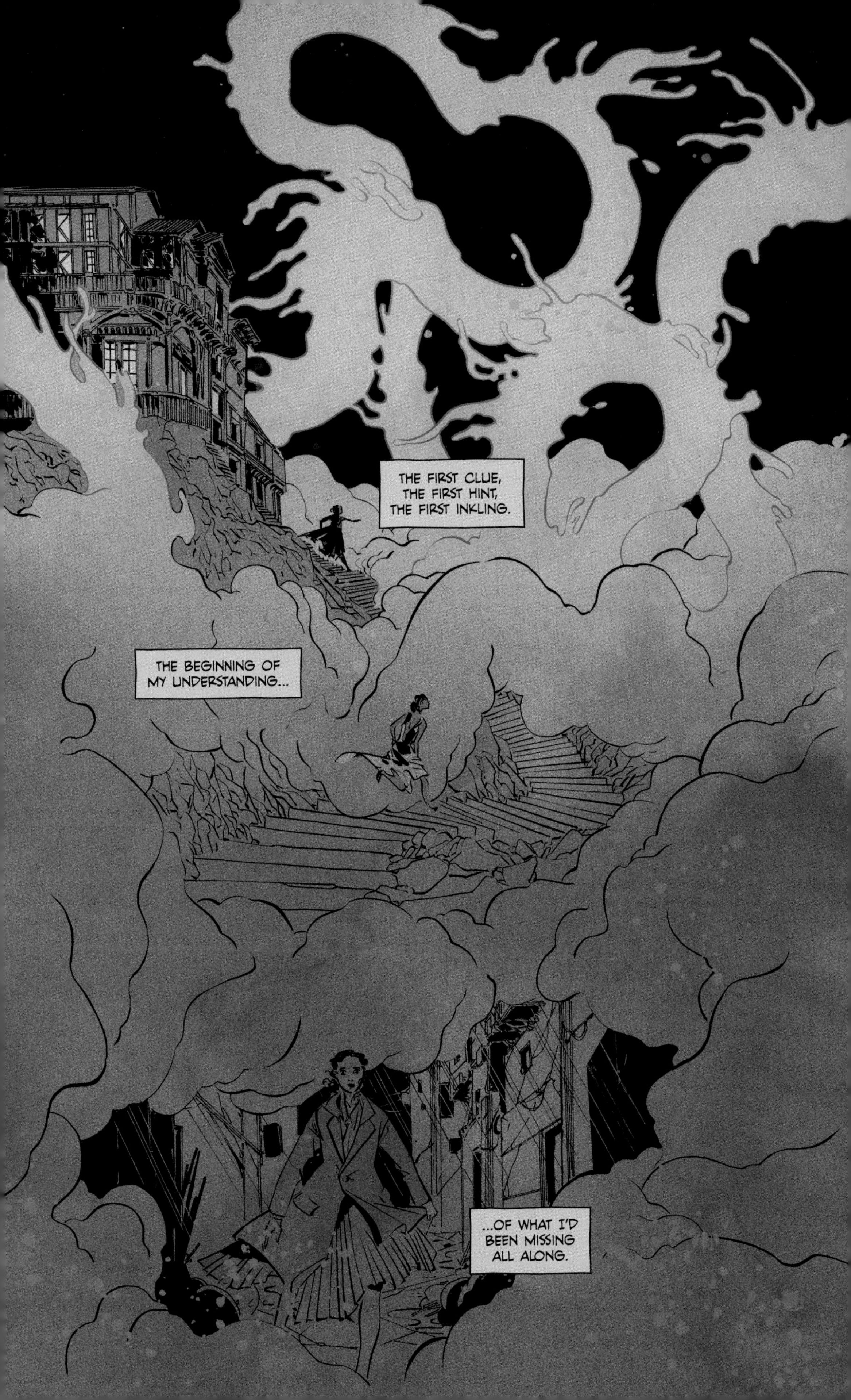
THE FIRST CLUE,
THE FIRST HINT,
THE FIRST INKLING.
THE BEGINNING OF
MY UNDERSTANDING...
...OF WHAT I'D
BEEN MISSING
ALL ALONG.

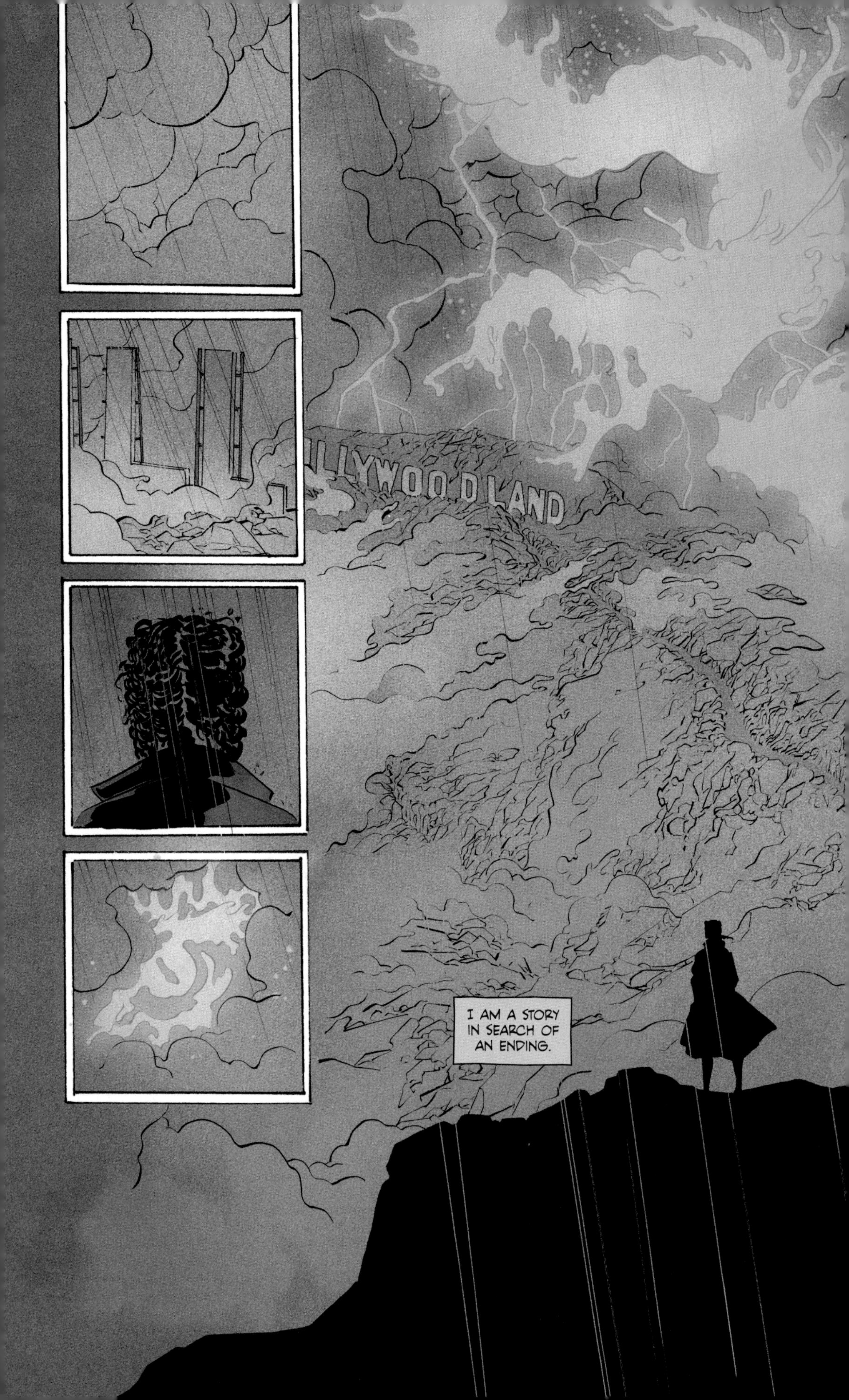
LLYWOO D LAND
I AM A STORY IN SEARCH OF AN ENDING.

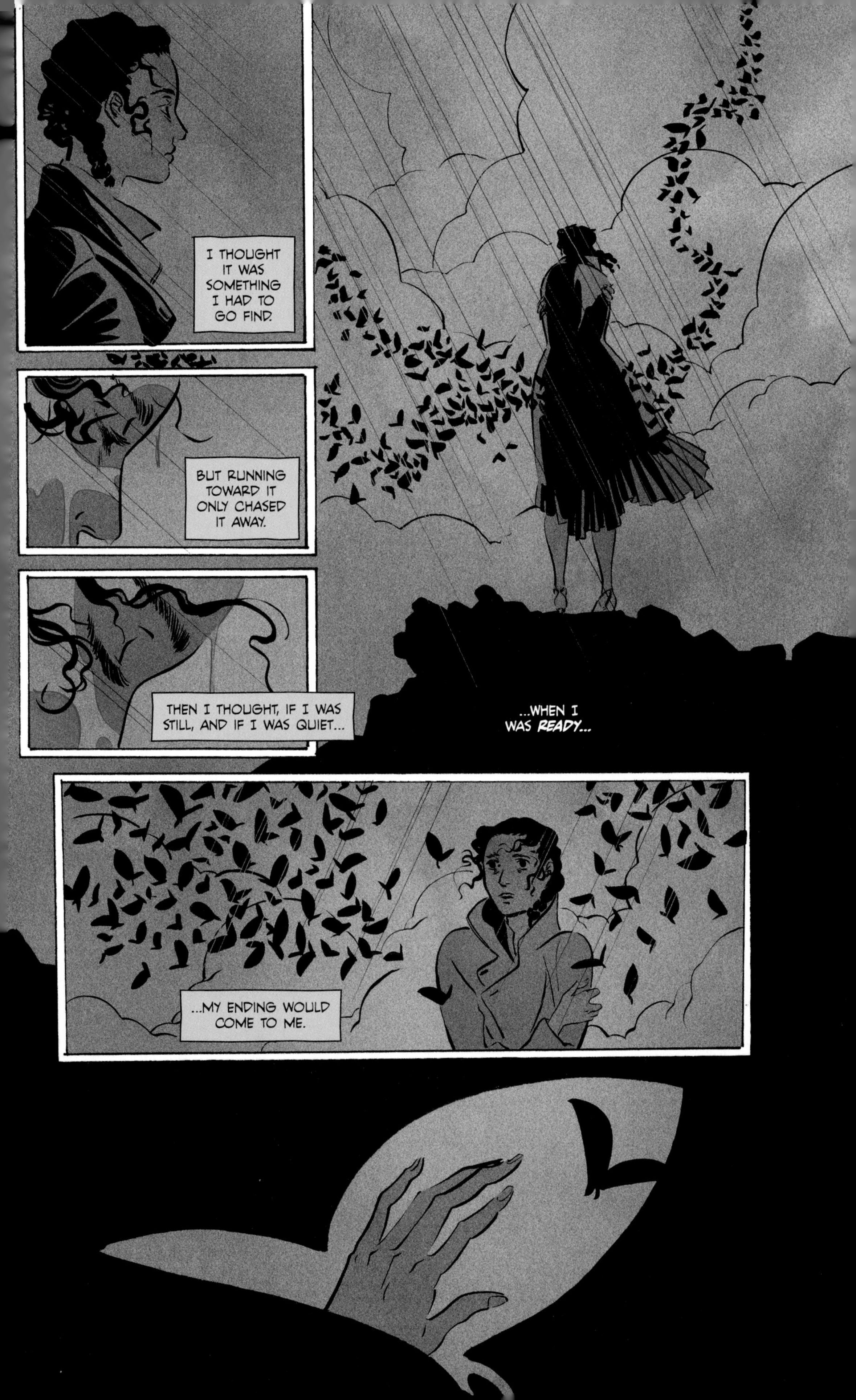
I THOUGHT IT WAS SOMETHING I HAD TO GO FIND.
BUT RUNNING TOWARD IT ONLY CHASED IT AWAY.
THEN I THOUGHT, IF I WAS STILL, AND IF I WAS QUIET...
...WHEN I WAS READY...
...MY ENDING WOULD COME TO ME.

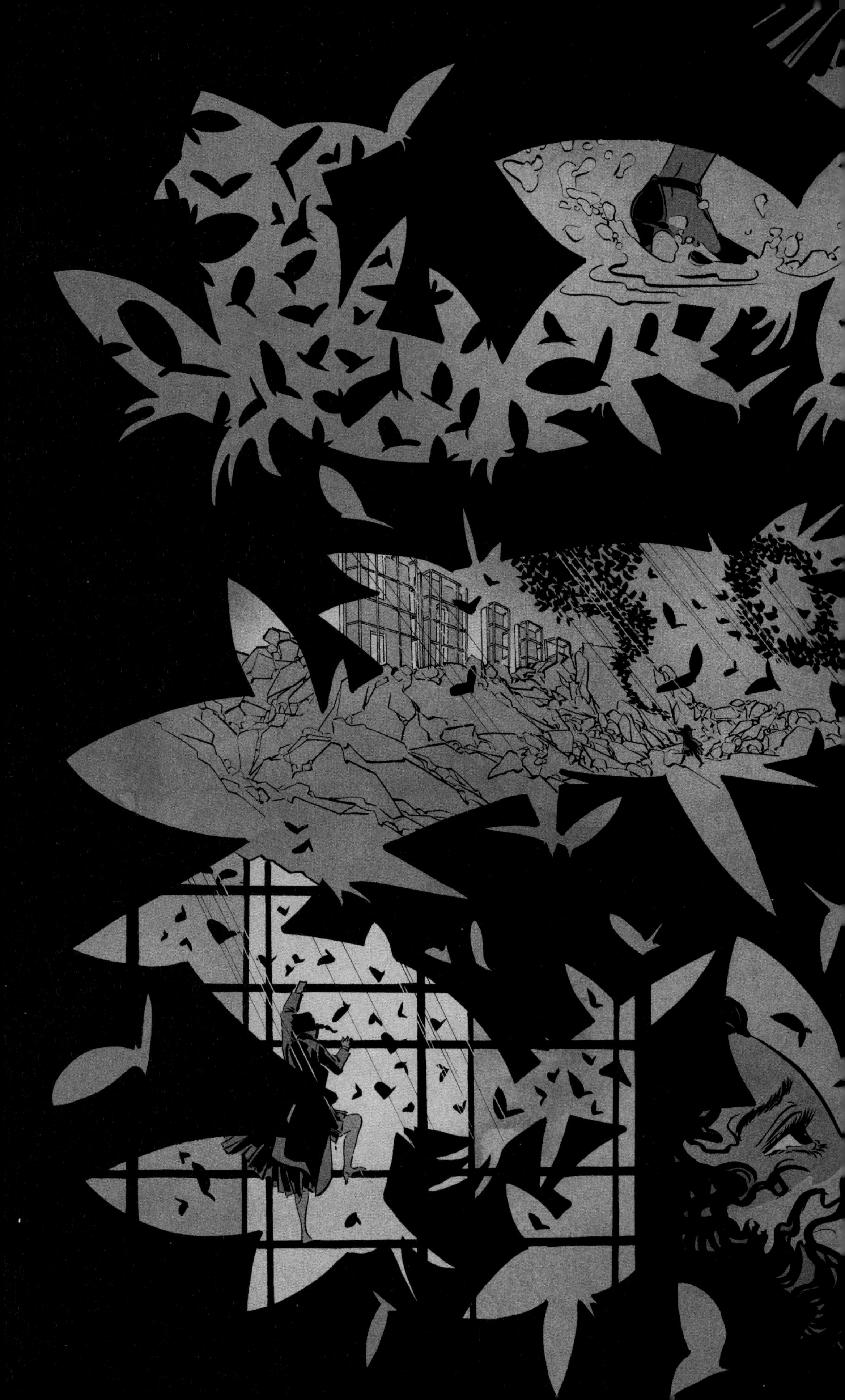

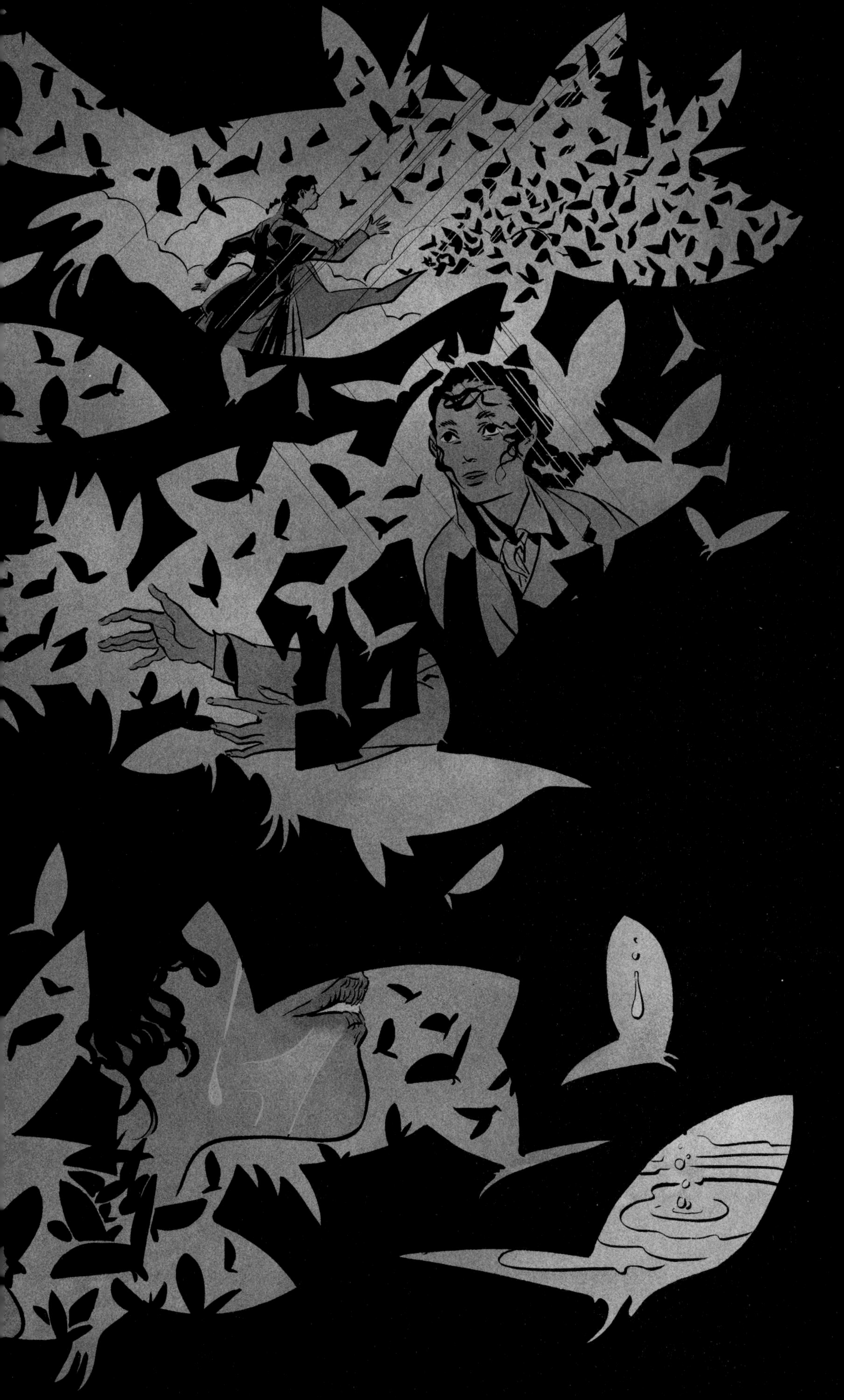

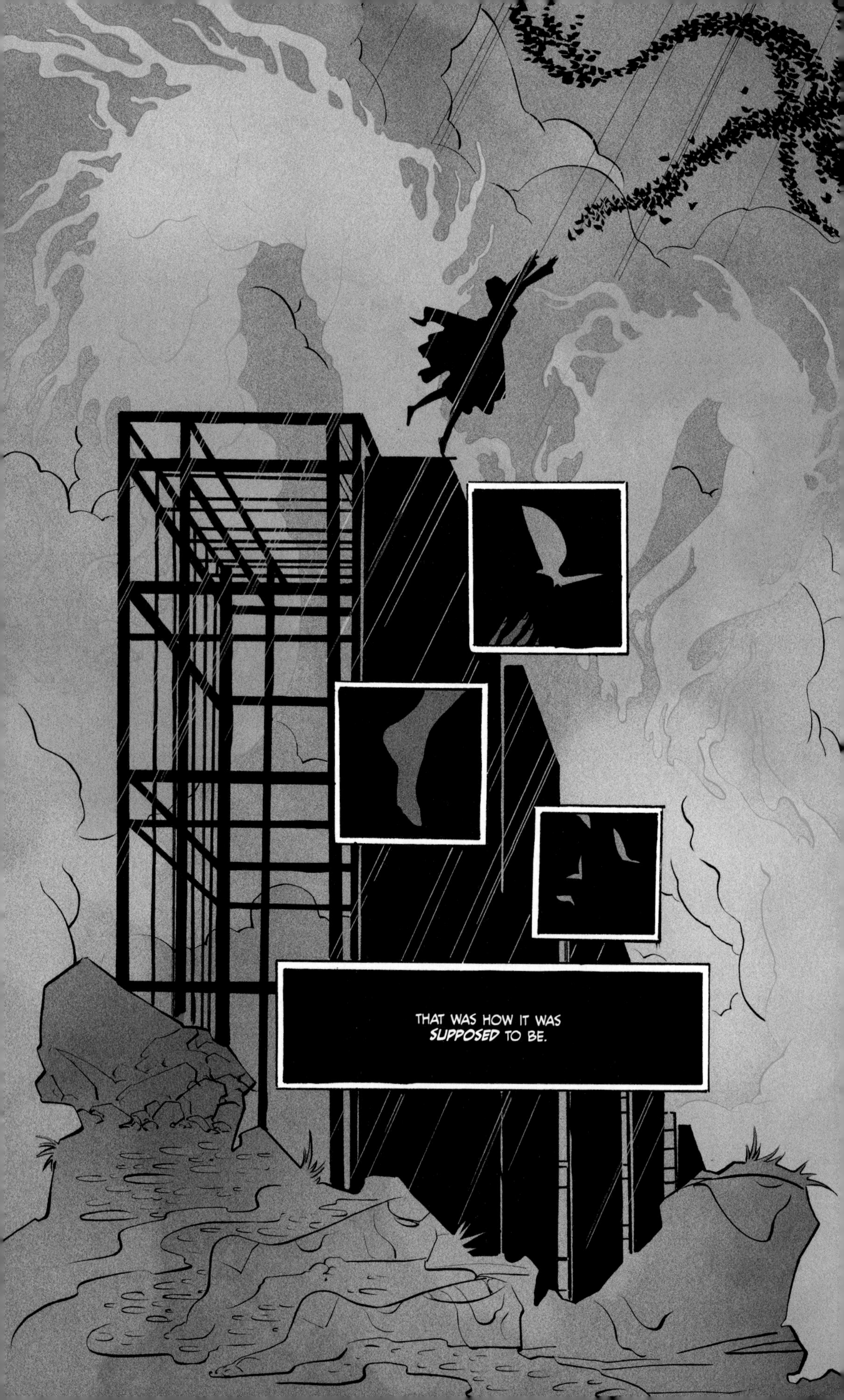
THAT WAS HOW IT WAS *SUPPOSED* TO BE.

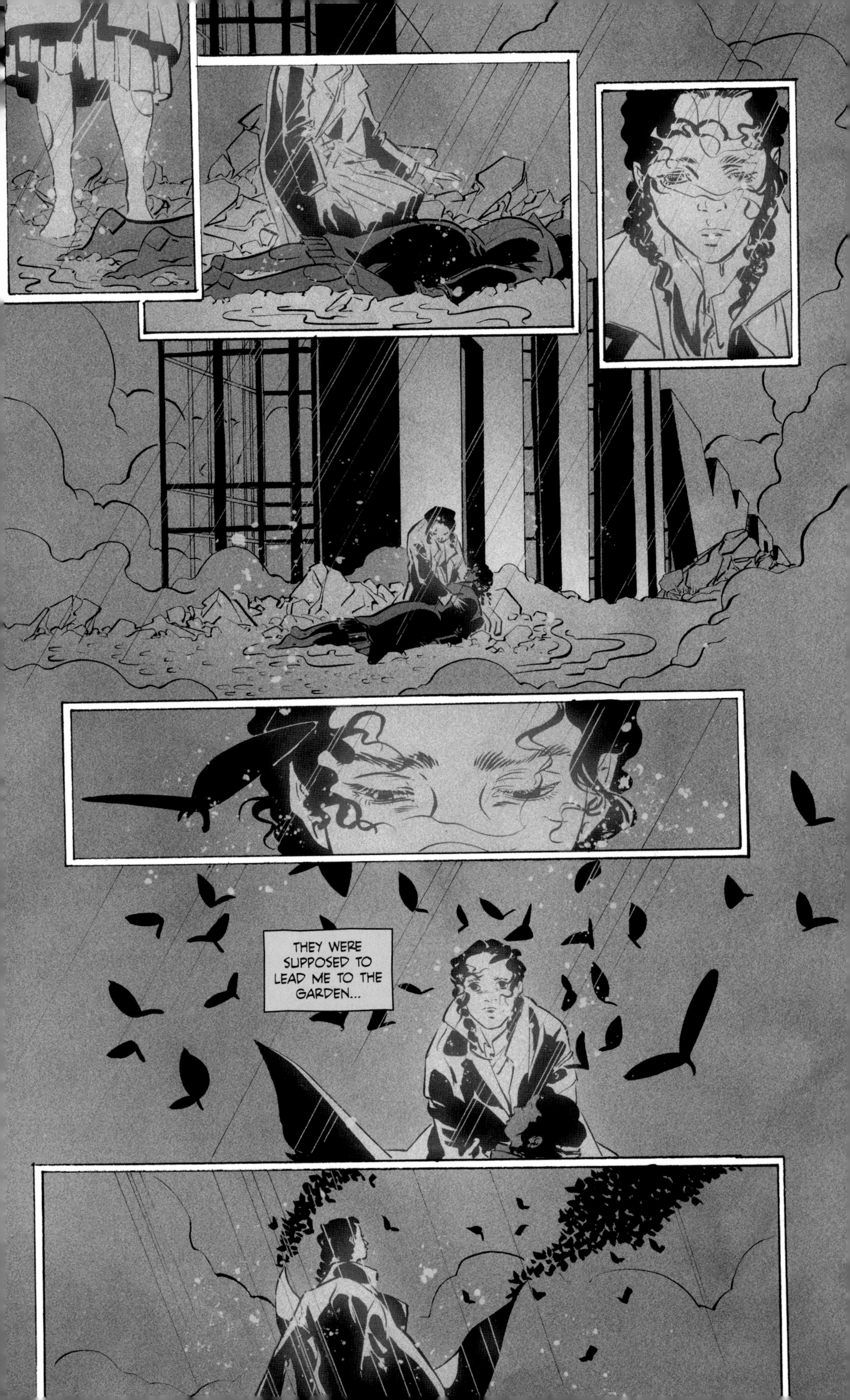
THEY WERE SUPPOSED TO LEAD ME TO THE GARDEN...

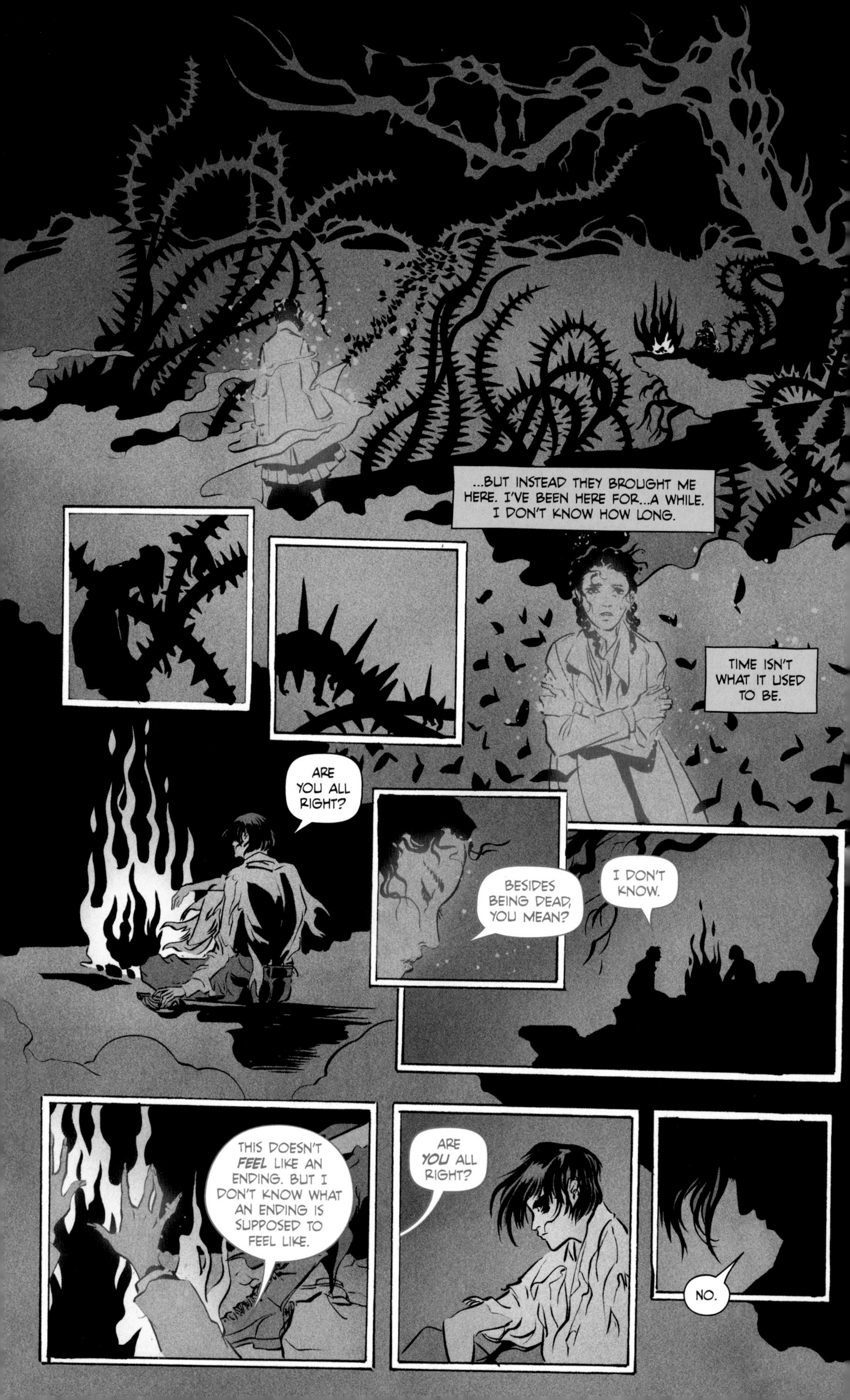
...BUT INSTEAD THEY BROUGHT ME HERE. I'VE BEEN HERE FOR...A WHILE. I DON'T KNOW HOW LONG.
TIME ISN'T WHAT IT USED TO BE.
ARE YOU ALL RIGHT?
BESIDES BEING DEAD, YOU MEAN?
I DON'T KNOW.
THIS DOESN'T *FEEL* LIKE AN ENDING. BUT I DON'T KNOW WHAT AN ENDING IS SUPPOSED TO FEEL LIKE.
ARE *YOU* ALL RIGHT?
NO.

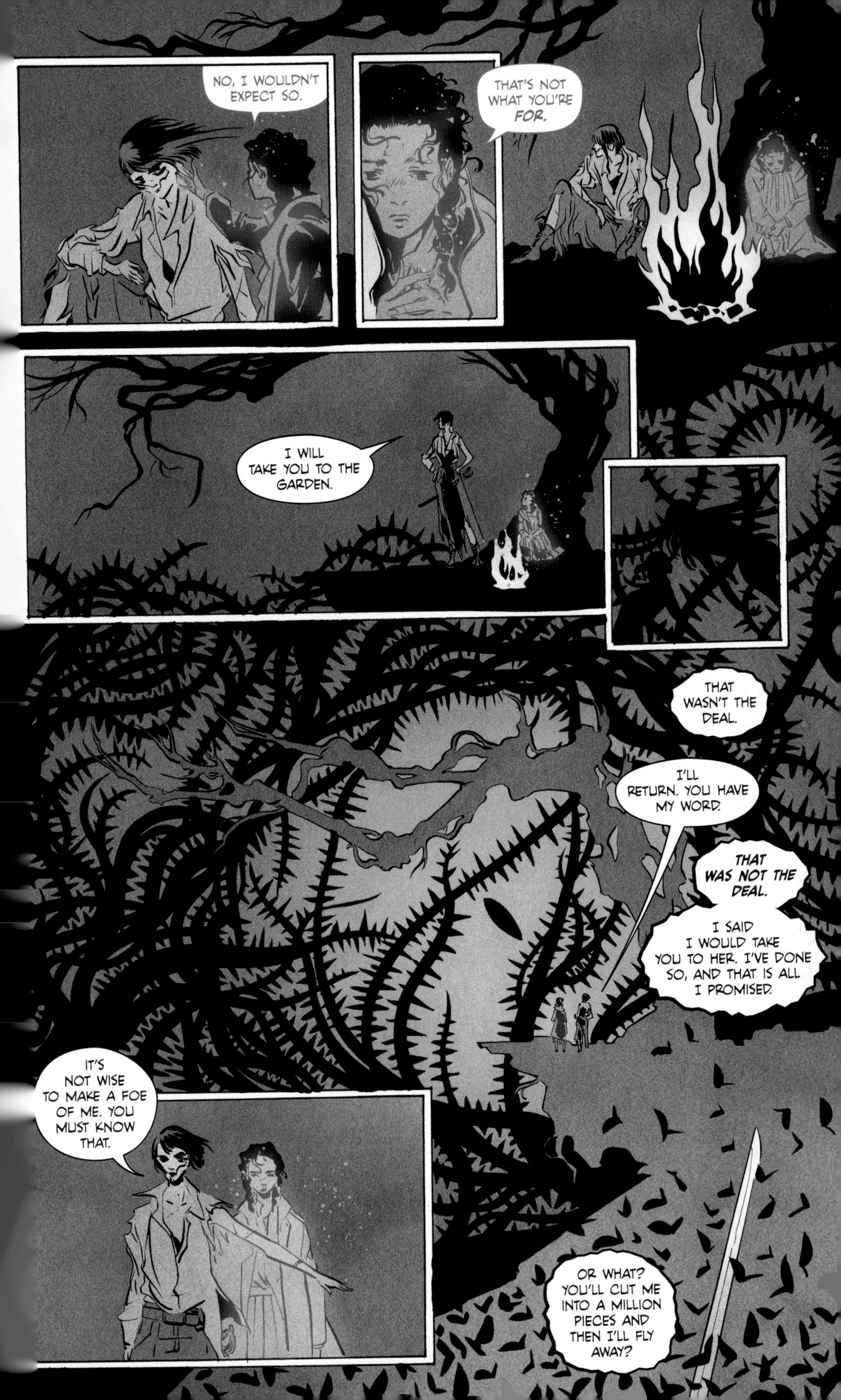
NO, I WOULDN'T EXPECT SO.
THAT'S NOT WHAT YOU'RE *FOR.*
I WILL TAKE YOU TO THE GARDEN.
THAT WASN'T THE DEAL.
I'LL RETURN. YOU HAVE MY WORD.
THAT WAS NOT THE DEAL.
I SAID I WOULD TAKE YOU TO HER. I'VE DONE SO, AND THAT IS ALL I PROMISED.
IT'S NOT WISE TO MAKE A FOE OF ME. YOU MUST KNOW THAT.
OR WHAT? YOU'LL CUT ME INTO A MILLION PIECES AND THEN I'LL FLY AWAY?

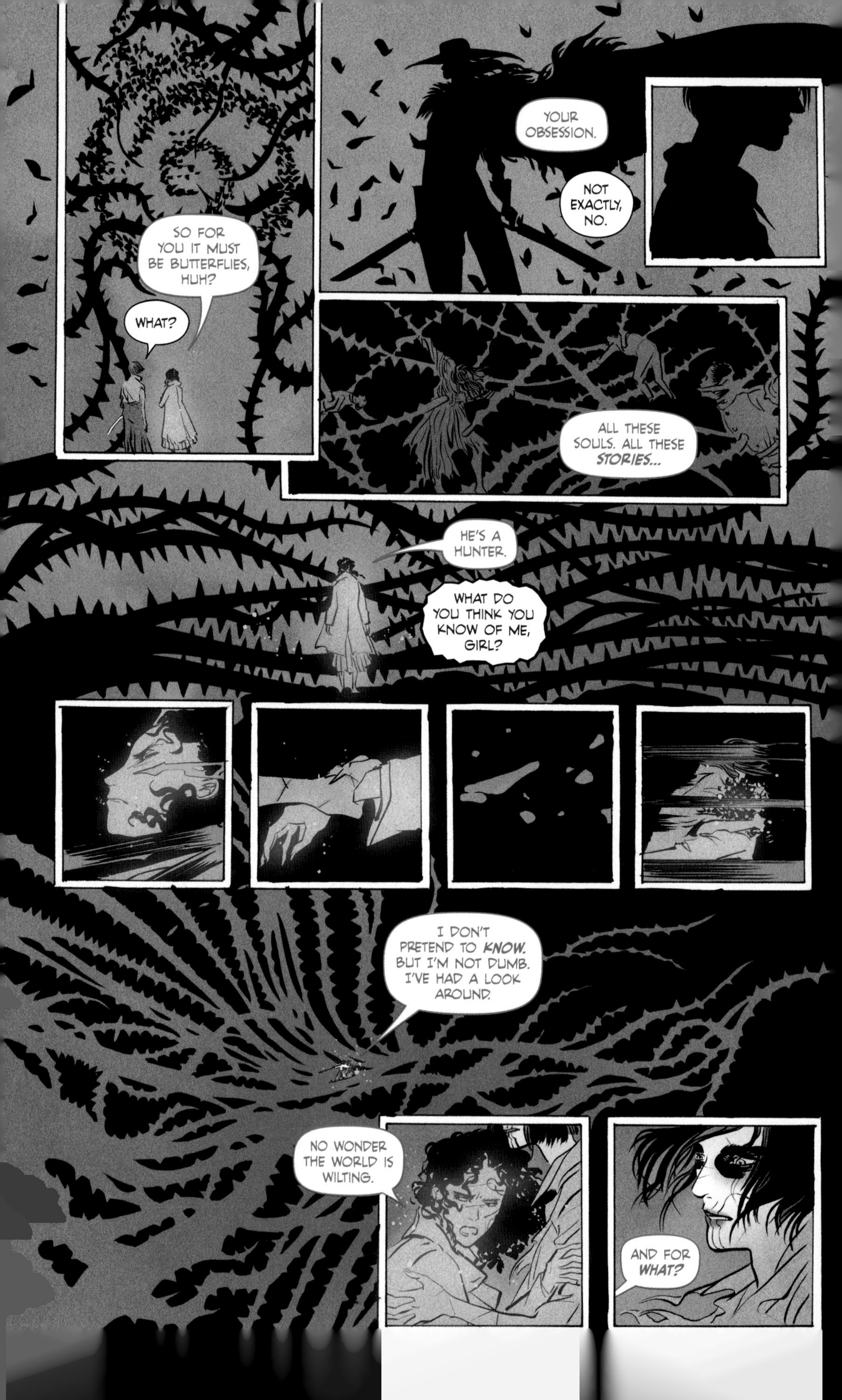
SO FOR YOU IT MUST BE BUTTERFLIES, HUH?
WHAT?
YOUR OBSESSION.
NOT EXACTLY, NO.
ALL THESE SOULS. ALL THESE STORIES...
HE'S A HUNTER.
WHAT DO YOU THINK YOU KNOW OF ME, GIRL?
I DON'T PRETEND TO KNOW. BUT I'M NOT DUMB. I'VE HAD A LOOK AROUND.
NO WONDER THE WORLD IS WILTING.
AND FOR WHAT?

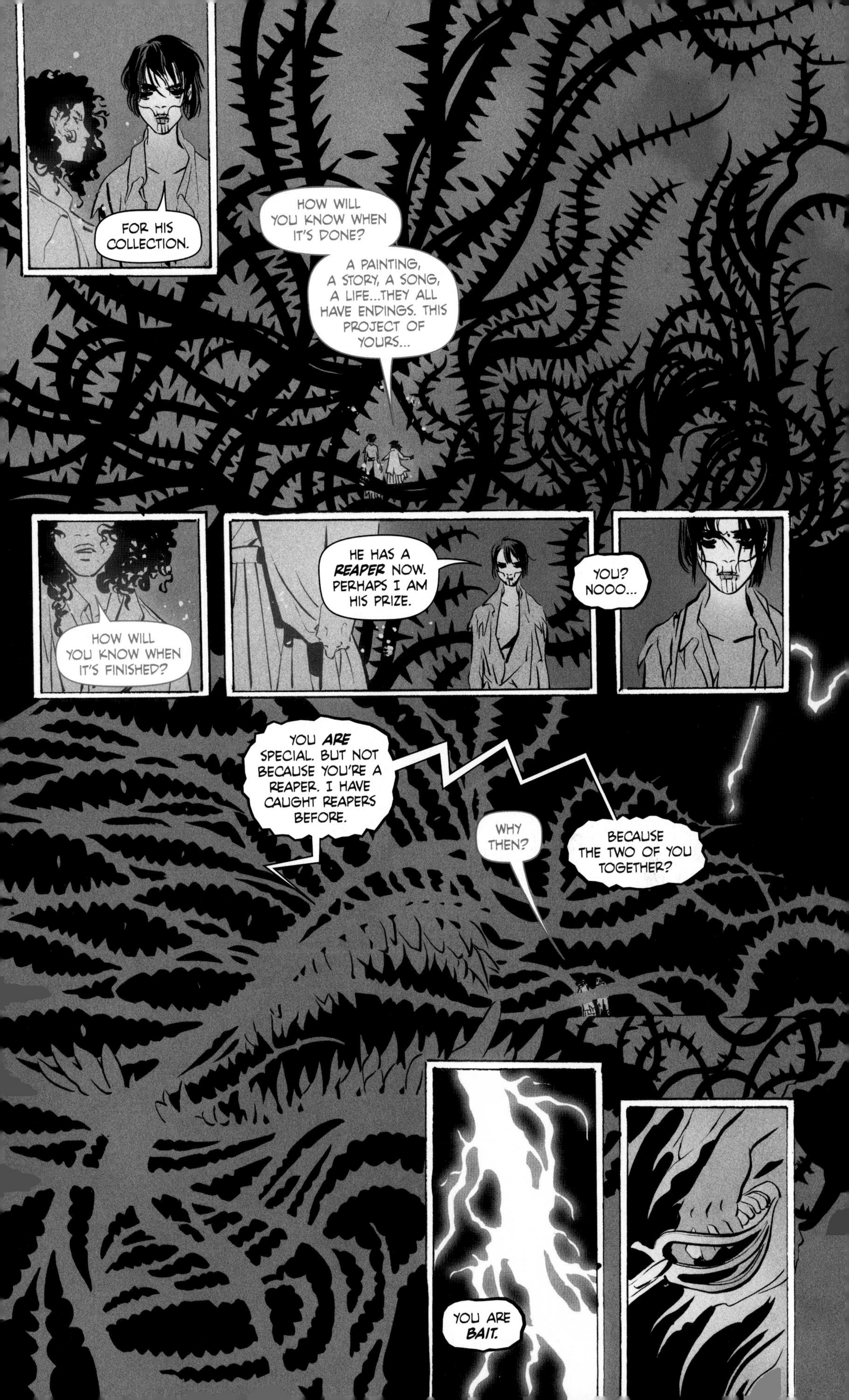
FOR HIS COLLECTION.
HOW WILL YOU KNOW WHEN IT'S DONE?
A PAINTING, A STORY, A SONG, A LIFE...THEY ALL HAVE ENDINGS. THIS PROJECT OF YOURS...
HOW WILL YOU KNOW WHEN IT'S FINISHED?
HE HAS A REAPER NOW. PERHAPS I AM HIS PRIZE.
YOU? NOOO...
YOU ARE SPECIAL. BUT NOT BECAUSE YOU'RE A REAPER. I HAVE CAUGHT REAPERS BEFORE.
WHY THEN?
BECAUSE THE TWO OF YOU TOGETHER?
YOU ARE BAIT.

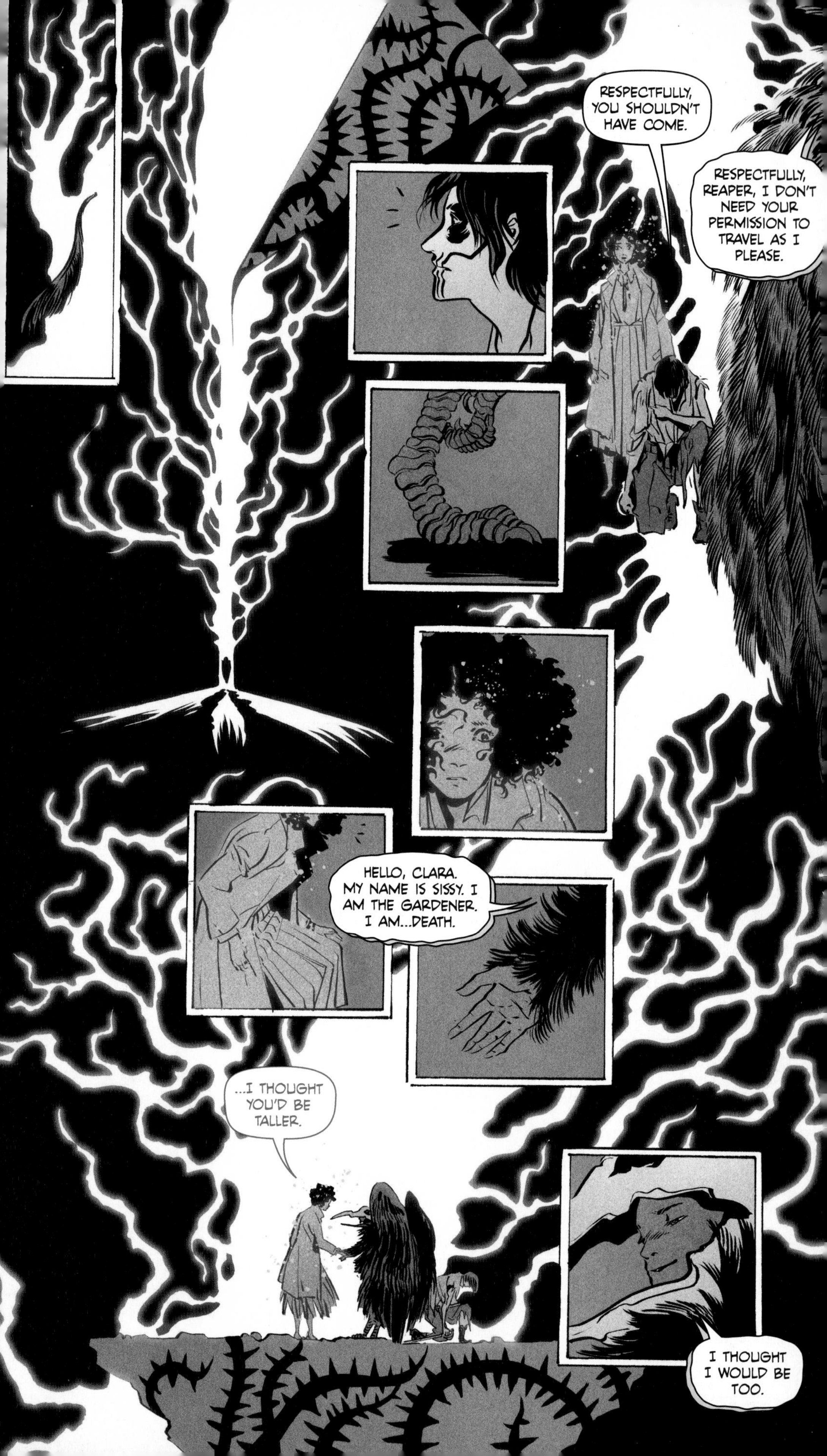
RESPECTFULLY, YOU SHOULDN'T HAVE COME.
RESPECTFULLY, REAPER, I DON'T NEED YOUR PERMISSION TO TRAVEL AS I PLEASE.
HELLO, CLARA. MY NAME IS SISSY. I AM THE GARDENER. I AM...DEATH.
...I THOUGHT YOU'D BE TALLER.
I THOUGHT I WOULD BE TOO.

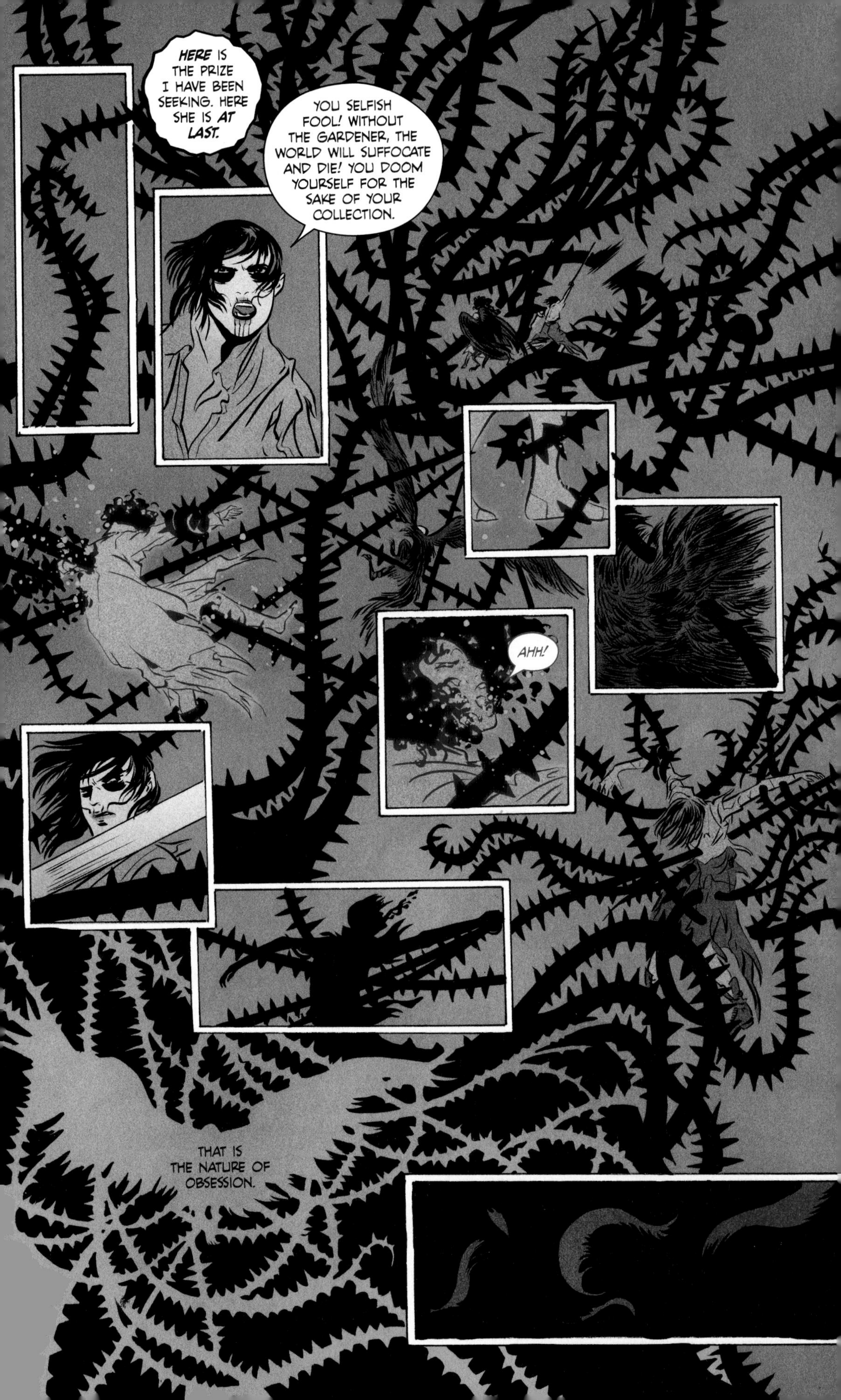
HERE IS THE PRIZE I HAVE BEEN SEEKING. HERE SHE IS AT LAST.
YOU SELFISH FOOL! WITHOUT THE GARDENER, THE WORLD WILL SUFFOCATE AND DIE! YOU DOOM YOURSELF FOR THE SAKE OF YOUR COLLECTION.
AHH!
THAT IS THE NATURE OF OBSESSION.

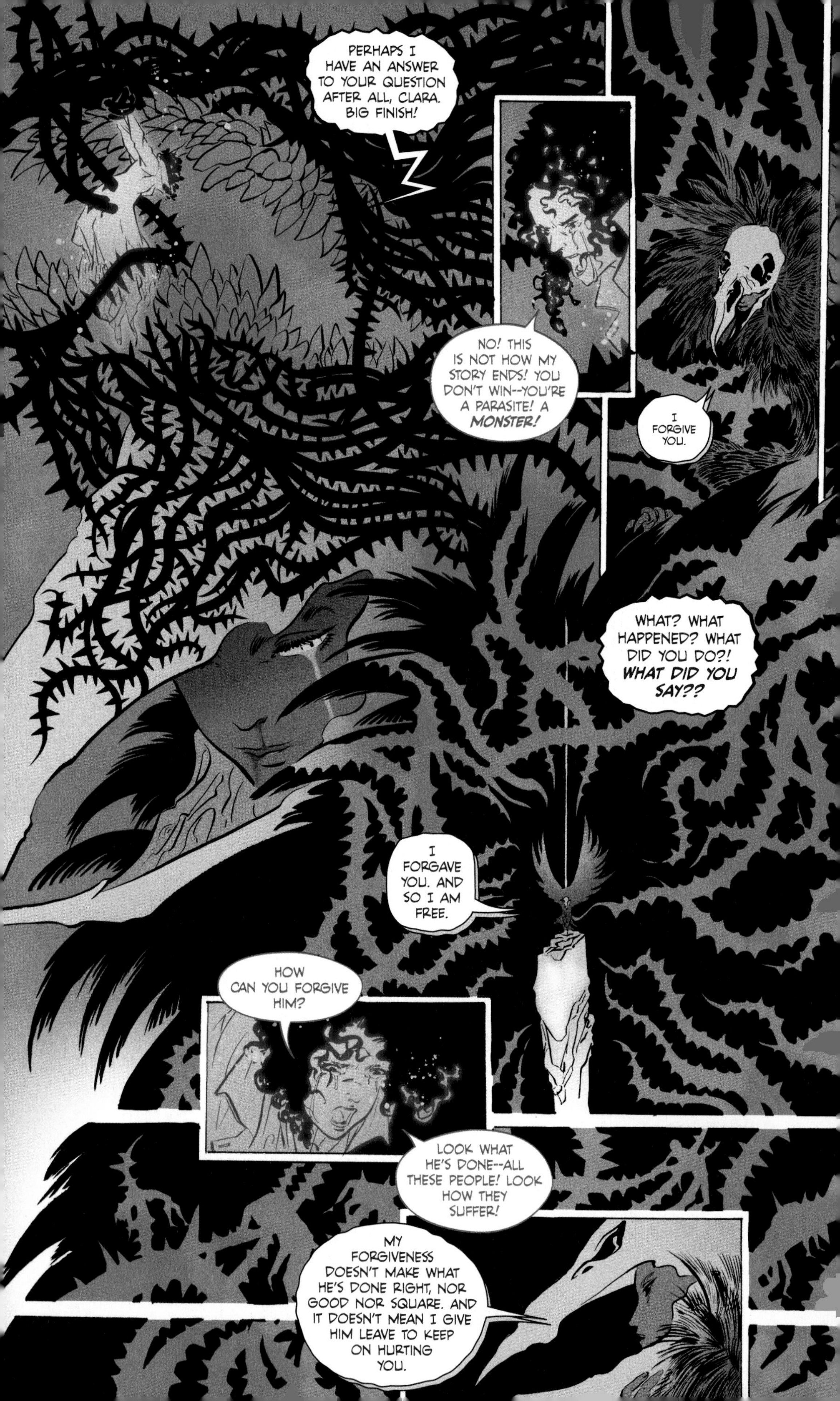
PERHAPS I HAVE AN ANSWER TO YOUR QUESTION AFTER ALL, CLARA. BIG FINISH!
NO! THIS IS NOT HOW MY STORY ENDS! YOU DON'T WIN--YOU'RE A PARASITE! A MONSTER!
I FORGIVE YOU.
WHAT? WHAT HAPPENED? WHAT DID YOU DO?! WHAT DID YOU SAY??
I FORGAVE YOU. AND SO I AM FREE.
HOW CAN YOU FORGIVE HIM?
LOOK WHAT HE'S DONE--ALL THESE PEOPLE! LOOK HOW THEY SUFFER!
MY FORGIVENESS DOESN'T MAKE WHAT HE'S DONE RIGHT, NOR GOOD NOR SQUARE. AND IT DOESN'T MEAN I GIVE HIM LEAVE TO KEEP ON HURTING YOU.

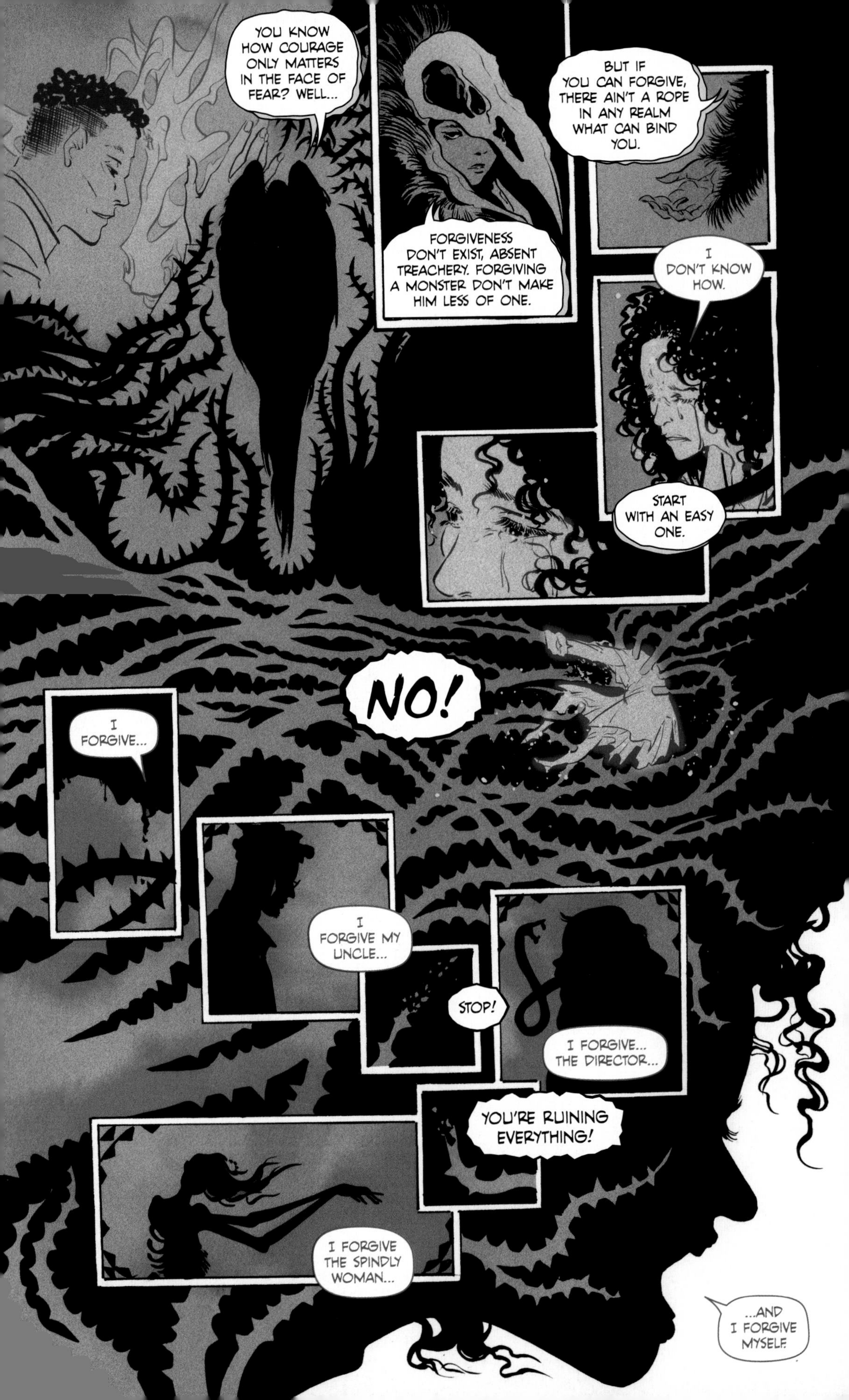
YOU KNOW HOW COURAGE ONLY MATTERS IN THE FACE OF FEAR? WELL...
FORGIVENESS DON'T EXIST, ABSENT TREACHERY. FORGIVING A MONSTER DON'T MAKE HIM LESS OF ONE.
BUT IF YOU CAN FORGIVE, THERE AIN'T A ROPE IN ANY REALM WHAT CAN BIND YOU.
I DON'T KNOW HOW.
START WITH AN EASY ONE.
NO!
I FORGIVE...
I FORGIVE MY UNCLE...
STOP!
I FORGIVE... THE DIRECTOR...
YOU'RE RUINING EVERYTHING!
I FORGIVE THE SPINDLY WOMAN...
...AND I FORGIVE MYSELF.

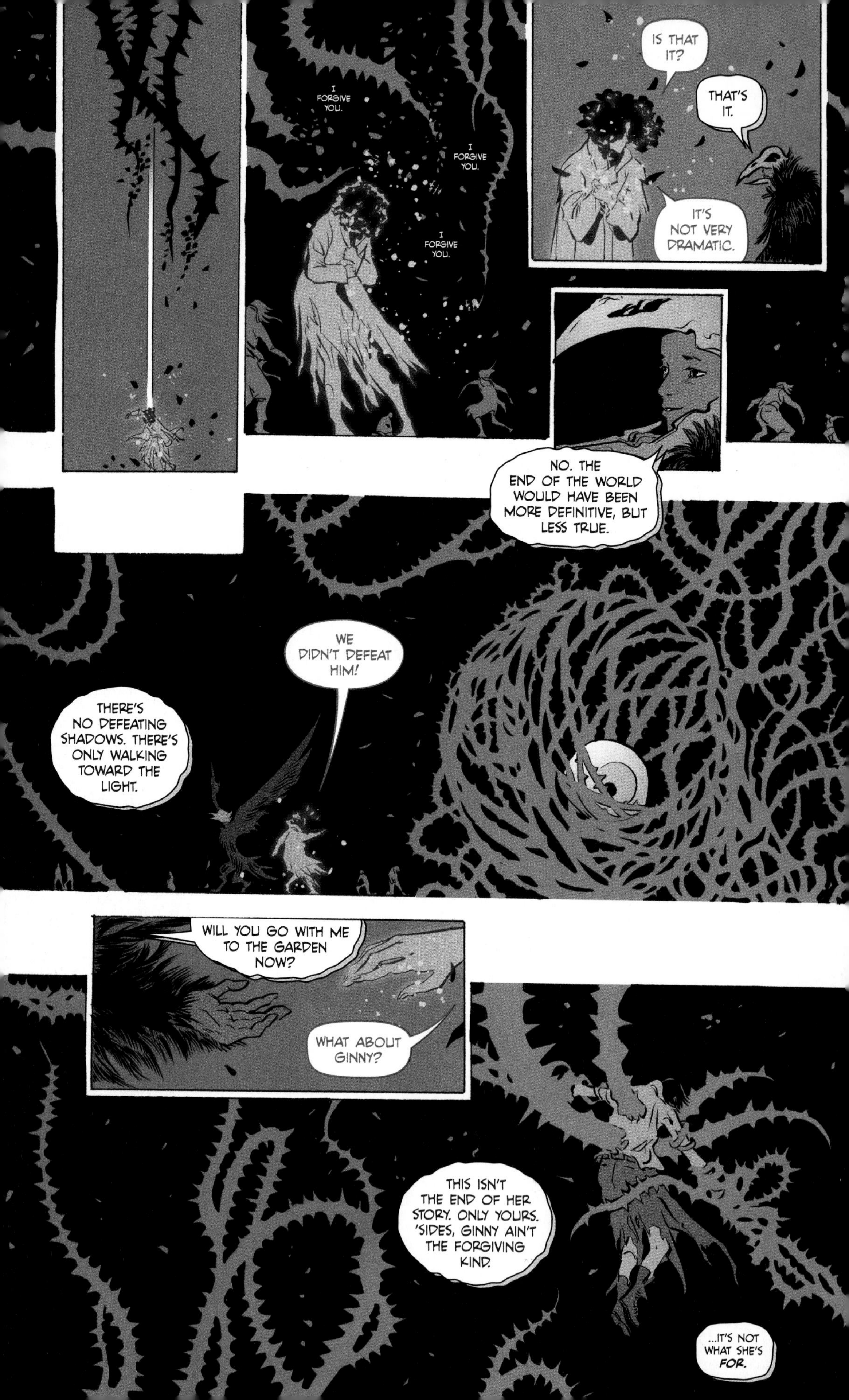
I FORGIVE YOU.
I FORGIVE YOU.
I FORGIVE YOU.
IS THAT IT?
THAT'S IT.
IT'S NOT VERY DRAMATIC.
NO. THE END OF THE WORLD WOULD HAVE BEEN MORE DEFINITIVE, BUT LESS TRUE.
WE DIDN'T DEFEAT HIM!
THERE'S NO DEFEATING SHADOWS. THERE'S ONLY WALKING TOWARD THE LIGHT.
WILL YOU GO WITH ME TO THE GARDEN NOW?
WHAT ABOUT GINNY?
THIS ISN'T THE END OF HER STORY. ONLY YOURS. 'SIDES, GINNY AIN'T THE FORGIVING KIND.
...IT'S NOT WHAT SHE'S *FOR.*

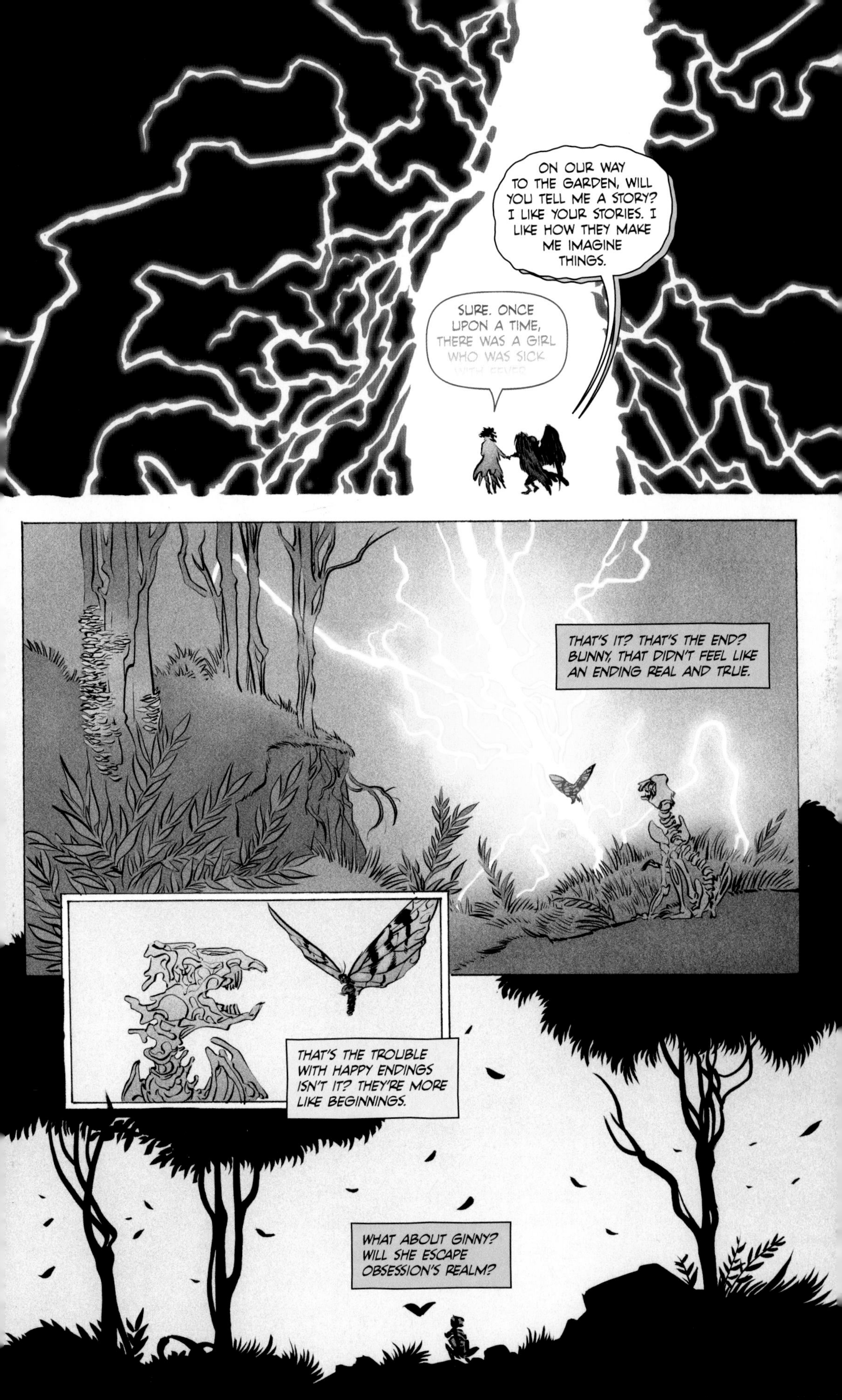

ON OUR WAY TO THE GARDEN, WILL YOU TELL ME A STORY? I LIKE YOUR STORIES. I LIKE HOW THEY MAKE ME IMAGINE THINGS.
SURE. ONCE UPON A TIME, THERE WAS A GIRL WHO WAS SICK
THAT'S IT? THAT'S THE END? BUNNY, THAT DIDN'T FEEL LIKE AN ENDING REAL AND TRUE.
THAT'S THE TROUBLE WITH HAPPY ENDINGS ISN'T IT? THEY'RE MORE LIKE BEGINNINGS.
WHAT ABOUT GINNY? WILL SHE ESCAPE OBSESSION'S REALM?

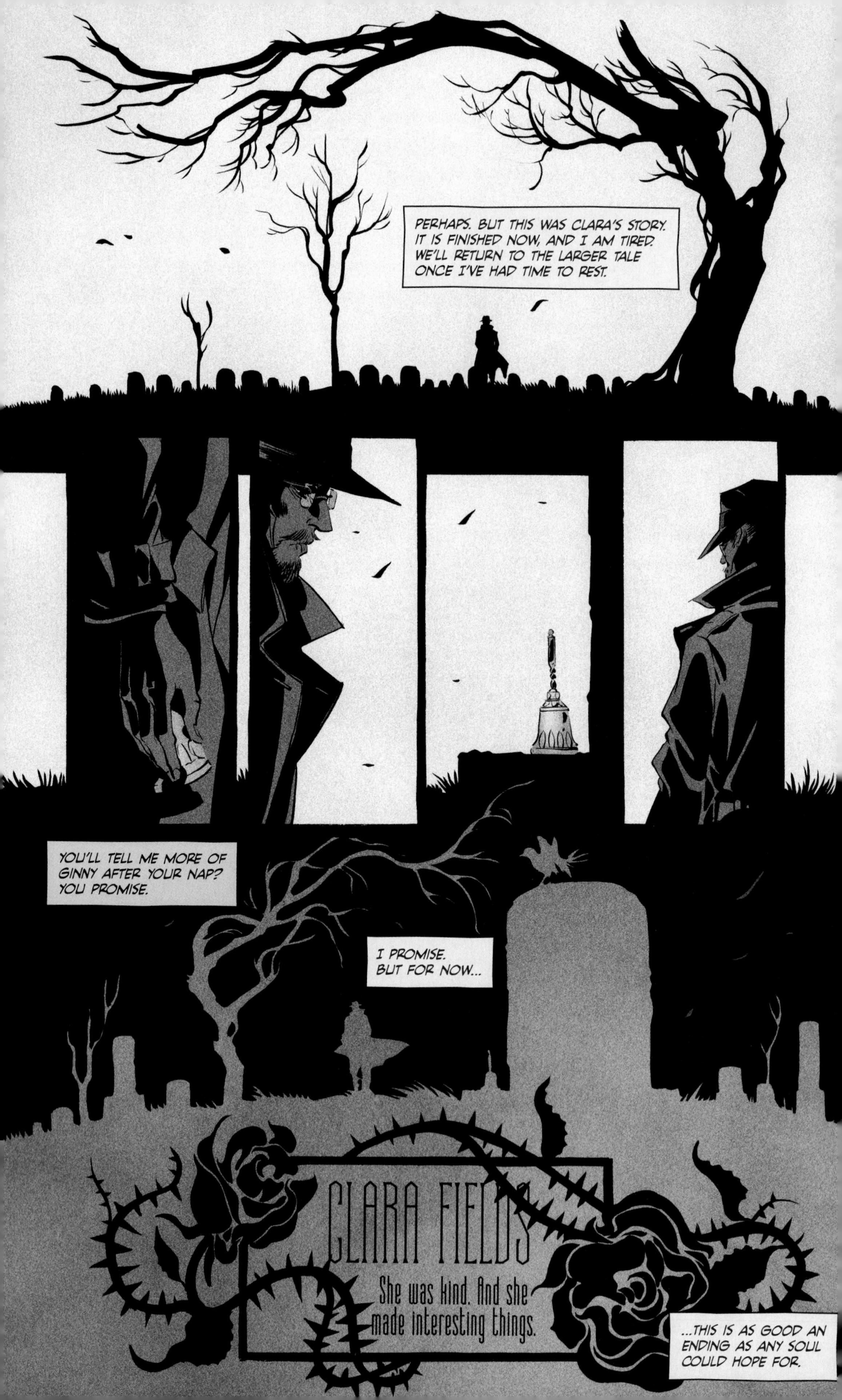
PERHAPS. BUT THIS WAS CLARA'S STORY. IT IS FINISHED NOW, AND I AM TIRED. WE'LL RETURN TO THE LARGER TALE ONCE I'VE HAD TIME TO REST.
YOU'LL TELL ME MORE OF GINNY AFTER YOUR NAP? YOU PROMISE.
I PROMISE. BUT FOR NOW...
CLARA FIELDS
She was kind. And she made interesting things.
...THIS IS AS GOOD AN ENDING AS ANY SOUL COULD HOPE FOR.

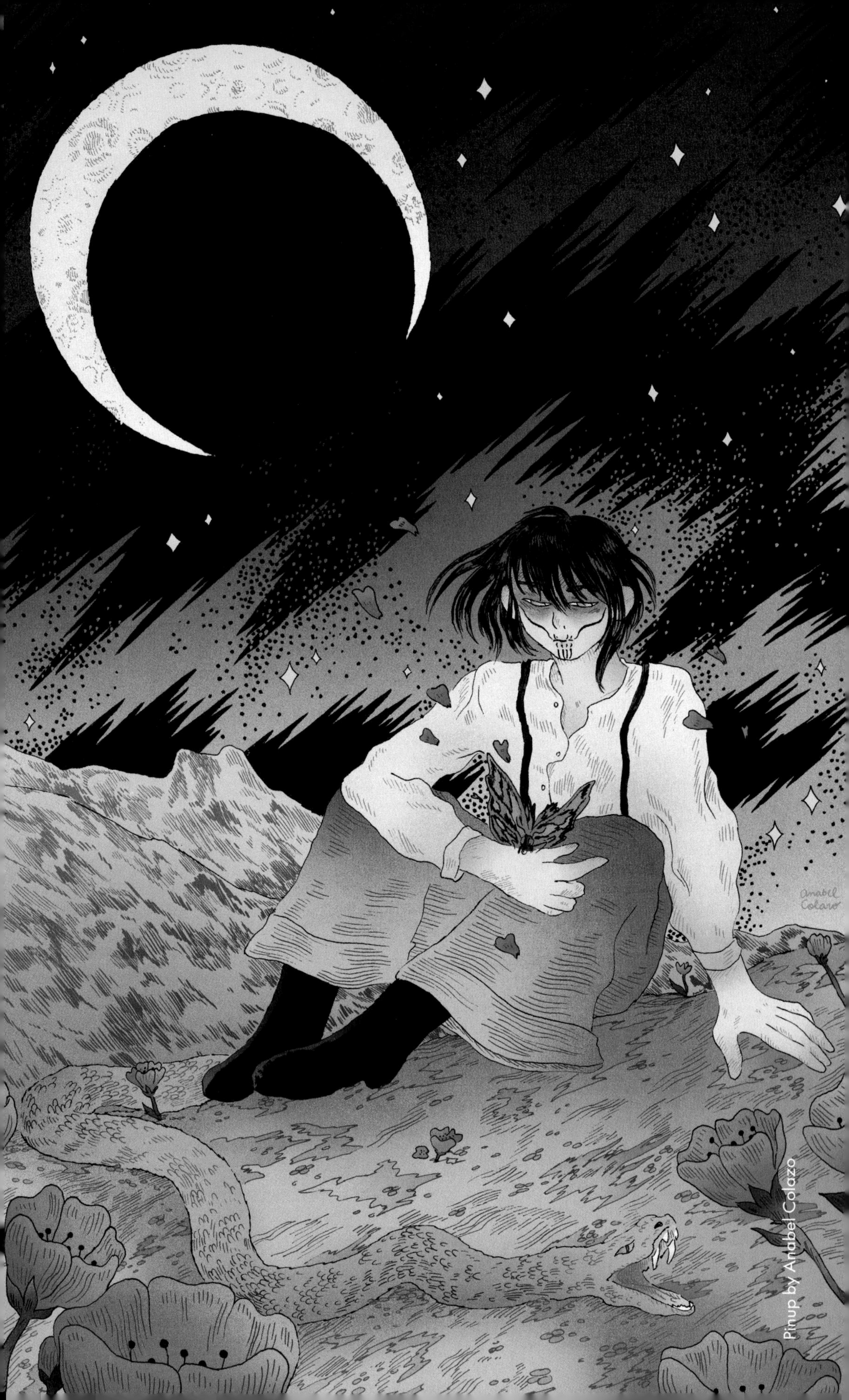
Anabel Colazo

Pinup by Anabel Colazo

DISCUSSION GUIDES FOR THE RAT

ISSUE ONE

In this issue, PRETTY DEADLY shifts from the old West of Volume 1 and wartime of Volume 2 to yet another kind of tale. As Conjure-Man investigates his niece's death, readers enter a noir story, with high-contrast imagery, urban landscapes, ambiguous female characters, and an anti-hero male on a quest for clarity. What we are dealing with here is a genre - or a socially recognized form for telling stories and communicating meaning[1]. Scholars from many fields - literature, rhetoric, linguistics, media studies, folklore, and otherwise – show that genres provide a basis from which to understand and enjoy the stories we tell. Genres like noir, war stories, and westerns give readers a framework for interpreting their meaning.

As a medium, American comics has a long history of western, war, and noir storytelling due to its evolution alongside pulp magazines, where these genres first flourished. Noir, in particular, became popular in film and literature after World War II - and reflected the difficulties of life after wartime. More recent works have critiqued the values that these works illustrated – especially through more complex storytelling and defiance of gender norms.

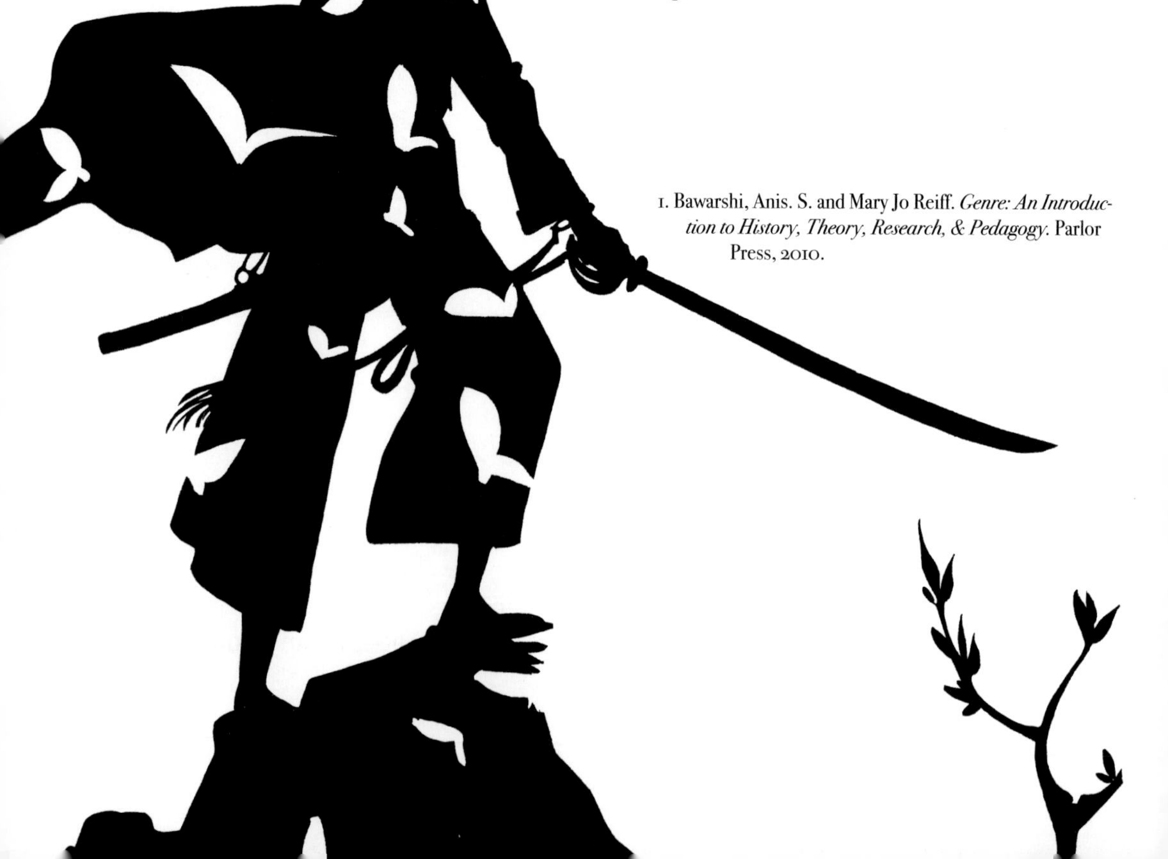

1. Bawarshi, Anis. S. and Mary Jo Reiff. *Genre: An Introduction to History, Theory, Research, & Pedagogy*. Parlor Press, 2010.

1. What expectations do we as readers have about noir stories? How does this issue fit or not fit into the genre of noir? What might the creators be attempting to show by telling a story that both does and does not meet expectations?

2. What comics, films, or similar noir stories does issue #1 relate to? How does comparing DeConnick, Ríos, Bellaire, and Cowles' story to them change our interpretation of it?

3. How does this issue portray gender? Feminist scholars like Yvonne Tasker analyze how noir can rely on potentially harmful gender norms. She specifically notes that "For feminist criticism, noir's most duplicitous female characters...are compelling constellations of Western culture's conflicted view of women"[2]. Noir can show us the social norms for womanhood, as well as how people might resist them. How might characters like Clara and Sissy both fit and not fit our expectations of women's roles?

4. As a series, PRETTY DEADLY is a serial story – one told over multiple issues and volumes. How does issue #1 relate to the past 2 volumes? How do you read the characters and story so far differently – knowing that it is grounded in the same story world(s)?

(And two additional questions from the PRETTY DEADLY Production Team:)

5. This issue introduces three new Reapers: Hunger, Thirst and Obsession. How do these three "concepts" interact with the notion of "Hollywood"? How does Conjure-Man's narration, specifically: "Why stop with enough when you can have too much?" fit into this discussion?

6. Given the omnipresence of the internet and media in our modern lives (a torrent of information, much like the unceasing rain in issue #1), how do ideas of consumption, excess, and abundance help us understand our relationship to mass media? What's similar or dissimilar about our experiences versus those our characters might have in the 1930s?

2. Tasker, Yvonne. 2013. "Women in Film Noir." In *A Companion to Film Noir,* edited by Andrew Spicer and Helen Hanson, Wiley Blackwell, 2013, pp. 353-368.

 ISSUE TWO

Previously, we discussed the nature of genre and noir. A central element of both noir and detective fiction is the pursuit of truth, from solving crimes to sending villains to jail. These kinds of stories come out of shifting social norms in 1940s America and the growing influence of media like the films of Golden Age Hollywood. As a result, there is a metaphysical tendency in such stories, where characters question their understanding of self, society, or even reality itself. As a field of thought, metaphysics concerns the nature of reality and our existence in the world, from the relationship between mind and matter to how people experience their lives. In detective and noir storytelling, as narrative scholar Jeanne C. Ewert notes, "The worlds...are strange, uncanny... and dangerous. They are worlds without happy endings, where protagonists are lost in mazes without exits, destroyed by ruthless cabals, or simply doomed to impotence and incompetence" (192). Such stories present worlds where characters question their personal identities and the nature of truth or even reality itself.

Similarly, in this issue, DeConnick, Ríos, Bellaire, and Cowles show our main characters questioning their roles and encountering experiences that distort the story world. Early on in the issue, Sissy laments that, as Gardener, she cannot bring order to the world, while Ginny pauses her pursuit of Alice to aid Conjure-Man, albeit for vengeance. Meanwhile, with imagery inspired by Busby Berkeley's *Footlight Parade*, Jack Kaufman's hallucinatory account of plagiarizing Clara's stories distorts the comics page and leaves many questions unanswered. A lack of clarity in social roles—where Sissy reflects on her position and Ginny sidesteps her duties—or in the nature of reality—where Kaufman's confession distorts the story—each reflect the concerns of noir storytelling and the confusion of an illusion-filled Hollywood of the 1940s.

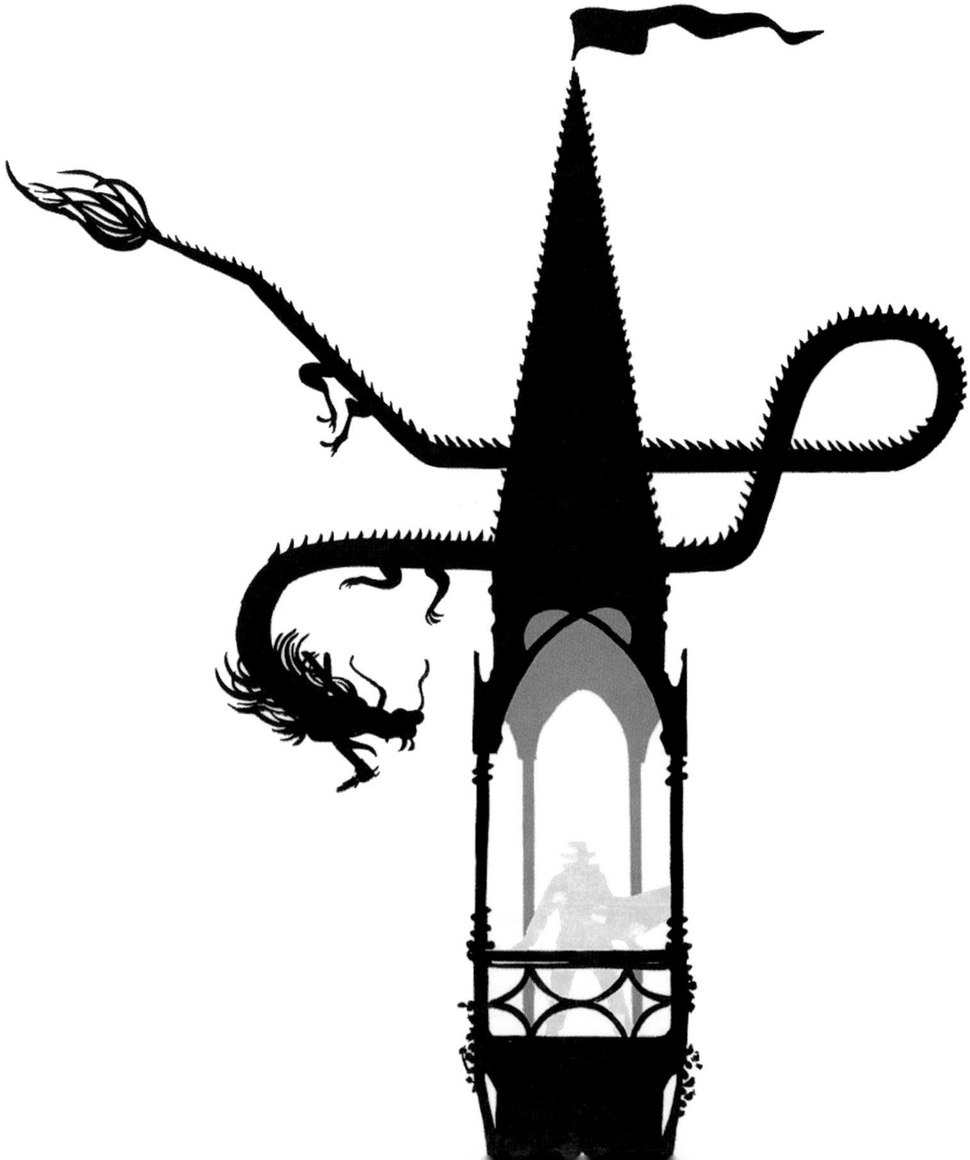

1. The detective in noir acts as a kind of archetype—or repeating character type with recognizable traits and associated meanings that together guide our expectations and interpretation of storytelling. How does Conjure-Man resemble or differ from a standard noir protagonist? How might his relationship with Ginny change his role in the story—or Ginny's role as a Reaper who defies expectation?

2. Another key archetype for noir is the femme fatale. She has a unique history, having evolved from British anxiety over women's emancipation into a standard of 1940s Hollywood. As Hanson and O'Rawe note, "Conventionally, the femme is...both unknowable and an index of unknowability, always representing more than can be articulated." In other words, she is an attractive archetype with hidden motivations that drive the narrative forward. How might characters like Ginny, Clara, or even Conjure-Man reflect or change this archetype? What is the relationship between gender and knowability—and how might that relationship reflect or change gender norms?

3. A common technique in noir and detective fiction is the nested narrative, where one story contains smaller ones. In this case, Issue #1 and #2 contain Clara's film of the Reapers and Kaufman's hallucination of Clara. How does this structure affect our understanding of the story? How does the fragmentation of page and narrative affect our reading of it?

4. In this issue, Ríos and Bellaire use innovative page composition to communicate Kaufman's hallucinatory account. On pages 18 and 19, his consciousness as he partially drowns is represented by his face breaking through the surface of the water and into a surreal sequence of swimming dancers. Since panels and page structure are so central to the comics form—providing, at base, a sense of perspective, pacing, and weight of moments—how do the creators use bodies of and in water to structure our sense of story? How might they be preparing readers for the nested narrative to come? And what might that framing show about Kaufman's reliability as narrator or the nature of truth in this arc?

References:

Hanson, Helen and Catherine O'Rawe. "Introduction." In *The Femme Fatale: Images, Histories, Contexts*. Palgrave MacMillan, 2010.

Ewert, Jeanne C. 20__. "'A Thousand Other Mysteries': Metaphysical Detection, Ontological Quests." In *Detecting Texts: The Metaphysical Detective Story from Poe to Postmodernism*, eds. Patricia Merivale & Susan Elisabeth Sweeney, University of Pennsylvania Press, 1999, pp. 179-198.

ISSUE THREE

As this issue ends, Conjure-Man and Ginny discover key information about Clara's fate, even as they continue to navigate surreal visions and half-truths. Their encounter with the Reaper of Thirst, in particular, both helps and hinders— as she only shares what she knows about Clara in a distorted dreamscape. In so doing, Thirst reveals herself to be a kind of trickster—or, as art historian Patricia Vettel Tom explains, "one who adapts to use or deceives to cheat the existing social structures."[1] Such outsider figures rely on their intellect and can serve a range of roles—from humorous ally to deceptive villain.

Whatever their purpose, tricksters drive plot and character development by revealing what is hidden and by catalyzing change. Here, the Reaper of Thirst deceives by playing on characters' desires—and so fulfills another key quality of tricksters by talking around questions and stoking others' desires. At the same time,

1. Vettel Tom, Patricia. "Felix the Cat as Modern Trickster." *American Art*, Vol. 10, No. 1 (Spring, 1996), pp. 64-87.

she also helps by revealing Conjure-Man's role in Clara's disappearance. In so doing, Thirst reveals to the reader that Clara is more than a virtuous contrast to Director Jack Kaufman—she is a fully fledged person with flaws, passions, and her own story to tell.

Another source of character definition is the concept of foils—or characters whose differences illustrate what defines each. The classic example is the protagonist and antagonist whose relationship helps flesh each character out. In this issue, Sissy attempts to fragment the World Garden to better understand it, while Clara has been fragmented to the point of destruction. Conjure-Man and Ginny link these two storylines together, even as they themselves foil one another's characteristics. While each seeks justice, Ginny wields her power responsibly, while Conjure-Man has seemingly ignored his duties—which may have led to Clara's destruction. DeConnick, Ríos, Bellaire, and Cowles use these relationships to show what defines each character—and how they manage the difficulties of a noir world where truth, fiction, and story are all intertwined.

1. What other foils are there in the story? How might additional contrasts—such as that between Conjure-Man and Clara or Fox and Sissy—show new meanings?

2. This issue includes multiple scenes that function much like Director Jack Kaufman's hallucination in issue #2—to indicate a change in consciousness and/or perception. In particular, on pages 8 and 9, Rios transforms the comics page into a freeform series of moments that can be read in many directions. How does this composition change our reading experience? How might it reflect the larger themes of this volume's arc?

3. Tricksters are important characters in storytelling because they provide a more holistic view of the world that includes both order and disorder. In particular, they often undermine authority and cause characters to walk less obvious paths. How might the Reaper of Thirst deepen our understanding of the story world in PRETTY DEADLY? What does she reveal about Clara, Conjure-Man, Ginny, and other characters? What does she reveal about us as readers—and the assumptions we make about storytelling?

4. The Reaper of Thirst clearly fits into the archetype of a trickster, alongside figures from world mythologies like African spider Anansi, cunning Japanese kitsunes, Indigenous American coyotes and ravens, and the infamous Norse god Loki. What other characters in PRETTY DEADLY might also fall into that category? For instance, both Fox and Ginny have played ambiguous roles at times in this story world—specifically in their unclear loyalties and motivations in Volume 1. How would classifying them as tricksters change our understanding of these characters and their roles in the story of PRETTY DEADLY?

References:

Waddell, Terrie. *Mis/takes: Archetype, Myth, and Identity in Screen Fiction.* Routledge, 2006.

ISSUE FOUR

This issue plays on the character tensions discussed in the previous guide, escalating the stakes as Ginny and Conjure-Man confront their emotions. It begins with the reciprocal relationship between coyote and badger, whose story shows the importance of not keeping score with kin. Then, we witness the confrontation with the Reaper of Obsession, a shift in the story that recalls the paranoia and half-truths of noir fiction. As Ginny returns Conjure-Man to his world, DeConnick, Ríos, Bellaire, and Cowles play with noir and comics conventions as they mediate the relationship between what the story is and how it is communicated to readers.

The medium of comics specifically adds the tension between what is seen on the page and the story that is created by the relationships between images. As cultural studies scholars Jan Baetens and Charlotte Pylyser note, comics has the unique ability to translate time into spatial forms: "The temporal unfolding of the material is made visible through panels and pages that can also be looked at as plastic constructions..." (2016, p. 303)[1]. In other words, creators build stories by placing panels in sequence, with each page acting as both a collection of panels and a full composition in and of itself. In so doing, they give moments weight based on their placement on the page and in relation to surrounding panels. For example, as Ginny faces the Reaper of Obsession and Conjure-Man his grief, multiple threads are interwoven – illustrating how, like coyote and badger or Sissy and Fox, each character's actions are key to their partnership and to the overarching story. How might a different layout have given these moments different weight? What would that have done to our understanding of the events in this issue and in this story arc?

Conjure-Man's grieving also displays the comics medium's ability to represent emotions. We see him mourning his niece as he returns to the real world – drowning in water as well as his grief as he finally sorts through her belongings. Literary scholar Hilary Chute theorizes that comics' fragmented form of pages composed of panels makes it "...adept at engaging the notion and matter of memory, and reproducing the effects of memory – its gaps, fragments, positions, layers, circularities".[2] The unique relationship between images in a sequence that creates a sense of story can allow tales to be told that are incomplete or that have no single meaning. In analyzing the autobiographical work of Lynda Barry, Chute specifically notes that comics creators are able to represent trauma through the layering of memories on the page. Similarly, DeConnick, Ríos, Bellaire, and Cowles portray Conjure-Man and Ginny each confronting a loss in different ways – by moving through the waters of grief or by combatting a manifestation of the inability to let go. Each approach is given time and weight on the page – and so is shown to be one way to process loss, albeit with varying results, as we'll see next issue. How else is grief or trauma represented in PRETTY DEADLY? What is the impact of different ways of representing emotion? How might we reflect on our own emotions or relationships in comics?

1. In this issue, the Reaper of Obsession is also the catalyst for an added layer of narrative, one that Ríos uses a paper-cut style to demarcate as the shadow world. How does this change in style push the story forward? How does this visual style make us feel or add to the overall mood of the story? What might it reveal about obsession, given that real life is rarely so clear cut as this black and white world? Finally, how might this visual metaphor change our understanding of specific characters – such as Ginny, who is partially transformed by her obsession, or Clara, who has appeared in paper-cut form in the previous three issues?

2. This issue ends with Ginny seemingly trapped in the shadow world and allied with the Reaper of Obsession, albeit in order to find Clara. When taunted by the Reaper, though, she notes that "I chose to free him. I am here because I chose to stay." How does Ginny's statement change our understanding of story events? How might it resist or fulfill standard archetypes like hero, villain, femme fatale, trickster, etc.?

1. Baetens, Jan and Charlotte Pylyser. "Comics & Time." In *The Routledge Companion to Comics*, eds. Frank Bramlett, Roy T. Cook, & Aaron Meskin: pp. 303-309. Routledge, 2016.
2. Chute, Hillary. "Materializing Memory: Lynda Barry's One Hundred Demons." In *Graphic Subjects: Critical Essays on Autobiography & Graphic Novels*, ed. Michael A. Chaney: pp. 282-309. Madison: The University of Wisconsin Press, 2011.

DeConnick, Ríos, Bellaire, and Cowles personify Obsession as multiple dragons that are a relatively un-traditional villain. In particular, the Reaper of Obsession forces Conjure-Man and Ginny to confront difficult truths – namely, the role that each fear they may have played in a loved one's fate. How does this confrontation fulfill or contradict our expectations of a noir story and its archetypes? Why might it be important that our characters' adventure leads them to confront their fears and grow through self-reflection?

Water has played an important role in this arc. The story opened with a torrential rain that the ground could not absorb, just as Conjure-Man was confronted with the loss of his niece. The second issue then saw Director Jack Kaufman forced to confront the painful truth of his own harmful actions by immersing himself in the waters of his distorted memories. Last issue, an "insatiable rain" poured down on Conjure-Man and Ginny as they visited the Reaper of Thirst and discussed the obsession that would take center stage this issue. Where else have you seen an emphasis on water in PRETTY DEADLY? What might it symbolize in terms of the characters' emotions – or the meanings of their actions?

ISSUE FIVE

As PRETTY DEADLY: THE RAT ends, we finally get Clara's side of the story, even as Sissy steps in to defeat the Reaper of Obsession and guide her into the Garden where she belongs. This issue continues many themes and techniques discussed in previous reading guides—defying the gender norms of noir while positioning characters as foils to define each other. Clara's account, though, expands the story by retelling it through the eyes of the character at its center.

As noted in issue #4's discussion guide, comics as a form allows for multiple perspectives through its combination of image and text in panels and pages. Here, DeConnick, Ríos, Bellaire, and Cowles use that ability to give Clara, a character who could be seen as a victim, her own role in the story. In the process, they question the nature of power—a concept sociologists understand as one's ability to affect others' actions. As sociologist Casey Brienza (2015) explains, power acts as a field or system of social relations that establishes one's position in society through interactions. So, Clara might seem to lack power, having been taken advantage of by characters and potentially killed by Obsession. However, in her telling, she is full of power. As "a story in search of an ending", she has the power to make her own choices, create her own art, and decide whether to allow the harm that Obsession has done to define her life in death.

DeConnick, Ríos, Bellaire, and Cowles thus make masterful use of the denouement, or final reveal of detective fiction. Not only does Clara's story provide a conclusive beat for Conjure-Man and Ginny's search for truth, but it also pushes us as readers to question our understanding of power. Communications scholar Eddah Mutua (2015) points to the importance of analyzing the stories we tell, especially about ourselves, as addressing one's position can unveil and disrupt power. In particular, a person's position shapes their experiences and their ability to hold and act on power—especially as part of larger systems of class, race, gender, orientation, ability/disability, and otherwise. In PRETTY DEADLY, Clara's realization of her power to forgive allows her to transform her position from someone lost—a kind of damsel in distress—to someone who has found herself and her ability to follow her own path. How might this transformation re-frame Clara as the hero of this story arc? What does her choice—to forgive and transform—show us as readers about the power of perspective?

1. As already noted, "The Rat" ends with forgiveness, as Clara and Sissy show the value of coming to terms with the actions of someone who has done harm. How do Clara's actions compare to those of other characters? How might she provide a foil not just to characters in PRETTY DEADLY—but to heroic archetypes in general? What can we learn as readers? How might the story challenge your own understanding of forgiveness?

2. In illustrating Clara's journey, Ríos continues to critically re-imagine the comics page, transforming panels into butterflies and thorns to communicate a range of emotions, from pain to forgiveness. For example, the spread on pages 10 and 11 uses a swarm of butterflies to narrow our view of the world much as Clara's perspective was narrowed through obsession. Similarly, the Reaper of Obsession is visualized with thorny vines that fracture the comics page, much as they attempt to fracture Ginny, Clara, and Sissy. How do these formal innovations affect our reading of the story and empathy for its characters? What was your reading experience like? How does Ríos push us as readers to move – slowly or quickly – through different moments, giving them different weights? How was this similar to or different from other comics that you've read?

3. As we come to the conclusion of "The Rat", we as readers bring certain expectations to the story. How should a story end? Where do we expect the conclusion to find different kinds of characters, and what experiences should they have had? What are our expectations for the end in noir genre storytelling and in comic book series like PRETTY DEADLY? How might this issue challenge some of those understandings?

4. Finally, this issue ends with a beginning of sorts. Even as Sissy guides Clara into the World Garden, she leaves Ginny to face her own inability to forgive. In so doing, DeConnick, Ríos, Bellaire, and Cowles not only set up the next arc of PRETTY DEADLY, but also challenge readers' expectation for resolution. How does our lack of resolution as readers parallel the conclusion of "The Rat", where Conjure-Man faces his grief without knowing Clara's fate and Ginny never finds Alice? What is the impact on us readers? How might it help us reflect on the power of story—and different ways of telling tales?

References:

Brienza, Casey. "Producing Comics Culture: A Sociological Approach to the Study of Comics." *Journal of Graphic Novels & Comics* Vol. 1, No. 2 (2010): pp. 105-119.

hooks, bell. "Community: Loving Communion." In *All About Love: New Visions*: pp. 129-144. Harper, 2000.

Mutua, Eddah M. "How I Came to Know: Moving Through Spaces of Post/Colonial Encounters." In *Globalizing Intercultural Communication: A Reader*, eds. Kathryn Sorrells & Sachi Sekimoto: pp. 95-101. Sage Publishing, 2015.

Dr. Jeremy Stoll is a comics creator and scholar whose research focuses on comics in India. He has a BA in Creative Writing & Fine Arts from University of Michigan and a PhD in Folklore from Indiana University. Stoll's articles have appeared in the *International Journal of Comic Art*; *Marg, A Magazine of the Arts*; *Cultures of Comics Work*; and the *Routledge Companion to Comics*. He is currently completing an edited volume on comics worlds (with Benjamin Woo) and a book manuscript on India's comics cultures.